San Francisco For Dummies
2nd Edition

S0-BCM-762

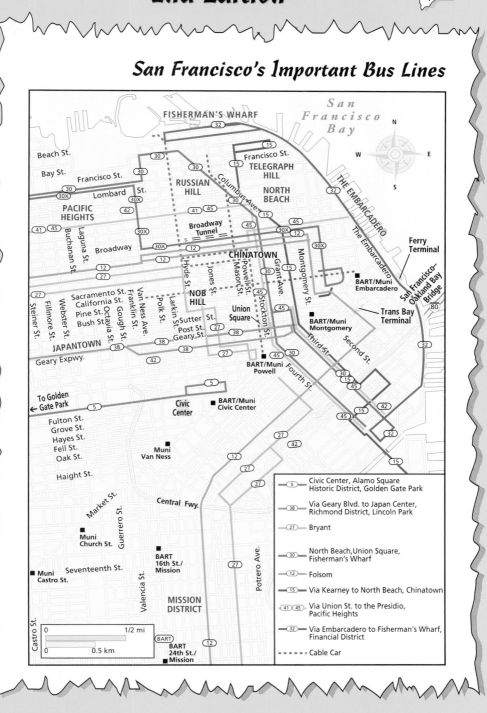

San Francisco's Important Bus Lines

5	Civic Center, Alamo Square Historic District, Golden Gate Park
38	Via Geary Blvd. to Japan Center, Richmond District, Lincoln Park
27	Bryant
30	North Beach, Union Square, Fisherman's Wharf
12	Folsom
15	Via Kearney to North Beach, Chinatown
41 45	Via Union St. to the Presidio, Pacific Heights
32	Via Embarcadero to Fisherman's Wharf, Financial District
·····	Cable Car

For Dummies: Bestselling Book Series for Beginners

San Francisco For Dummies, 2nd Edition

Cheat Sheet

The Napa Valley

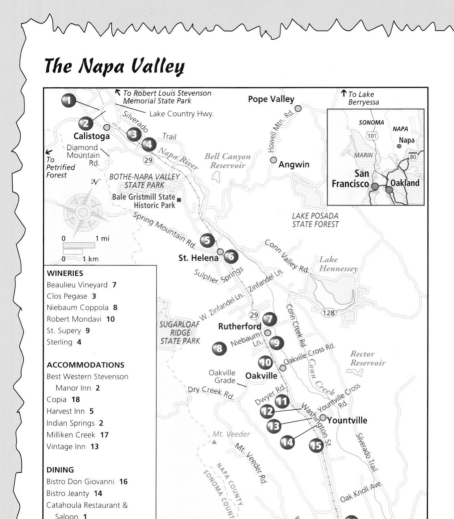

To Robert Louis Stevenson Memorial State Park

Pope Valley

To Lake Berryessa

Lake Country Hwy.

Silverado

Calistoga

Trail

Diamond Mountain Rd.

To Petrified Forest

Napa River

Bell Canyon Reservoir

Howell Mtn. Rd.

Angwin

BOTHE-NAPA VALLEY STATE PARK

Bale Gristmill State Historic Park

LAKE POSADA STATE FOREST

Spring Mountain Rd.

0   1 mi
0   1 km

St. Helena

Sulpher Springs

Conn Valley Rd.

Lake Hennessey

SONOMA   NAPA
101
Napa
MARIN
San Francisco   Oakland
80

W. Zinfandel Ln.   Zinfandel Ln.

128

SUGARLOAF RIDGE STATE PARK

Rutherford

Niebaum Ln.

Conn Creek Rd.

Rector Reservoir

Oakville Cross Rd.

Oakville Grade

Oakville

Dry Creek Rd.

Conn Creek

Dwyer Rd.

Yountville Cross Rd.

Mt. Veeder

Mt. Veeder Rd.

NAPA COUNTY
SONOMA COUNTY

Washington St.

Yountville

Silverado Trail

Oak Knoll Ave.

Redwood Dr.

Trancas St.

NAPA

Napa Valley Wine Train

SONOMA

WINERIES
Beaulieu Vineyard **7**
Clos Pegase **3**
Niebaum Coppola **8**
Robert Mondavi **10**
St. Supery **9**
Sterling **4**

ACCOMMODATIONS
Best Western Stevenson Manor Inn **2**
Copia **18**
Harvest Inn **5**
Indian Springs **2**
Milliken Creek **17**
Vintage Inn **13**

DINING
Bistro Don Giovanni **16**
Bistro Jeanty **14**
Catahoula Restaurant & Saloon **1**
French Laundry **15**
Gordon's Cafe & Wine Bar **12**
Julia's Kitchen **18**
Mustards Grill **11**
Tra Vigne **6**

Copyright © 2002 Wiley Publishing, Inc.
All rights reserved.

Item 5450-6.

For more information about Wiley Publishing, call 1-800-762-2974.

For Dummies: Bestselling Book Series for Beginners

San Francisco

FOR

DUMMIES®

2ND EDITION

by Paula Tevis

Wiley Publishing, Inc.

San Francisco For Dummies, 2nd Edition

Published by
Wiley Publishing, Inc.
909 Third Avenue
New York, NY 10022
www.wiley.com

Copyright © 2002 by Wiley Publishing, Inc., Indianapolis, Indiana

Published simultaneously in Canada

For general information on our other products and services or to obtain technical support, please contact our Customer Care Department within the U.S. at 800-762-2974, outside the U.S. at 317-572-3993, or fax 317-572-4002.

Wiley also publishes its books in a variety of electronic formats. Some content that appears in print may not be available in electronic books.

Library of Congress Control Number: 2002110276

ISBN: 0-7645-5450-6

ISSN: 1528-2120

Manufactured in the United States of America

10 9 8 7 6 5 4 3 2 1

2B/QZ/QZ/QS/IN

About the Author

A California native, **Paula Tevis** made many treks to San Francisco as a young girl before moving to her favorite city in 1983. After an eclectic but blessedly brief career that included stints in the computer and nonprofit sectors, she and her husband produced a couple of children in quick succession, and Paula happily relinquished the 9-to-5 world for the 24/7 one that parenting brings. Upon regaining consciousness, Paula recalled a childhood ambition and declared herself a writer. From her humble beginnings word processing cookbook manuscripts for a local publisher, Paula metamorphosed into a freelance copy editor and soon received her first break as a professional writer with *Parenting* magazine, crafting a column on kids who cook. Over the years, she has contributed articles and essays to *Family Fun* magazine, the *San Francisco Chronicle, Citysearch.com, Frommer's Las Vegas, Frommer's New Orleans,* and *Variety.* She is the co-author of *California For Dummies,* 2nd Edition, and author of the *Berlitz Vancouver Pocketguide* and the soon-to-be-released *Frommer's San Francisco with Kids.*

Dedication

To Mark, Madeleine, and Lili.

Author's Acknowledgments

Many thanks to my exceedingly calm editor, Christine Ryan; to my cousins Irene Levin Dietz and Ina Levin Gyemant, who add so much to my life in the city; to the UK Ladies; to Germaine and Jonathon Arginteanu; and to Bev Chin. And a long-overdue thank you to Bonnie Monte for providing me with my first assignment.

Publisher's Acknowledgments

We're proud of this book; please send us your comments through our Dummies online registration form located at www.dummies.com/register/.

Some of the people who helped bring this book to market include the following:

Editorial

Editors: Elizabeth Kuball, Christine Ryan

Cartographer: Roberta Stockwell

Editorial Supervisor: Michelle Hacker

Editorial Assistants: Stephen Bassman, Carol Strickland

Senior Photo Editor: Richard Fox

Assistant Photo Editor: Michael Ross

Cover Photos: Front: John Elk III Photography; Back: Donovan Reese/ Getty Images

Production

Project Coordinator: Regina Snyder

Layout and Graphics: Joyce Haughey, Jackie Nicholas, Julie Trippetti

Proofreaders: Susan Moritz, Linda Quigley, Charles Spencer, TECHBOOKS Production Services

Indexer: TECHBOOKS Production Services

Publishing and Editorial for Consumer Dummies

Diane Graves Steele, Vice President and Publisher, Consumer Dummies

Joyce Pepple, Acquisitions Director, Consumer Dummies

Kristin A. Cocks, Product Development Director, Consumer Dummies

Michael Spring, Vice President and Publisher, Travel

Brice Gosnell, Publishing Director, Travel

Suzanne Jannetta, Editorial Director, Travel

Publishing for Technology Dummies

Andy Cummings, Acquisitions Director

Composition Services

Gerry Fahey, Vice President of Production Services

Debbie Stailey, Director of Composition Services

Contents at a Glance

Maps at a Glance

Table of Contents

Introduction

Many years ago, long before mandatory seatbelt laws, my mother would occasionally squeeze my sister Patience and me into her little red sports car and literally zoom up Highway 101 for a weekend in San Francisco. We lived 350 miles south, in Santa Barbara, but due to my mom's lead foot, we'd be cruising along the bay in no time, past a hill filled with rows of boxy pastel-colored houses, then onto the boulevard that led to our cousin Mildred's beautiful home. My desire to live in a big city (and drive really fast) no doubt developed during these trips, and during many subsequent ones in my teens, but my ties to San Francisco actually extend back farther. My grandmother, Sarah, and her sister, Lottie, grew up here. At 18 and 20 years of age they camped in Golden Gate Park after the 1906 earthquake, and in later years they lived in a series of houses in the outer Richmond District.

When I had the chance to move to San Francisco in 1982, I didn't think twice. My future husband and I first lived near Haight Street, then moved to a small neighborhood near the Mission District and Bernal Heights. Eventually I found myself working at one time or another around the Richmond District, Civic Center, Potrero Hill, and South of Market. I loved getting well-acquainted with different areas of the city, and in hindsight I realize my early, admittedly dilettantish, professional life helped prepare me for the greatest (and perhaps longest) job I've ever had — writing about San Francisco.

The San Francisco of my grandmother's day was elegant enough to attract the most famous people of its time, yet still wild enough to garner an exciting reputation. The multicultural, expansive, and liberal city of today continues in that tradition, and even improves upon it. Even after 20 years of familiarity, I still continue to marvel at everything San Francisco has to offer, and I'll bet that after a day or two spent here, you'll do the same.

About This Book

San Francisco For Dummies, 2nd Edition, is foremost a reference guide for people who intend to vacation in San Francisco and need basic, clear-cut information on how to plan and execute the best possible trip. If you like, you can begin reading from Chapter 1 and head straight through to the appendix. But if you turn directly to the restaurant section or to the chapter on the wine country, because that's the piece that interests you at the moment, the book will work just as well. I haven't included absolutely everything San Francisco has to offer in the way of attractions, hotels, restaurants, or diversions — a book that size would be too heavy to pack and probably too bothersome to read. What I've done is picked and chosen what I believe to be worth your time and your money, while still offering enough variety to please a range of tastes, budgets, and family configurations.

Let me underscore that travel information is subject to change at any time — and this is especially true of prices. I therefore suggest that you write or call ahead for confirmation when making your travel plans. The authors, editors, and publisher cannot be held responsible for the experiences of readers while traveling. Your safety is important to us, however, so we encourage you to stay alert and be aware of your surroundings. Keep a close eye on cameras, purses, and wallets, all favorite targets of thieves and pickpockets.

Conventions Used in This Book

So, San Francisco, here you come! You've picked a stunner of a destination, with a wide variety of wonderful sites to see, fabulous foods to try, and interesting places to visit. But don't be overwhelmed. You've made a smart decision in buying *San Francisco For Dummies,* 2nd Edition. This book walks you through all the nitty-gritty details to make sure that planning your trip goes smoothly, and that the trip itself is memorable.

In this book I've included lists of hotels, restaurants, and attractions. As I describe each, I often include abbreviations for commonly accepted credit cards. Take a look at the following list for an explanation of each:

> **AE:** American Express
>
> **CB:** Carte Blanche
>
> **DC:** Diners Club
>
> **DISC:** Discover
>
> **JCB:** Japan Credit Bank
>
> **MC:** MasterCard
>
> **V:** Visa

I've divided the hotels into two categories — my personal favorites and those that don't quite make my preferred list but still get my hearty seal of approval. Don't be shy about considering these "runner-up" hotels if you're unable to get a room at one of my favorites or if your preferences differ from mine — the amenities that the runners-up offer and the services that each provides make all these accommodations good choices to consider as you determine where to rest your head at night.

I also include some general pricing information to help you as you
decide where to unpack your bags or dine on the local cuisine. I've
used a system of dollar signs to show a range of costs for one night in a
hotel or a meal at a restaurant (including appetizer, main course,
dessert, one drink, tax, and tip). Check out the following table to deci-
pher the dollar signs:

Cost	SF Hotels	Wine Country Hotels	SF and Wine Country Restaurants
$	under $125	$100 or less	$25 or less
$$	$125–$175	$100–$150	$25–$40
$$$	$175–$300	$150–$200	$40–$60
$$$$	$300 or more	$200 or more	$60 or more

Foolish Assumptions

As I wrote this book, I made some assumptions about you and what
your needs may be as a traveler:

 ✔ You may be an inexperienced traveler looking for guidance on
   whether to take a trip to San Francisco and how to plan for it.

 ✔ You may be an experienced traveler, but you don't have a lot of
   time to devote to trip planning or you don't have a lot of time to
   spend in San Francisco after you get there. You want expert advice
   on how to maximize your time and enjoy a hassle-free trip.

 ✔ You're not looking for a book that discusses the history and architecture of the city, provides all the data available about San
   Francisco, or lists every hotel, restaurant, or attraction available
   to you. Instead, you're looking for a book that focuses on the
   places that will give you the best or most unique experience in
   San Francisco.

If you fit any of these criteria, then *San Francisco For Dummies,* 2nd
Edition, will give you the information you're looking for!

How This Book Is Organized

Like all *For Dummies* guides, this book is organized in parts that contain anywhere from two to five chapters of related information. You
don't need to start at the very beginning (though it's a very good place
to start); feel free to turn directly to the chapter that intrigues you the
most.

Part 1: Getting Started

This part gives you an overview of San Francisco and discusses the details that you need to think about, such as when to come, what the trip may cost, and how to budget. The calendar of events in Chapter 2 may influence your decision on when to arrive, and the text on San Francisco seasons may dissuade you from showing up in August. Because this book is intended for a varied audience, I include specific advice for family travelers, the disabled, seniors, and gay/lesbian visitors.

Part 11: Ironing Out the Details

Because you're reading this, you probably aren't the type to just show up without an appointment — you intend to do a good bit of pre-planning before your arrival. That's a good idea, and this part covers what you need to know about getting to San Francisco, particularly if you plan to fly. When it comes to figuring out where to sleep, I include a rundown of the major neighborhoods where visitors stay, offering tips on getting the most room for your money and a brief but informative description of my favorite hotels. Then I help you decide whether to rent a car, and finally I tell you which activities you'll need advance reservations for — like Alcatraz and the American Conservatory Theater (see Chapter 9).

Part 111: Settling Into San Francisco

In an unfamiliar city, figuring out where you are can take days, but Part III saves time by explaining how to get to town from the airport and around the most important neighborhoods. A thorough chapter on local transportation options follows, including everything I know about parking — although luck and patience usually play a more important role than mere words. And because money is an integral part of any trip, I provide a few choice paragraphs on where to get it and what to do if it disappears.

Part 1V: Dining in San Francisco

An entire section devoted to food? You betcha. If not in a book devoted to the culinary center of the universe (or at least a good three-quarters of the U.S.), then where? Read these chapters and you'll soon be able to discuss the intricacies of the local food scene as if you spent all your weekends dining in these parts. And if you prefer to eat and run, you'll get a head start with a chapter on food to go — and I don't mean fast food.

Part V: Exploring San Francisco

You likely have an idea of what you want to see, and this part provides the information you need to conquer the most popular sites. Along with the big stuff, I've categorized other fun and interesting options under lots of different interests. My three– and five-day itineraries at the end of the part will help you focus and plan your days with all the precision you care to muster up.

Part VI: Living It Up After the Sun Goes Down: San Francisco Nightlife

As my husband says during his annual pilgrimage to JazzFest in New Orleans, "You can sleep when you're dead." But first, you need to figure out where to go after dinner, and that's what you'll discover in Part VI. From opera to swing dancing to barhopping, you can always find something stimulating to do around town.

Part VII: Exploring beyond San Francisco: Great Day and Overnight Trips

Leaving already? Don't stay away long, but have a wonderful time investigating a few of the beautiful areas an hour or less from the city. In this part, I help you plan a day trip to Berkeley, an overnighter to the coast, and a getaway to Wine Country, including winery tours and a mud bath.

Part VIII: The Part of Tens

This is where I get to lurch from the sublime (the best views) to the practical (what to do if it's raining) to the ridiculous (how not to look like a tourist). But there's plenty of useful information to be gleaned.

You can also find two other elements near the back of this book. I've included an appendix — your Quick Concierge — containing lots of handy information you may need when traveling in San Francisco, like phone numbers and addresses, emergency personnel or area hospitals and pharmacies, contact information for baby-sitters, lists of local newspapers and magazines, protocol for finding taxis, and more. Check out this appendix when searching for answers to lots of little questions that may come up as you travel.

I've also included a bunch of worksheets to make your travel planning easier — among other things, you can determine your travel budget, create specific itineraries, and keep a log of your favorite restaurants so you can impress your friends or hit them again next time you're in town. The worksheets are printed on yellow paper to make them easy to find.

Icons Used in This Book

These five icons appear in the margins throughout this book:

Find out useful advice on things to do and ways to schedule your time when you see the Tip icon.

Watch for the Heads Up icon to identify annoying or potentially dangerous situations such as tourist traps, unsafe neighborhoods, budgetary rip-offs, and other things to beware of.

Look to the Kid Friendly icon for attractions, hotels, restaurants, and activities that are particularly hospitable to children or people traveling with kids.

Keep an eye out for the Bargain Alert icon as you seek out money-saving tips and/or great deals.

Part of the fun of traveling to a city other than your own is finding all the things that you can't find anywhere else — especially when so much of the landscape is dotted with chains that are the same wherever they're located. This icon highlights sights or activities that really help you get a feel for San Francisco and why it's so unique.

Where to Go from Here

Grab some sticky notes to mark the pages that you may want to refer back to later, clear your calendar, check the condition of your suitcase, and get ready to hit the road.

Part I
Getting Started

The 5th Wave — By Rich Tennant

"Yeah, I can tell you how to get there. First, you go down here to Lombard Street, then you take a right, then you take left, then you take a right, then you take a left, then you take a right..."

In this part . . .

San Francisco may appear a formidable place to visit, at least the first time, but let me assure you that it's not. The city is small and friendly, so it won't take long for you to figure out which way is which. Of course, the more you discover about any destination, the more familiar it will seem when you arrive. This part of the book is designed to "raise your comfort level," as we like to say in Northern California.

Chapter 1

Discovering the Best of San Francisco

*W*ith a wink and a wave to the past, San Francisco continues to reinvent herself. In her brief role as the heartbeat of the Internet economy, the city sashayed into the 21st century with an energy and style that caused even the old-timers to gasp in admiration. But before there was time to dump all the stock options, the bubble burst, the old-timers scrambled to diversify their portfolios, and commercial real estate brokers and Web designers returned to graduate school. Fortunately, some things stayed the same: The beautiful scenery continues to dazzle, the top-flight dining continues to garner raves, and the entertainment possibilities continue to grow in sophistication.

No matter how the economy fares, San Francisco consistently rates as one of the top tourist destinations in the world, and it's no secret why. The city's treasured cable cars provide both thrills and great views as they whiz down and around our hills; a majestically golden bridge suspends travelers over the deep blue of the bay; hidden staircases lead to lovely gardens and eye-catching homes. And where else can you savor freshly-made miniature chocolate truffles, meander down the crookedest street in the world, and escape from Alcatraz — all in one action-packed day?

The Bay Area

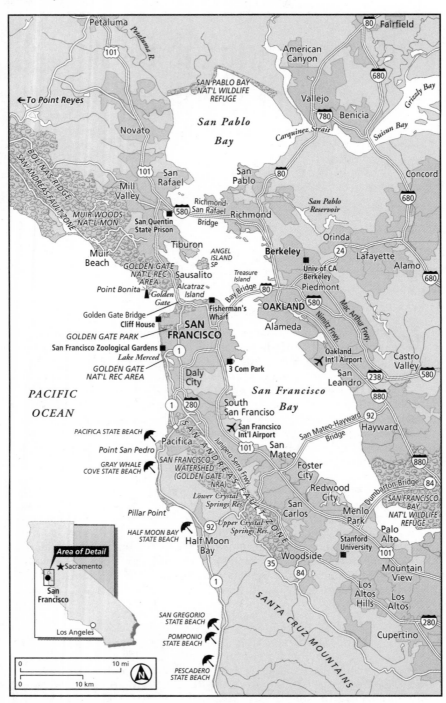

Summarizing San Francisco is not easy. When it comes to culture, we deliver everything from grand opera to leather-clad, fire-dancing performance artists. As for dining, we can down a burrito for lunch and polish off a multi-course designer meal for dinner, but critique both with equal passion. Our neighborhoods can more accurately be called villages, each with its own shopping blocks, parks, and highly distinct personalities. For in the face of rampant cultural homogeneity — the malling of America, so to speak — San Francisco is holding on tight to its individualism and enthusiastically applauds, or quietly salutes, those who do the same. What is consistent about the city, from the top of Telegraph Hill to the newly paved sidewalks of South Park, is constant surprise. As you round a bend in the road, a lovely vista unexpectedly pops into your line of sight. As you savor a glass of chardonnay, a Chinese funeral cortege may suddenly glide past your cafe table, the band playing a pop classic. Or the smell of roasting coffee beans may waft down the street and completely erase any thought but where to find an espresso.

If You Cook It, They Will Come

San Francisco's reputation as a food-lover's paradise is both well-deserved and tested on a daily basis. You can find thousands of restaurants around town, from dives to divas, all with their loyal followings and all under constant scrutiny by critics and self-proclaimed gourmands. Between the competition and the narrowed eyes of the food patrol, a restaurateur has to stay sharp, or at least hire a crackerjack public relations firm, to make it through the first year in business. The constant buzz and change in the food scene can be a little nerve-wracking to track, but it serves to make dining an event for locals and tourists alike. In the end, fortunately, it all comes down to ingredients. And where else but here do you find the freshest, most beautiful, and even the most politically correct fruits, veggies, fish, and organically raised meats? Well, Berkeley, maybe, but certainly nowhere else.

The Hills (And the Views) Are Alive

The clatter and hum of cable cars, the huffing and puffing of out-of-shape joggers, the wooden stairways leading to hidden gardens — San Francisco's famous hills are most certainly alive and well. They serve as the main attraction, as well as the backdrop, for sightseers in the city, and they've worked their way into our collective imagination through the myriad books and films that have immortalized them.

But these hills, gathered between the orange-hued **Golden Gate Bridge** and the silvery **Bay Bridge,** the hypnotic Pacific Ocean and the icy waters of the bay, are just one part of the scenery. For equally breath-taking, if less lofty, views seek out the **Palace of Fine Arts,** the **Museum of Modern Art,** or **Golden Gate Park.** Ride the streetcar down **Market**

Street to **Fisherman's Wharf** or in the opposite direction to the Giants' fabulous **baseball stadium.** Revel in the urban gardens at **Yerba Buena Center** and in the crowded sidewalks of **Chinatown.** In these places, you can catch a glimpse of what San Francisco was like during its formative years and where the city is headed in the 21st century.

The Lowdown on the After Hours

San Francisco has matured greatly from its rough and tumble years during the gold rush. There's no chance you'll get shanghaied on a boat to China any longer, nor are you apt to witness any vigilante groups patrolling the streets as they did during the Barbary Coast heydays. But if you're looking for excitement, the city still delivers. The music and club scene, especially around **North Beach** and **South of Market**, is thriving, for those who want to shimmy as well as those who prefer to groove silently with the horn section. There's no lack of places to relax and make a toast to your vacation, and theater, dance, and classical music lovers can find a great many venues in which to laugh, cry, or clap wildly. We're not exactly an all-nighter town, but we have plenty of activities to keep you occupied.

Day Trading

From the hallowed picture windows of **Union Square** to the curio-packed sidewalks of **Chinatown**, from the boutiques along **Fillmore**, **Sacramento**, and **Union streets** to the discounters of **SoMa**, if shopping is your bag, San Francisco can fill 'er up. Do you fancy fine wines? Do handmade chocolate truffles have you making promises you have no intention of keeping? Would a unique objet d'art be just the right pick-me-up for your old coffee table? This is the town for you!

Urban Renewal

San Francisco never seems to sit still. Neighborhoods are developing in areas that at best were ignored prior to the dot-com revolution. Traffic, which will forever be a problem, hasn't lightened up, but public transportation is improving and expanding. With more and more people determined to call San Francisco home, gentrification is reaching every nook and cranny with both fortunate and unfortunate consequences. Skid row as a definable geographic location is disappearing slowly, but homelessness seems entrenched. Nary a downtown street nor a median strip is empty of some poor soul holding a sign asking for handouts. Although comparing San Francisco to Calcutta, as one travel writer did, is a stretch (and a nasty dig), be prepared psychologically and/or financially — whichever suits you. Underneath it all, San Francisco stays remarkably the same — youthful, vibrant, beautiful, and a lot of fun.

Chapter 2

Deciding When to Go

● ●

In This Chapter

▶ Choosing the best season to visit

▶ Finding events that suit your interests

● ●

*Y*ou may not have much choice when it comes to scheduling your trip, especially if you have to plan around school vacations and holidays. But for those who do have some leeway, in this chapter I outline what's going on in San Francisco at different times of the year in terms of weather, crowds, and special events. The kind of weather we locals long for are days of balmy temperatures and clear skies. I can only hope you find the same, but just in case, bring a warm jacket and a hat no matter when you're visiting. And remember, a little fog never hurt anybody.

The Secret of the Seasons: When to Go and What to Do

Because of its temperate California address, San Francisco hosts tourists and business travelers year-round. However, San Francisco is the most crowded between June and October. Push spontaneity aside and plan ahead if you visit during this time of the year. In other words, make hotel and car reservations at least six weeks in advance, reserve a table at the more well-known restaurants three to four weeks in advance, and purchase your tickets to Alcatraz (see Chapter 16) before you leave home. Don't think you can arrive in the city with just a suitcase, a camera around your neck, and a bright smile. You don't want to waste your time and energy making phone calls, searching for accommodations, or waiting for a table at Slanted Door (see Chapter 14) for hours and hours.

Something to remember about the San Francisco "summer" is that it may not be the summer you're expecting. (All those people wearing shorts failed to read a guidebook like this one.) Temperatures rarely top 70 degrees Fahrenheit and are often quite cool. Bring a sweater and be prepared for fog — at any time of year.

The city is at its warmest and most glorious in September and October. In an average year, these are also the busiest months. It's when Fisherman's Wharf is packed to the gills, every cable car is overflowing with bodies, and there's not an available hotel room in sight. Don't even think about trying to get a discount on accommodations during this time.

School vacation schedules will probably dictate your travel dates if you're bringing the kids. The days start out with heavy fog in July and August but eventually clear up enough for you to lose the jacket or sweatshirt. Prepare for big crowds, especially at the most popular tourist destinations. Fortunately, a little imaginative planning can help you entertain your kids while avoiding some (though not all) of the crowds. (See Chapter 17 for some offbeat sightseeing ideas.)

During the winter, the visitors do thin out considerably. (Those seeking a tan in the winter should try Florida or maybe Singapore.) November through March, when the weather can be damp and chilly, is considered down time for tourists in San Francisco. But if you don't mind sightseeing with an umbrella, or bundled up in sweaters and a hat, you can get a great deal at a nice hotel during these months. You may even be pleasantly surprised by blue skies and low 60s temperatures in the middle of February (and no fog!). In general, room rates are lowered between November and mid-April, unless a big convention is in town (check with the **Convention and Visitors Bureau** at ☎ **415-391-2000**). A few attractions even reduce their entrance fees at this time.

Wintertime can be a great time to visit San Francisco, in spite of the weather. A good number of the larger hotels offer packages, and some have special events for kids. The Ritz-Carlton hosts a Teddy Bear Tea throughout December, a popular affair that sells out early in the season. Along with sightseeing, you can admire the Christmas windows decorating Union Square, skate around the Embarcadero Center's outdoor ice rink, and take in one of many *Nutcracker* ballet or music performances.

In the following sections, I fill you in on the good and the bad of each season. For information on average temperatures and rainfall, take a look at Table 2-1 (for Fahrenheit and inches) or Table 2-2 (for Celsius and centimeters).

Table 2-1   San Francisco's Average Temperatures (°F) and Rainfall (Inches)

	Jan	Feb	Mar	Apr	May	June	July	Aug	Sept	Oct	Nov	Dec
High	56	59	60	61	63	64	64	65	69	68	63	57
Low	46	48	49	49	51	53	53	54	56	55	52	47
Rain	4.5	2.8	2.6	1.5	0.4	0.2	0.1	0.1	0.2	1.1	2.5	3.5

Table 2-2   San Francisco's Average Temperatures (°C) and Rainfall (Centimeters)

	Jan	Feb	Mar	Apr	May	June	July	Aug	Sept	Oct	Nov	Dec
High	13	15	16	16	17	18	18	18	21	20	17	14
Low	8	9	9	9	11	12	12	12	13	13	11	8
Rain	11.5	7	6.5	4	1	0.5	0.25	0.25	0.5	3	6.5	9

Winter

You're unlikely to see snow, but the weather won't exactly be balmy either. Still, a winter visit to San Francisco has its advantages. Here are the pros and cons:

   ✓ The skies may be gray and the air damp.

But . . .

   ✓ Hotel prices will be lower, especially on weekends.
   ✓ Cable cars aren't jam-packed.
   ✓ Store windows are decorated for the holidays.
   ✓ Restaurants won't be as busy.

Spring

Spring is a popular time for travel, but in San Francisco, it's also a popular time for conventions. Here's what to expect if you're considering a springtime visit:

   ✓ Convention season starts, bringing hotel costs up.

But . . .

- ✓ Flowers are in bloom in the parks.
- ✓ The weather can be glorious.
- ✓ The major sites will be less crowded than in summer.

Summer

Many travelers are surprised at how cool and foggy San Francisco summers are. Here's what else to expect if you're planning a summer trip:

- ✓ Pier 39 and Fisherman's Wharf are madhouses.
- ✓ Hotels are packed.
- ✓ Foggy mornings are downers.

But . . .

- ✓ Mimes are out in full force.
- ✓ Kids are out of school and it's the best time to plan a family vacation.

Fall

If reliably warm, sunny days are a top priority for you, this is the best time to visit. Here are some other things to consider if you think you may want to plan your trip for the autumn months:

- ✓ Napa Valley is booked.
- ✓ The heavy events calendar lures additional crowds.

But . . .

- ✓ It's the finest weather available all year on average.
- ✓ The cultural season begins.

Mark Your Calendar

I list San Francisco's most popular special events and festivals in the following sections. However, tons of other street fairs and happenings are scheduled during the year that I don't have room to mention. For more events, check out the *Bay Guardian* Web site (www.sfbg.com), the *San Francisco Chronicle* site (www.sfgate.com), or the Citysearch Web site (www.bayareacitysearch.com), or send $3 to the Convention and Visitors Bureau for their Festivals and Special Events calendar (see the appendix). Call the phone numbers included with each event for exact dates and ticket prices.

You pay no charge for street fairs and holiday festivals, but bring along some cash for the crafts booths and food. How do you keep a festival festive? Don't drive. Parking is always impossible, and you'll just get frustrated driving around in circles. Walk, take public transportation, or if all else fails, take a cab — it's well worth the expense.

January/February

Chinese New Year, Chinatown. This is an important, well-attended, two-week event in San Francisco, with lots of free entertainment, an exciting parade, and colorful sights. Dates vary. ☎ **415-391-9680;** Internet: www.chineseparade.com.

March

St. Patrick's Day Parade, Downtown. A fair number of Irish ex-pats live in San Francisco, making St. Patrick's Day a big holiday. The parade is one of San Francisco's largest. ☎ **415-731-0924.**

April

San Francisco International Film Festival, at the Castro Theater on Castro Street and AMC Kabuki 8 Theatres at Fillmore and Post streets. This festival, one of the oldest in the United States, features more than 100 films and videos from over 30 countries. April through early May. Call for a schedule. ☎ **415-561-5000** or 415-931-FILM; Internet: www. sffs.org.

Cherry Blossom Festival, Japantown. Celebrate Japanese culture with flower arranging, sumo wrestling, traditional drumming, and a parade. Two weekends mid– to late April. ☎ **415-563-2313.**

May

Cinco de Mayo Celebration, Mission District. Festivities and a parade are held around the Mission District on the first Sunday of May. ☎ **415-826-1401.**

Carnival, Mission District. If you like crowds and scantily dressed samba dancers, this spectacle is a must-see. More than a half-million revelers turn out for this two-day celebration. Memorial Day weekend. ☎ **415-920-0125.**

June

Lesbian/Gay/Bisexual/Transgender Pride Celebration Parade, Embarcadero to Civic Center. This is a major gathering, and the parade, held on Sunday morning, is quite entertaining. Last weekend in June. ☎ 415-864-FREE; Internet: www.sfpride.org.

Ethnic Dance Festival, Palace of Fine Arts Theater, next to the Exploratorium. Three weekends of world dance and music perform-ances. ☎ 415-392-4400.

Union Street Arts Festival, on Union from Fillmore to Gough streets. Music and entertainment, food and drink, arts and crafts, yuppies — this fair has it all. First weekend in June. ☎ 415-381-8198.

North Beach Festival, Grant Street in North Beach. Come for the music, the arts and crafts, and the people-watching. Organizers claim that this festival is the oldest urban street fair in the country. ☎ 415-989-6426.

July

San Francisco Chronicle **Fourth of July Waterfront Festival,** Fisherman's Wharf. A day-long party culminating in fireworks. ☎ 415-705-5500.

August

Comedy Celebration Day, Golden Gate Park. Four hours of free chuck-les and guffaws. ☎ 415-386-5035.

A La Carte, A La Park, Sharon Meadow, in Golden Gate Park. Check out this festival for samplings from the city's best wine cellars, micro-breweries, and restaurants, and for some great music, too. Labor Day weekend. ☎ 415-459-1988.

September

Autumn Moon Festival, Chinatown. Grant Street between California and Pacific streets. This Chinese festival features moon cakes (which are round pastries with eggs inside), children's activities, and traditional dances. Dates vary. ☎ 415-982-6306; Internet www.moonfestival.org.

Latino Summer Festival, 24th Street between Mission and York streets in the Mission. A celebration of Central and South American independ-ence, with international food, arts and crafts, and four stages with live music. Date varies. ☎ 415-826-1401.

San Francisco Blues Festival, Fort Mason. Both national and local musicians perform on the Great Meadow, in the biggest outdoor blues event on the West Coast. Late September. ☎ 415-979-5588.

Folsom Street Fair, Folsom Street between 7th and 12th Streets. This adult-oriented arts-and-crafts street fair attracts the black-leather and dog-collar crowd. Usually the last Sunday in September. ☎ **415-861-3247.**

San Francisco Fringe Festival, Exit Theater and various venues downtown. A ten-day marathon of experimental theater and performance art starting the first weekend in September. ☎ **415-931-1094;** Internet: www.sffringe.org.

October

Artspan/San Francisco Open Studios. Hundreds of local artists invite the public into their studios every weekend throughout this month. Call for information, including how to obtain a studio map. ☎ **415-861-9838.**

Castro Street Fair, Market to 19th streets between Noe and Collingwood streets. Community organizations and local merchants entertain a few hundred thousand people at this street fair, which takes place in the Castro District. The first Sunday in October. ☎ **415-467-3354.**

San Francisco Jazz Festival. Held in various venues around the city, this eclectic two-week jazz fest sells out fast. Last week of October, beginning of November. ☎ **800-850-7353** or 415-788-7353; Internet: www.sfjazz.org.

November

San Francisco International Automobile Show, Moscone Center. Cars, and lots of 'em. ☎ **415-331-4406;** Internet: www.sfautoshow.com.

December

Teddy Bear Tea, Ritz-Carlton. Starting after Thanksgiving and continuing through Christmas, this event reserves fast. Reservations open in August and are recommended, especially for weekends. ☎ **415-773-6198.**

Chapter 3

Planning Your Budget

● ●

In This Chapter

▶ Figuring out the cost of things

▶ Knowing where to go for money

▶ Cutting your expenses down to size

● ●

Money may or may not make the world go 'round, but nothing spoils a vacation faster than stressing over a higher-than-expected dinner tab or running out of dough altogether. This chapter covers everything from figuring the cost of your trip to the nitty-gritty of how to obtain your cash while you're in town.

Adding Up the Elements

Creating a travel budget is easy: You write down everything that's going to incur a charge and add it up. But sticking to your budget can be difficult, especially if it's unrealistic to begin with. A worksheet at the end of this book may help you get a handle on approximately what your vacation will cost. The Bay Area is not a cheap date, and you'll likely spend the largest proportion of your funds on lodging. You can spend as lavishly as you like on food, but you can also easily eat well inexpensively. I don't recommend that you rent a car (see Chapter 9 for my reasons), so that will save a bundle. Other expenses to consider include transportation to and around the city, snacks and beverages, attractions, shopping, entertainment, and incidentals such as telephone calls. After you figure your expenses, follow my general rule and add an extra 15%. (Unless you're unusually disciplined, you won't come in under budget.)

Transportation

Most people arriving in San Francisco do so by plane or car. If you're driving, be aware that gas prices in Northern California are among the highest in the country.

The cost of things to come

Knowing what to expect ahead of time is always helpful, but especially when it comes to all things financial. Here are some average prices for goods and services you're likely to want on your trip:

- Lemonade: $1.95
- Latté in North Beach: $2.50
- 12-ounce microbeer at Blue Bar: $4
- Lunch for one at Citizen Cake (moderate): $18
- Lunch for one at Pancho Villa (inexpensive): $8
- Three-course dinner for one at Spoon (moderate): $40
- Three-course dinner for one at U.S. Restaurant (inexpensive): $21
- Super Shuttle from airport to hotel (excluding tip): $12.50
- Taxi from airport to city center (excluding tip): $35
- One-way Muni/bus fare to any destination within the city (adult): $1
- One-way Muni/bus fare to any destination within the city (senior/child): 35¢
- Movie ticket at the Metreon for an adult: $9.25
- Ticket to *Beach Blanket Babylon:* $25 to $62

Airline ticket prices depend on so many variables that I would be foolish to suggest what you'll pay to fly here. See Chapter 5 for tips on how to get the best deal, and I'll remind you now to always contact low-cost carriers, such as Southwest Airlines, that don't show up on most travel Web sites. At press time, a roundtrip flight in the summer from Raleigh/Durham to Oakland on Southwest was $428. Checking on Expedia.com, roundtrip flights from Raleigh/Durham to San Francisco started at $410. Factoring in a Southwest promotion, two roundtrips from Baltimore to San Francisco cost $430 on Southwest, whereas two tickets on American Airlines for the same cities was priced at $798. If you have time to troll the airline sites, it can pay off.

Lodging

Chapter 6 discusses everything you need to know about local hotels, but to summarize, the only bargains you'll find in this town are relative. I've included a range of rooms to suit pocketbooks large and small, but the most spartan is $65 per night in the dead of winter. From there, prices only go up, and up, and up, so keep that in mind when you sharpen your pencil.

Dining

Dining out is a big deal in the Bay Area. If your hometown is bereft of decent restaurants, budget for at least one blow-out meal. In between, study Chapter 15 for ideas on where to eat swell on the cheap.

Sightseeing

Many of San Francisco's enduring attractions are absolutely free — like the Golden Gate Bridge, the parks, the hidden staircases, and neighborhood walks — and others, such as the cable cars, are fairly inexpensive. Part V includes lots of ways to see the city without draining your bank account, and a worksheet in the back is a fine place to note which attractions you're dying to see and how much, if anything, they'll cost to experience.

Shopping

Souvenirs both annoy and inspire me. I fondly recall a small replica of the Eiffel Tower on a bookcase in my childhood home left by an older sister, but still I cluck disparagingly over the useless trinkets my family brings home from trips (and vice versa). My best suggestion is to give any kids in your party a sum of money to spend and gentle reminders that when it's gone, it's gone. Adults should pat themselves on the back for contributing to the local economy, which is much appreciated, I'm sure.

On the other hand, if you consider giving your credit card a major workout a necessary part of vacation, you've come to the right place. Plenty of upscale chains and pricey boutiques exist in San Francisco that you may not be able to find back home. Chapter 19 discusses where to shop no matter what your budget, and gives a few suggestions for finding low-cost gifts.

Nightlife

You can live large with seats for the ballet or nurse a beer in a North Beach music club for very little — it just depends on your predilections (and your budget). Chapters 21 and 22 covers some of the entertainment options and tells you where to find all the local listings.

Unearthing those hidden expenses

My credit card bill never ceases to amaze me. I often wonder where half those charges came from, then reminisce fondly about the recent past as I dig through the statement. You may not want to be reminded of your vacation in such a potentially harsh manner — better to stick with photographs — but that means paying attention to expenses that are less obvious than shelter and sustenance. For example, remember that the cost of your hotel is more than the stated room rate. A steep hotel tax of 14% is added on, plus any minibar, telephone, bar, and room service charges. Parking in San Francisco can bankrupt you. Remember, too, minor items such as film and developing; bridge tolls; SF sweatshirts times the number of people in your family who forgot to pack a jacket; and tips for the bellmen, parking garage attendants, waiters, and tour bus drivers . . . they add up quickly. Do you have to kennel your dog? May as well include that on the list.

Finding the Payment Method That's Best for You

From traveler's checks to cash to credit cards, knowing what to bring on a trip and what to leave at home is difficult. You want security, but you also want flexibility. Read on for a rundown of what each money method entails.

A check of all trades

Traveler's checks were a great invention in the days before ATMs — a sound alternative to filling your wallet with cash at the beginning of a trip because they could be replaced if lost or stolen. If you prefer the security of traveler's checks and don't mind the hassle of showing identification every time you want to cash one, you can get them at almost any bank. Here's a listing of companies to contact:

- **American Express** offers checks with service charges ranging from 1% to 4%, but AAA members can obtain checks without a fee at most AAA offices. You can also get American Express traveler's checks over the phone by calling ☎ **800-221-7282;** AmEx Gold and Platinum cardholders who call this number are exempt from the 1% fee.

- **Visa** also offers traveler's checks, available at Citibank locations across the country and at several other banks. For the location nearest you, call ☎ **800-227-6811.** The service charge ranges from 1.5% to 2%.

- **MasterCard** also offers traveler's checks. Call ☎ **800-223-9920** for a location near you.

The ABCs of ATMs

Traveler's checks are less necessary these days because most cities have 24-hour ATMs linked to a national network that most likely includes your bank at home. **Cirrus** (☎ **800-424-7787** or 800-4CIRRUS) and **Plus** (☎ **800-843-7587**) are the two most popular networks. You can look on the back of your ATM card to see which network your bank belongs to. The toll-free numbers give you specific locations of ATMs where you can withdraw money while on vacation. If you like using cash, using an ATM while in San Francisco may be the route for you. However, making several withdrawals while you're in town, so you don't have a lot of money on you at one time, may be in your best interest. Paying the $1.50 ATM fee a few times is smarter than walking through Fisherman's Wharf with a bulging wallet in the seat of your pants as an incentive for pickpockets.

Charge it!

Credit cards are invaluable while traveling: They're a safe way to carry money and they provide a convenient record of all your travel expenses when you arrive home. In a pinch, you can also get cash off your credit card with a cash advance transaction at any bank (though you'll start paying high interest charges on the advance the moment you receive the cash, and you won't receive frequent-flier miles on an airline credit card). At most banks, you can bypass the teller and go straight to the ATM for a cash advance — if you know your PIN. If you don't know your PIN, call the phone number on the back of your credit card and ask the bank to send it to you. It usually takes five to seven business days, though some banks will give you your PIN over the phone provided you give them certain information to verify your identity.

 If a problem comes up, you can reach American Express at ☎ **800-221-7282,** Citicorp Visa at ☎ **800-645-6556,** and MasterCard at ☎ **800-307-7309.**

Cutting Costs: 12 Surefire Money-Saving Strategies

If you're still worried about how you can go on vacation without going into debt, here are some tried-and-true strategies for reducing sticker shock:

✔ **Change your date of travel.** You can save big time on airfare and hotel costs if you travel during the off-season — winter or early spring. Yes, it may be cold and/or wet, but you may also luck out. Remember, we're talking California — if El Niño doesn't alter the weather patterns, maybe we'll have a drought.

✔ **Travel on off days of the week.** Airfares vary depending on the day of the week you travel: If you can travel on a Tuesday, Wednesday, or Thursday, you may find a cheaper flight. When you inquire about airfares, ask if flying on a different day is less expensive. Staying over a Saturday night can reduce airfares by more than half.

✔ **Always ask for corporate, weekend, senior citizen, or other discount rates.** Membership in AAA, frequent-flier plans, trade unions, AARP, or other groups may qualify you for discounted rates on car rentals, plane tickets, hotel rooms, and even meals. Ask about a possible discount every time you open your wallet; you may be pleasantly surprised.

✔ **Try a package tour.** For many destinations, including San Francisco, you can book airfare, hotel, ground transportation, and even some sightseeing just by making one call to a travel agent or packager, for a lot less than if you tried to put the trip together yourself. (See the section on package tours in Chapter 5 for specific suggestions of companies to contact.)

✔ **Reserve a hotel room with a kitchenette and use it.** It may not feel as much like a vacation if you have to do your own cooking, but you can save a lot of money by not eating out three times a day. Even if you only make breakfast and an occasional lunch in your room, you'll still save. And you won't have to worry about any unexpected room-service bills.

✔ **Ask whether kids stay free.** A room with two double beds usually doesn't cost any more than a room with a queen-size bed. And many hotels won't charge you the additional-person rate if the additional person is pint-sized and related to you. Even if you have to pay $10 or $15 for a rollaway bed, you can save hundreds of dollars by taking one rather than two rooms.

✔ **Find out which days attractions offer free admission.** Take advantage of free museum entry days and other free admission days.

✔ **Skip the souvenirs.** Your photographs and memories should be the best mementos of your trip. Forgo the T-shirts, key chains, salt-and-pepper shakers, and other trinkets, and save a bundle.

✔ **Don't rent a car.** The city is easily navigable on foot or by public transportation. You save a fortune on parking by not having a car, too.

✔ **Ride public transportation, such as Muni or BART.** Purchase a Muni passport and use it often (see Chapter 11).

✔ **Dine out at expensive restaurants for lunch instead of dinner.** Lunch tabs are usually a fraction of what a dinner costs at most top-notch restaurants, and the menu often boasts many of the same specialties.

✔ **Don't drink a lot of alcohol at meals.** A restaurant's wine and spirits list is a tidy profit center. Buying some wine or liquor and having a pre-dinner cocktail in your hotel room is a lot cheaper.

Chapter 4

Planning Ahead for Special Travel Needs

A h, don't you long for the good old days when you could grab a backpack, throw in a pair of jeans, and venture out into the world? Now there's the family to consider, with Junior needing to run around and let off steam every few hours, your teenage daughter needing to check out just one more store, and your spouse needing a break and maybe a beer. Or perhaps you have a physical limitation that makes traveling a challenge. Or maybe you want to take advantage of your status as an elder statesperson. Read on, friend. I like nothing better than to dispense advice.

San Francisco is already well known as a haven for gay and lesbian visitors. If you're gay or lesbian, the resources I've listed will help you find areas of the city and entertainment venues that will be of special interest to you.

Focusing on the Family

Babes in backpacks and strollers are a common sight on the streets of San Francisco, so you can be assured that munchkins are welcome here. But taking a vacation with your kids can sometimes mean *you're* not exactly on vacation, at least in my experience. Here are some tried-and-true ways to make your trip as stress-free as possible.

Looking at the trip from a kid's point of view

Before you board the plane or pack up the car, sit down with your family and this book and go over the sights and activities listed in Chapters 16 and 17. Let your kids choose three to six things to see and do (based on the number of days you plan to stay in San Francisco), and then have them rate their choices in order of preference. You do the same for the places you want to visit. Next, plot a worksheet (see the yellow pages at the back of this book) with the days or times you plan to do a kid activity and the times you plan to do something more adult-oriented, such as enjoying the Museum of Modern Art (see Chapter 16) or joining a walking tour (see Chapter 18). Block out time for eating, snacking, resting, and dropping by neighborhood parks.

Family trips are supposed to be fun, but kids turn cranky when exhaustion sets in (doesn't everybody?), so don't pull them in a hundred different directions. Neither you nor they need to see everything in one day. A long afternoon in Golden Gate Park watching the squirrels may be more memorable than dashing from Coit Tower to Alcatraz. Bring along books, paper, crayons and pencils, perhaps an inexpensive camera, a Walkman, or any other unobtrusive, portable toys and games your children can easily carry in their backpacks. Give kids their own copy of the itinerary that your family worked out together to remind them that their time will come.

Finding kid-friendly sleeps, eats, and entertainment

Most hotels are more than happy to accommodate your entire clan. Chapter 6 offers tips for figuring out what kind of accommodations are right for you and yours.

Chapter 17 describes various places to go and things to do with young kids as well as teenagers. But if you'd still like more direction, consider the itinerary in Chapter 20 or look for the new Frommer's guide *San Francisco with Kids.* And don't forget to look out for the Kid Friendly icon to point you toward hotels, restaurants, and attractions that may especially appeal to kids. You'll have no trouble planning the perfect trip for tots, teens, and in-betweens.

Locating a baby-sitter

You and your spouse or a friend may want to go out on the town without the little, or not-so-little, ones in tow. Many hotels (particularly the pricey ones) offer baby-sitting services for their guests. If yours isn't one of them, you can find a handful of agencies that will send a carefully screened sitter to your hotel. Rates vary, as do add-ons, such as transportation and agency fees, but you can expect to pay at least $63 for an evening out without the kids. **A Bay Area Child Care Agency** (☎ 650-991-7474) used by many of the downtown hotels, charges $12 per hour (four-hour minimum) for two siblings, plus a $15 agency fee. Call at least a day in advance.

Seeing San Francisco as a Senior

People over the age of 60 are traveling more than ever before, and being a senior citizen entitles you to some terrific travel bargains. If you become a member of **AARP,** you can save even more. For starters, you can get discounts on car rentals and hotels. Contact AARP at 601 E St. NW, Washington, DC 20049 (☎ **202-434-AARP**) for information on joining.

A popular resource for seniors, *The Mature Traveler* is a 12-page monthly newsletter on senior-citizen travel. Subscribe for $30 a year by writing to GEM Publishing Group, Box 50400, Reno, NV 89513-0400. GEM also publishes *The Book of Deals,* a collection of more than 1,000 senior discounts on airlines, lodging, tours, and attractions around the country. You can order it for $9.95 by calling ☎ **800-460-6676.** See also the helpful publication *101 Tips for the Mature Traveler,* available from Grand Circle Travel, 347 Congress St., Suite 3A, Boston, MA 02210 (☎ **800-221-2610** or 617-350-7500; Fax: 617-350-6206).

Seniors get automatic discounts on public transportation fares in San Francisco. Just present identification showing your age for reduced admission at movies, museums, and many other attractions. Many tour companies also offer a discount for those over 62.

Getting the Scoop for Travelers with Disabilities

Traveling can be a challenge when you're disabled, but don't let that stop you from seeing the world. There are more resources out there than ever before. Check out many of these resources with *A World of Options,* a 658-page book of resources for travelers with disabilities. For $45 you can find out about adventures from biking trips to scuba outfitters. Order it from Mobility International USA, P.O. Box 10767, Eugene, OR 97440 (☎ **541-343-1284,** voice and TTY; Internet: www.miusa.org). For more personal assistance, call the **Travel Information Service** at ☎ **215-456-9603** or 215-456-9602 (for TTY).

If you're a traveler with a disability, you can also consider joining a tour that caters specifically to travelers with your needs. Check out Flying Wheels Travel, 143 West Bridge (P.O. Box 382), Owatonna, MN

55060 (☎ **800-535-6790;** Internet: www.flyingwheelstravel.com), which offers escorted tours and cruises, as well as private tours in minivans with lifts. Another great find is FEDCAP Rehabilitation Services, 211 W. 14th St., New York, NY 10011. Call ☎ **212-727-4200** or fax 212-721-4374 for information about membership and summer tours.

If you are a vision-impaired traveler, contact the American Foundation for the Blind, 11 Penn Plaza, Suite 300, New York, NY 10001 (☎ **800-232-5463**) for information on traveling with seeing-eye dogs.

The Bay Area–based Center for Independent Living publishes a 25-page booklet called *San Francisco Access,* covering hotels, transportation options, and other information helpful to disabled travelers. You can obtain a copy for free by contacting the San Francisco Convention and Visitor's Bureau (see "Where to Get More Information" in the appendix). The organization also has a fine Web site, www.accessnca.com, with detailed information on traveling all around Northern California.

Touring on wheels

If you're a wheelchair user, you'll find San Francisco's public areas quite accessible. All sidewalks have curb cuts, and ramps for easy on/off access have been erected throughout the municipal railway system (Muni). You can find some buses equipped with wheelchair lifts as well. For specific information on public transportation accessibility, request a free copy of the **Muni Access Guide** from Muni's Accessible Services Program by phoning ☎ **415-923-6142** or writing the program at 949 Presidio Ave., San Francisco, CA 94115. If you need a ramped taxi, phone **Yellow Cab** at ☎ **415-282-3737,** ext. 240 — there's no extra charge.

Many of the major car rental companies now offer hand-controlled cars for drivers with disabilities. Avis can provide such a vehicle at any of its locations in the U.S. with 48-hour advance notice; Hertz requires notice between 24 and 72 hours in advance at most of its locations. **Wheelchair Getaways** (☎ **800-642-2042;** Internet: www.wheelchairgetaways.com) rents specialized vans with wheelchair lifts and other features for travelers with disabilities in more than 100 cities across the U.S.

Staying accessible

The Americans with Disabilities Act requires hotels built within the past 15 years to be much more handicapped-friendly. However, lodgings that are housed in old buildings may have entry stairs, tiny elevators, narrow hallways, and minuscule bathrooms, making them unsuitable for anyone having to maneuver in a wheelchair.

You can enjoy the **Tuscan Inn** near Fisherman's Wharf (see Chapter 8), which is a somewhat newer property that's fully accessible. Also, look for the chain hotels, such as the **Embarcadero Hyatt** (see Chapter 8), that are equipped to provide certain services such as TTY phones.

Let the reservation clerk at your hotel know what your needs are when making reservations to make your stay more comfortable, be it TTY phones or grip bars.

All newly built or restored restaurants are also up-to-date when it comes to meeting requirements for accessible bathrooms and entrances. If you have any doubts about access, ask when you call for a table.

Getting to the sights

You won't have any problem accessing the main attractions in San Francisco. **Golden Gate Park** is completely accommodating, as are the museums, the **Exploratorium,** and many other sites. Some areas are not very accessible, though (for example, places that have a series of stairs, such as the **Filbert Street Steps**). **Fort Point** has a wheelchair ramp, and its first floor is easily maneuverable; a walk or roll above **Fort Funston** is also accessible for travelers with disabilities.

Anyone who would prefer to admire the hills without actually trekking over them will appreciate the easy, flat walks that shun both stairs and vertical climbs detailed by **On the Level San Francisco Excursions.** The company publishes 20-page color booklets of self-guided walking tours in various neighborhoods and parks, with historical highlights and helpful hints on parking and obstacles. Each booklet is $3.95 and can be purchased online at www.onthelevelsf.com. Guided walks are also available. Call ☎ **415-776-1253** or check the Web site for information on locations and schedules.

Traveling Tips for Gay and Lesbian Visitors

San Francisco remains an important and historic destination for gay travelers. You'll find the majority of gay bars and inns in **The Castro,** the heart of San Francisco's gay community. The lesbian community resides mostly in portions of **Noe Valley** and the **Mission District** (with Valencia Street as the main drag).

Check out these great Web sites for your trip planning: www.gay.com and Citysearch (www.bayareacitysearch.com), which has a complete section devoted to gay and lesbian nightlife and an interesting history of the Castro. Also take a look at these handy print guides: *Betty and Pansy's Severe Queer Review of San Francisco,* which is updated yearly, and *The Official San Francisco Gay Guide.* You can order these books through A Different Light bookstore, 489 Castro St., San Francisco, CA

94114 (☎ **415-431-0891**) or on their Web site (www.ad1books.com). When you get to the city, pick up a copy of the *Bay Area Reporter* for comprehensive entertainment listings. It's free and available in coffeehouses, bookstores, and around the Castro.

For information on specific hotels that cater to gay visitors, check out *Frommer's San Francisco*. But there aren't any compelling reasons to plunk yourself down in such a hotel unless you don't intend to leave the Castro. And if that's the case, you'll be missing out on the alternative gay scene **South of Market** (see Chapter 22).

Part II
Ironing Out the Details

In this part . . .

Back in his student days, my husband was the kind of traveler who would blithely show up in some foreign destination without any notion of where he would sleep, expecting that something would come along. I, however, prefer the security of knowing a pillow, an airplane, or a theater seat has my name on it — so go ahead and guess which one of us does the travel planning.

The hard truth, especially for people like my devoted spouse who aren't, shall we say, detail-oriented, is that you need to consider a lot of things when it comes to planning a vacation, and most of them arise before you set foot off the airplane. This part of the book lays out your traveling options, including which airport to use if you're flying — an important decision whether you use a travel agent or let your fingers do the walking and do your own fare hunting. I also prod you to think about what you require in accommodations so you can make a good match with a hotel or motel. The other particulars — renting a car, reserving theater or sightseeing tickets, and even knowing what to pack — are covered as well.

Chapter 5

Getting to San Francisco

*T*he Internet has made it possible for anyone to play travel agent. You want to compare flight schedules and ticket prices? You want to take a virtual tour of a hotel? You want to purchase theater tickets online? Or would you rather let your local travel agent make the calls? If you do use a travel agent, make sure the agent has in-depth knowledge of the destination and isn't just reserving the hotel that will give him the largest commission. Relatives of mine (who shall remain nameless) let their travel agent recommend the hotel on their last trip to San Francisco, which turned out to be a dump. The sad look on their faces made me want to hit them over the head — with a guidebook of course.

Using a Travel Agent

Word-of-mouth is the best way to find a good travel agent — use the information someone else has already gone to the trouble of finding out. Any travel agent can help you find the basics: airfare, hotel, and rental car information. A good travel agent also stops you from ruining your vacation by trying to save a few dollars. The best travel agents have actually visited the cities you're going to and can tell you how much time you need to budget for a certain destination, find you a reasonable flight that doesn't require you to leave at 3:30 a.m. and change planes in Dallas and Denver, get you a better hotel room than you could find yourself for about the same price, arrange for a competitively priced rental car, help you deal with airlines and hotels if something goes wrong, and even give you tips on where to eat.

Take advantage of all your travel agent has to offer (and find out how much he really does have to offer about a destination) by starting out with your own research first. Read about San Francisco (you've already made a sound decision by buying this book) and choose some accommodations and attractions you're interested in. You can do extra research by getting a more comprehensive travel guide like *Frommer's San Francisco*. If you have access to the Internet, check prices on the Web in advance to get an idea of the airfare price ranges you'll encounter (see the section, "Getting the best airfare" later in this chapter for ideas). Then take your guidebook and Web information with you to the travel agent and ask him to make the arrangements for you. Travel agents have access to more resources than even the most complete Web travel site; therefore, they should be able to get you a better price than you could get by yourself. And they can issue your tickets and vouchers on the spot.

Travel agents work on commission. What's good about that is that you don't pay the commission; the airlines, accommodations, and tour companies do. What's bad about that is that unscrupulous travel agents may try to persuade you to book the vacations that give *them* the biggest kickbacks, regardless of whether they're appropriate for *you*. Recently, some airlines and resorts have begun to limit or eliminate travel agent commissions altogether. The immediate result has been that some travel agents won't take the time or trouble to book certain services unless the customer specifically requests them. Others have started charging customers fees for their services. Paying a fee isn't necessarily a bad thing: Agents who can count on a fee regardless of where they book you are more likely to have your best interests at heart. But before you hand over your money, be sure you know exactly what services that fee entitles you to, and do your research so you know if your agent is actually getting you a deal or just doing what you could have done yourself.

Evaluating Escorted Tours: Freedom or Confinement?

Do you like to let a bus driver worry about traffic while you sit in comfort and listen to a tour guide explain everything? Or do you prefer to rent a car and follow your nose, even if you don't catch all the highlights? Do you like to have events planned for each day, or would you rather improvise as you go along? The answers to these questions will determine whether you should choose the guided tour or travel à la carte.

Some people love escorted tours. The tour company takes care of all the details and tells you what to expect at each attraction. You know your costs up front, and there aren't many surprises. Escorted tours can take you to the maximum number of sights in the minimum amount of time with the least amount of hassle.

Other people need more freedom and spontaneity. They prefer to discover a destination by themselves and don't mind getting caught in a thunderstorm without an umbrella or finding that a recommended restaurant is no longer in business. That's just part of the adventure.

If you decide you want an escorted tour, think strongly about purchasing travel insurance, especially if the tour operator asks to you pay up front. But don't buy insurance from the tour operator — if they don't fulfill their obligation to provide you with the vacation you've paid for, there's no reason to think they'll fulfill their insurance obligations either. Get travel insurance through an independent agency (see Chapter 9).

When choosing an escorted tour, ask a few simple questions before you buy:

- ✔ **What is the cancellation policy?** Do you have to put a deposit down? Can the company cancel the trip if there aren't enough people? How late can you cancel if you're unable to go? When do you pay? Do you get a refund if you cancel? If the company cancels?

- ✔ **How jam-packed is the schedule?** Do they try to fit 25 hours into a 24-hour day, or will you have ample time to relax by the pool or shop? If getting up at 7 a.m. every day and not returning to your hotel until 6 or 7 p.m. sounds like a grind, certain escorted tours may not be for you.

- ✔ **How big is the group?** The smaller the group, the less time you'll spend waiting for people to get on and off the bus. Tour operators may be evasive about this, because they may not know the exact size of the group until everybody has made their reservations. But they should be able to give you a rough estimate. Some tours have a minimum group size and may cancel the tour if they don't book enough people.

- ✔ **What exactly is included?** Don't assume anything. You may have to pay to get yourself to and from the airport. A box lunch may be included in an excursion, but drinks may cost extra. Beer may be included but not wine. How much flexibility do you have? Can you opt out of certain activities, or does the bus leave once a day, with no exceptions? Are all your meals planned in advance? Can you choose your entree at dinner, or does everybody get the same chicken cutlet?

Booking Package Tours: Wrap It Up, I'll Take It

Package tours are not the same as escorted tours. They're a way of buying your airfare and accommodations at the same time, allowing you to travel independently at group prices.

For popular destinations like San Francisco, package tours can be the smart way to go. In many cases, a package that includes airfare, hotel, and transportation to and from the airport will cost less than just the hotel alone if you booked it yourself. That's because packages are sold in bulk to tour operators, who resell them to the public.

A wide variety of package options exists, so you'll have to do some research to figure out which package is right for you. Some package tours offer a better class of hotels than others. Some offer flights on scheduled airlines; others book charters. In some packages, your choice of accommodations and travel days may be limited. Some let you choose between escorted vacations and independent vacations; others will allow you to add on just a few excursions or escorted day-trips (also at discounted prices) without booking an entirely escorted tour.

Each destination usually has one or two packagers that are better than the rest because they buy in even bigger bulk. The time you spend shopping around will be well rewarded.

The best place to start looking is the travel section of your local Sunday newspaper. Also check the ads in the back of national travel magazines like *Travel & Leisure, National Geographic Traveler,* and *Condé Nast Traveler.* **Liberty Travel** (☎ 888-271-1584; Internet: www.libertytravel.com) is one of the biggest packagers in the Northeast and usually boasts a full-page ad in Sunday papers. **American Express Vacations** (☎ 800-346-3607; Internet: http://travel.american express.com/travel) is another option.

The airlines themselves are another good resource — they often package their flights together with accommodations. When you pick the airline, you can choose one that has frequent service to your hometown and the one on which you accumulate frequent-flier miles. Among the airline packages, your options include: **American Airlines Vacations** (☎ 800-321-2121; Internet: www.aavacations.com), **Continental Airlines Vacations** (☎ 888-898-9255; Internet: www.coolvacations.com), **Delta Vacations** (☎ 800-872-7786; Internet: www.deltavacations.com), and **US Airways Vacations** (☎ 800-455-0123; Internet: www.usairways vacations.com). American, in particular, tends to have good packages to San Francisco, because it's one of the airline's hubs.

The biggest hotel chains also offer packages. If you already know where you want to stay, call the hotel itself and ask if it offers land/air packages.

Going It Alone: The Independent Planner

In the following sections, I talk about planning your own trip without the aid of a travel agent.

Getting the best airfare

Competition among the major U.S. airlines is unlike that of any other industry. A coach seat is virtually the same from one carrier to another, yet the difference in price may run as high as $1,000 for a product with the same intrinsic value.

Business travelers who need the flexibility to purchase their tickets at the last minute or change their itinerary at a moment's notice, or who want to get home before the weekend, pay the premium rate, known as the *full fare.* Passengers who can book their ticket long in advance, who are able to stay over Saturday night, or who are willing to travel on a Tuesday, Wednesday, or Thursday pay the least, usually a fraction of the full fare. On most flights, even the shortest hops, the full fare is close to $1,000 or more, but a 7-day or 14-day advance-purchase ticket can be closer to $300. Obviously, it pays to plan ahead.

The airlines also periodically run fantastic sales where they lower the prices on their most popular routes. These fares have advance-purchase requirements and date-of-travel restrictions, but you can't beat the price — usually you'll pay no more than $400 for a cross-country flight. Keep your eyes open for these sales as you're planning your vacation. The sales tend to take place during the off-seasons, when travel volume is low. Don't plan on seeing a sale around the peak summer vacation months — July and August — or around Thanksgiving or Christmas, when people have to fly regardless of the airfares.

Consolidators, also known as *bucket shops,* are a good place to check for low fares. They often (though not always) offer prices that are much better than the fares you can get yourself and may be even lower than what your travel agent can get you. Scan the Sunday travel section — you can find consolidators' ads in the small boxes at the bottom of the page. Before you pay, request a confirmation number from the consolidator and then call the airline to confirm your seat. Be aware that bucket shop tickets are usually nonrefundable or rigged with stiff cancellation penalties. Keep in mind that if an airline sale is going on, or if it's high season, you can often get the same or better rates by contacting the airlines directly, so do some comparison shopping before you buy. Here are some of the most reliable consolidators:

- ✔ **Cheap Tickets (☎ 800-377-1000;** Internet: www. cheaptickets.com).
- ✔ **Fly Cheap (☎ 800-FLY-CHEAP;** Internet: www.flycheap.com).
- ✔ **Travac Tours & Charters (☎ 877-872-8221;** Internet: www. thetravelsite.com).
- ✔ **Council Travel (☎ 800-226-8624;** Internet: www.counciltravel. com). This one caters to young travelers, but their great prices are available to people of all ages.

Booking your ticket online

Surfing the Internet can be a great way to comparison-shop. Put your PC to work by letting it search through millions of pieces of data for the information you want, in the order you want it. But keep in mind that Web fares aren't always the lowest fares — always call the airline directly before booking online to find out if they have a better price on the flights you want.

Too many travel booking sites exist out there to list here, but check out a few of the more respected (and more comprehensive) ones:

- **Travelocity:** www.travelocity.com
- **Microsoft Expedia:** www.expedia.com
- **Yahoo! Travel:** http://travel.yahoo.com
- **Orbitz:** www.orbitz.com

Each site has its own unique quirks but all provide variations of the same service. All you do is enter the dates you want to fly and the cities you want to visit, and the computer looks for the lowest fares. Several other features have become standard to these sites:

- The ability to check flights at different times or dates in hopes of finding a cheaper fare
- E-mail alerts when fares drop on a route you have specified
- A database of last-minute deals that advertise super-cheap vacation packages or airfares for those who can get away at a moment's notice

You can get great last-minute deals directly from the airlines themselves through a free e-mail service called **E-savers.** Each week, the airline sends you a list of discounted flights, usually leaving the upcoming Friday or Saturday, and returning the following Monday or Tuesday. You can check out the deals on all the major airlines at the same time by logging on to **Smarter Living** (www.smarterliving.com), or you can simply go to each individual airline's Web site. These Internet sites offer schedules and information on late-breaking bargains, and allow you to book tickets.

- **Air Canada:** www.aircanada.ca
- **Alaska Airlines:** www.alaskaair.com
- **America West:** www.americawest.com
- **American Airlines:** www.aa.com
- **British Airways:** www.british-airways.com
- **Continental Airlines:** www.continental.com

✔ **Delta:** www.delta.com

✔ **National Airlines:** www.nationalairlines.com

✔ **Northwest Airlines:** www.nwa.com

✔ **Southwest Airlines:** www.southwest.com

✔ **United Airlines:** www.ual.com

✔ **US Airways:** www.usairways.com

You can fly into two airports in the Bay Area: **San Francisco International** (SFO), which is 14 miles south of downtown, and **Oakland International Airport,** which is across the Bay Bridge off Interstate 880. SFO is closer, and more airlines fly into this major hub. Oakland is smaller and easier to get in and out of, but you'll pay about 50% more for cab fares and shuttle fees. You can sometimes get a lower fare or a more convenient flight flying into Oakland, so always compare fares and travel times for each airport. Oakland also generally enjoys better weather than San Francisco. Flights are frequently delayed due to foggy conditions at SFO, a fact worth remembering as you mull over just how much reading material to bring with you on the plane.

Getting through security

In the wake of the terrorist attacks of September 11, 2001, the airline industry began implementing sweeping security measures in airports. Expect a lengthy check-in process and extensive delays. Although regulations vary from airline to airline, you can expedite the process by taking the following steps:

✔ **Arrive early.** Arrive at the airport at least two hours before your scheduled flight.

✔ **Don't count on curbside check-in.** Some airlines and airports have stopped curbside check-in altogether, whereas others offer it on a limited basis. For up-to-date information on specific regulations and implementations, check with the individual airline.

✔ **Be sure to carry plenty of documentation.** A government-issued photo ID (federal, state, or local) is now required. You may need to show this at various checkpoints. With an E-ticket, you may be required to have with you printed confirmation of your purchase, and perhaps even the credit card with which you bought your ticket. This varies from airline to airline, so call ahead to make sure you have the proper documentation. And be sure that your ID is up-to-date. An expired driver's license, for example, may keep you from boarding the plane altogether.

✔ **Know what you can carry on — and what you can't.** Travelers in the United States are now limited to one carry-on bag, plus one personal bag (such as a purse or a briefcase). The Transportation

Security Administration (TSA) also has issued a list of newly restricted carry-on items; you can find it on the Internet at www.tsa.gov, or check with your airline.

✔ **Prepare to be searched.** Expect spot-checks. Electronic items, such as a laptop or cellphone, should be readied for additional screening. Limit the metal items you wear on your person.

Using other ways to get from there to here

Don't like to fly? The following sections provide some other alternatives to getting to San Francisco.

Going by car

You can get to San Francisco by car along three major highways. **Interstate 5** runs through the center of the state. If you drive this route, you'll hit **Interstate 80,** which goes over the Bay Bridge into the city. It takes about six hours to reach San Francisco from Los Angeles along Interstate 5. The other major route you can take is **Highway 101,** which heads up from Los Angeles through San Francisco (about seven hours) to Marin County, Napa/Sonoma, and other points north. **Highway 1** is the more scenic coastal route that takes you closer to Monterey and Santa Cruz. It's really lovely, but the trip up from Los Angeles will take a lot longer — approximately eight to ten hours.

Going by train

Amtrak (☎ **800-872-7245** or 800-USA-RAIL) doesn't stop in San Francisco proper, but it does stop in Emeryville, a small town just south of Berkeley. Passengers then ride an Amtrak bus (scheduled to depart shortly after each train arrives) from Emeryville to the Ferry Building or the CalTrain station in downtown San Francisco. (The Ferry Building is more convenient to the hotels recommended in this book.)

Traveling by train may seem romantic, but don't assume it's cheaper than flying. At this writing, the lowest round-trip train fare from Los Angeles to San Francisco is $120, which is still more expensive than a 14-day advance-purchase ticket from one of the airlines serving the Los Angeles–San Francisco corridor. The trip by rail from New York (through Chicago) takes almost four days and costs anywhere from $320 to $582. But consider taking the train for the experience of chugging across the country, if you have the time, or if you're like my mother-in-law, who flunked a workshop on getting over one's fear of flying. (She wouldn't take the graduation flight the last day of class.)

Chapter 6

Deciding Where to Stay

● ●

In This Chapter

▶ Getting the rundown on the city's neighborhoods

▶ Picking out the best room for your family

▶ Securing accommodations that are right for you at the right price

● ●

*I*n a city like San Francisco, accommodations take the biggest bite out of your travel budget. If you don't stay in hotels very often, you may not know what level of service or quality of room you really need to enjoy your stay. Try to consider, among other variables, whether you really care if your room resembles something out of *Condé Nast Traveler* magazine, overlooks the bay, is vulnerable to street noise, or has a bathtub large enough for you and a close friend. Will you feel despondent if the hotel can't supply a cup of herbal tea at 10 p.m.? Will it throw off your whole day if you can't hit the treadmill first thing in the morning? Make a list of questions to ask before you call the reservations desk.

In this chapter, you can find descriptions of the various kinds of accommodations available; what the various city neighborhoods are like in San Francisco; and an idea of what to expect in the different room rate price ranges. See Chapter 8 for lists of accommodations, their range of room rates, and what neighborhoods they're located in, as well as a detailed description of each hotel.

Determining the Kind of Place That's Right for You

If you've started budgeting for your trip, you may have an idea of how much you're willing to pay for a room. Hotels come in many shapes, sizes, and price ranges. There are chain hotels, independent hotels, and hotels that serve business travelers rather than vacationers. So what is the difference between these various accommodations?

Choosing between chain hotels and independent hotels

Hotels belonging to huge chains, such as Holiday Inn, Sheraton, Marriott, and Hyatt, can sometimes be monolithic structures that are a bit on the boring side, and are usually pretty much the same wherever you go. But there's a comfort in that. For travelers who like the assurance of a well-known brand name, chains are a fine choice. In San Francisco, business people and conventioneers often make up the clientele at these hotels. Chapter 8 describes a few of the most noteworthy chain hotels, but you can find many other reliable choices in the city. The appendix at the back of this book contains a list of toll-free telephone numbers for the major chains.

Independent hotels (also called *boutique hotels*) are smaller in scope than other types of hotels and motels. They often target travelers who desire a more unique, perhaps quaint, atmosphere with a local slant. Some appeal to older couples seeking quiet and cozy budget lodgings, while other independents seek to attract a sophisticated traveler with hip furnishings and wild color schemes. San Francisco is currently a leader in the boutique hotel scene, with a great assortment to choose from. If you want more intimate surroundings, where your fellow guests may be movie fans, literati, musicians, or shopaholics, you would probably enjoy a stay in an independent hotel.

 Make sure you know what you're getting into, though — boutique hotels are not for everyone. The needs of a business traveler are typically not met at an independent hotel, and you don't always find a staff person available to answer questions or provide services. Room service is also iffy unless a restaurant is connected to the property.

Do I really get breakfast in bed?: Unpacking in a B&B

B&Bs, or bed-and-breakfast inns, can come in the form of an extra bedroom or two in a private home to a house renovated for the purpose of providing accommodations to visitors. Some B&Bs are lavishly decorated with antiques and extravagant fabrics, with an owner who prides himself on serving gourmet breakfasts and afternoon sherry. Other owners put less effort into the business, keeping some food in the fridge and engaging in casual conversation with guests about the local sites, rather than providing any official tour guidance. Accommodations at a B&B usually come with a continental or full breakfast. You may have to share the bathroom with fellow guests. Rooms at B&Bs are usually more economical than hotel accommodations, but there are a few high-end B&Bs out there with equally high-end prices.

Some small hotels advertise as B&Bs. In general, these properties have a dozen or so bedrooms, include continental breakfast with the room, and often offer wine in the afternoon.

I recommend only a few stellar B&Bs in this book, but there are plenty more in the city. For more information on bed-and-breakfasts and lists of properties, the following resources can help:

- ✔ **Bed & Breakfast International** (☎ **800-872-4500** for reservations or 415-696-1690 for information; Internet: www.bbintl.com).

- ✔ **California Association of Bed and Breakfast Inns,** 2715 Porter St., Soquel, CA 95073 (☎ **831-462-9191;** Internet: www.InnAccess.com). Their directory ($7 by mail) advertises B&Bs throughout California.

- ✔ **Bed and Breakfast Inns of Napa Valley** (☎ **707-944-4444;** Internet: www.napavalley.com/lodging/index.html). This is a great resource if you plan to take a side trip to Wine Country.

Family Ties: Choosing a Kid-Friendly Hotel

If you're taking your kids along on this trip, you have three choices: Share a room with them, rent two rooms, or rent a suite.

Sharing a room with your family means reserving a *double/double* — one room with two double beds. Double/doubles are the least expensive option and work best for a family of four with kids too young to have a room of their own. If you come to terms with the fact that you won't be staying up late, you won't be sleeping in, and life will revolve around the kids' needs, you can have a calm holiday.

Renting two rooms that are either connected by an interior door or are across the hall from each other is a great option if you have a large family or are traveling with older kids. Although you end up spending twice the money, renting two rooms ensures that you can get some R & R from the rigors of parenting, if only for a few blissful hours.

Reserving a suite may seem like an extravagant way to give yourself a little space while keeping a close eye on the children, but it's really a clever way to enjoy a high-quality hotel experience. Look at it this way: $260 buys you two rooms at the Golden Gate Hotel on Union Square, but at the Lambourne, $285 sets the nuclear family up in a two-room suite complete with a stereo system, compact kitchenette, and continental breakfast in the relaxed environs of Nob Hill.

Finding the Perfect Location

No matter where you stay in San Francisco, you're no more than 20 minutes by cab from all the major sites, shopping areas, and restaurants. The majority of the city's hotels are located in a few of the main, central neighborhoods of the city.

This book covers the best accommodations in the most convenient neighborhoods in terms of sightseeing, dining, shopping, and nightlife. Pick the neighborhood you want to stay in based on your interests and needs — for example, are you hoping to shop the major stores? Are you an enthusiastic museum-goer? Do you hope to find peace and quiet? Or do you want to be close to the bay? Whatever your lodging preferences, this chapter can help you find the perfect accommodations for you and your family. (See the index in Chapter 8 for a list of hotels in each neighborhood.)

Refer to *Frommer's San Francisco* for suggestions on accommodations in neighborhoods outside of the central part of the city that aren't covered here, or go to Citysearch on the Internet (www.bayareacity search.com), where you can search for hotels by area and price.

The following sections give you a general outline of the six most popular neighborhoods to tour and lodge in and the advantages and disadvantages of staying in each. See the "San Francisco Neighborhoods" map in Chapter 10 to orient yourself, and Chapter 16 for more on the major attractions in these areas.

Union Square

Union Square is about as convenient as it gets. You can find theaters, lots of great restaurants, fancy department stores, boutiques, and the greatest concentration of hotels in the city in varying price ranges, all within a few blocks. Chinatown, SoMa (South of Market Street), and the Financial District are within easy walking distance, and public transportation can take you just about anywhere from Union Square. Buses, Muni, BART, and the Powell Street cable cars all run through the area. You can even hail a cab from street corners in Union Square, whereas in other parts of town you usually need to call for one. Urbanites will love it.

The square itself is a welcome bit of green space that tops the very first underground garage in the U.S. A $25-million renovation, which should be finished by the time you read this, is designed to make Union Square much more inviting than in the past. Features will include a central plaza with a stage for live performances, a cafe, the TIX Bay Area outlet for half-price tickets, palm trees, and gardens.

On the down side, be prepared for heavy traffic. Hotel rooms are generally quiet, but you can often hear emergency vehicle sirens piercing through the walls. Most of the hotels are in older buildings, which lends a lot of charm; however, this means that the rooms and baths often are somewhat small. Parking in the area costs $18 to $30 a day.

Although Union Square sits next to the Tenderloin, a low-income neighborhood of immigrant families, druggies, and the down-and-out, the area is basically safe, as are most neighborhoods in San Francisco (see the appendix for more information on safety). Because of the many locals and tourists out and about, you do see plenty of street people and vagrants looking for handouts. Pickpockets can be a problem in the area, and women are advised to avoid walking around unescorted at night. Certain sections of the Tenderloin should be avoided any time of the day or night.

The benefits of staying in Union Square include the following:

- ✔ Chinatown is around the corner.
- ✔ You have dining, shopping, and nightlife all in one place.
- ✔ Public transportation is excellent.

But here are the drawbacks:

- ✔ You're right near the Tenderloin.
- ✔ The traffic is horrendous.
- ✔ The panhandling can get on your nerves.

Nob Hill

Just above Union Square is Nob Hill, which boasts beautiful, upper-crust residential apartments and the majestic Grace Cathedral. You can find the swanky Pacific Heights neighborhood (home to the Gettys and author Danielle Steele) to the west. A small selection of plush hotels cascades down the hill toward the Financial District, along with the California Street cable car line.

Nob Hill accommodations are pricey, with good reason. They offer a quiet, sophisticated, residential atmosphere that contrasts with the hustle and bustle of Union Square and Fisherman's Wharf. Here you see well-dressed business travelers and tourists going about their business, in contrast to the panhandlers and down-and-outers hanging around Market Street. Nob Hill is also quite safe, even at night. Although you may be walking up and down very steep grades, Nob Hill is really just a short stroll from Union Square. Muni buses and the California Street cable car provide any needed public transportation connections. And access to some of the city's finest bars and restaurants is often just an elevator ride away. Nob Hill streets also offer breathtaking views of downtown.

The benefits of staying in Nob Hill include the following:

- ✔ The area is very safe.
- ✔ It's more peaceful and residential than Union Square.

But here are the drawbacks:

- ✔ You need to be in good physical condition to walk up and down the hills.
- ✔ It's very expensive.
- ✔ Fewer shops and restaurants are nearby.

SoMa

The George Moscone Convention Center, on Howard Street between Third and Fourth, pioneered the renaissance of a major section of downtown. South of Market Street, or SoMa for short, particularly between Second and Fifth streets, has exploded in the past ten years with new hotels, restaurants, and cultural and entertainment stops.

Moscone Center is one part of the larger Yerba Buena Gardens. An entertainment hub set among lovely landscaping and fountains, it was fortified by the opening of Sony Corporation's Metreon (see Chapter 16); Zeum, an extremely cool technology center for older kids; an indoor ice-skating rink; and a bowling alley. San Francisco's Museum of Modern Art on Third Street (see Chapter 16) and the Cartoon Art Museum on Mission between Second and Third streets (see Chapter 17) add a dollop of culture to the festivities. Throughout SoMa, restaurants can't seem to debut fast enough.

Still, vestiges of the old neighborhood remain. Nearby Sixth Street is the purview of seedy residential hotels and corner stores specializing in extremely cheap wine. Market Street itself is pretty depressing west of Sixth Street — a combination of low-rent tourist shops, peep shows, and check-cashing counters, combined with a few legitimate theaters. The farther south you venture toward I-80, the more industrial things get. And you're competing for space in hotels with thousands of guys wearing plastic nametags and rushing to Moscone for that panel discussion on skeletal malocclusions.

The benefits of staying in SoMa include the following:

- ✔ It's the center for cutting-edge art and performance.
- ✔ You can find lots of worthy ways to spend time.
- ✔ There are some great restaurants and clubs.

But here are the drawbacks:

- It still has a fringe element about it.
- The hotel choices are limited.
- You get lots of convention traffic.

The Embarcadero

Once cut off from civilization by the cement pylons of the Embarcadero Freeway, which was damaged by the 1989 Loma Prieta earthquake and subsequently torn down, the Embarcadero now glows in the light reflected off the waters of the bay. The views along the lovely stretch of road that wraps around the northeast side of the city are some of the most sigh-inducing — the Bay Bridge soars above you, Alcatraz seems a mere stone's throw away, and on sunny weekends sailboats blissfully glide around the bay.

This is a very safe area and is generally quiet in the evenings, except during rush hour, when it's a major thoroughfare for bridge traffic. The most popular activities at the Embarcadero consist of promenading slowly down Herb Caen Way (a stretch of sidewalk near the Ferry Building named for the *San Francisco Chronicle*'s legendary columnist), jogging, biking, skateboarding, and any number of other outdoor activities. You won't feel the pulse of the town as distinctly as you do at Union Square, but don't think there isn't a good time to be had. Some of the hottest kitchens around town are based here, and you can find music and nightlife in unexpected venues.

Locals trek to the Embarcadero Center, a collection of five multi-use buildings connected by bridges and walkways, to check out the upscale chain stores and movie theaters. You can catch BART and Muni streetcars from the Embarcadero underground station to just about anywhere. A Muni extension from the Embarcadero to the CalTrain station rolls down past the magnificent new downtown ballpark, and charming old streetcars now breeze all the way down Market Street to Fisherman's Wharf and back. As for accommodations, the hotels are expensive and few and far between. And the neighborhood's popularity means continued building and remodeling around the waterfront, which, unfortunately, adds noise and confusion along the boulevard.

The benefits of staying in the Embarcadero include the following:

- It has beautiful bay views.
- It's a great location for strollers and joggers.
- Public transportation options are excellent.
- It's convenient to shopping and dining.

But here are the drawbacks:

- ✔ Rush-hour traffic is heavy.
- ✔ Hotel choices are limited (and expensive).
- ✔ Walks to other neighborhoods are relatively long.

North Beach/Fisherman's Wharf

Although just a few blocks separate North Beach from Fisherman's Wharf, the two neighborhoods are as different from one another as focaccia is from sourdough. North Beach is the most European of any neighborhood in town, and the one in which I'd most like to wake up. Ducking into a cafe for a latté, choosing a pastry from any number of Italian bakeries, watching elderly Chinese practicing T'ai Chi in Washington Square Park — what a heavenly way to pass the morning. Stores sell goods you haven't already seen a thousand times over, and the food is divine and diverse.

And then there's Fisherman's Wharf. I suppose 13 million tourists can't all be wrong, but just between you and me, I don't get it. Once it was the center of the city's harbor and fishing industries. Now, waterfront life is limited to a few sport-fishing boats, and tourist attractions have taken over. A group of chain hotels huddle around Northpoint Street, about two blocks off the Hyde Street cable car turnaround. A walk west along the waterfront, through the most tourist-oriented section, ends at the delightful Aquatic Park, but along the way, you pass a gauntlet of T-shirt emporiums, fast-food eateries, knick-knack shops, and beggars, one of whom camouflages himself with branches and jumps out at unsuspecting pedestrians — I kid you not.

As you may guess, prices are slightly lower in both North Beach and Fisherman's Wharf, but so is the safety factor. Watch your wallet, particularly around Fisherman's Wharf. Auto break-ins are also a problem. Depending on the weather, North Beach can be raucous during the evenings, and blocks of Broadway pulsate with bars and girlie clubs. Parking in either district is impossible unless you head for the nearest garage, which can get expensive.

The benefits of staying in Fisherman's Wharf/North Beach include the following:

- ✔ You can navigate your way through either location on foot.
- ✔ You can find plenty of great meals in North Beach.
- ✔ You have access to convenient public transportation.

But here are the drawbacks:

- ✔ You're surrounded by tourists on Fisherman's Wharf.

> ✔ The parking is a nightmare.
>
> ✔ Hotel choices are limited.

The Marina/Cow Hollow

If you're driving to San Francisco or renting a car while you're here, this neighborhood has its advantages. Outdoorsy types love the location, which is close to the Presidio and Crissy Field. Most, but not all, of the accommodations here include free parking. You can walk to several great sights from the Marina/Cow Hollow area, including the Exploratorium, the Palace of Fine Arts, and the Golden Gate Bridge. Nearby Union Street, with its trendy shops, offers a decent assortment of good restaurants and a movie theater, and Chestnut Street is only a block away, with more of the same. This is a good neighborhood for families, because the prices are more reasonable than in more tourist-oriented areas.

The downside of staying here is also the location. Most of the lodgings in the area are motels along Lombard Street, a four– to six-lane conduit to the Golden Gate Bridge and Van Ness Avenue and the busiest street in the city. Most visitors find the traffic horrendous in this area. There are a few hotels off the main drag (I review a few in Chapter 8), but pickings are lean.

The benefits of staying in the Marina/Cow Hollow include the following:

> ✔ It's near Chestnut and Union Street shopping.
>
> ✔ Hotel/motel parking is usually free.
>
> ✔ It's within walking distance of the Marina and the Golden Gate Bridge.

But here are the drawbacks:

> ✔ Accommodation choices are limited to motels and B&Bs.
>
> ✔ Traffic is heavy on Lombard Street.
>
> ✔ The immediate surroundings are less scenic.

Getting the Most for Your Money

Every accommodation that I recommend in this book is marked with one to four dollar signs. Here's a quick breakdown of the price categories, and what amenities and services you should expect in each range. All rates are for a standard double-occupancy room, excluding taxes.

> ✔ **$ (under $125):** Accommodations in this category are often in older buildings that may show their age. Room service, valet parking, and porters do not come with the package; but the rooms are carefully

tended, and the properties themselves exhibit some charm. The least expensive rooms may not have their own bathrooms.

The rooms I recommend in this price category tend to be on the "cozy" side and are typically furnished with inexpensive bed-spreads, towels, and curtains. You won't find hair dryers, little toiletries, or robes in the closet. Air-conditioning is also considered a luxury, although you rarely need it in mild San Francisco. A concierge won't be at the ready to cater to your every whim, but most desk clerks are delighted to help you arrange tours, tickets for shows, and dinner reservations. Many of the budget hotels recommended in this book offer a free continental breakfast, making them especially good deals.

✔ **$$ ($125–$175):** In this price category, I recommend some wonderful, charming places with stylish (but still small) rooms, handsome lobbies, and good to great service. Antique armoires and marble-tiled bathrooms are standard-issue in a few picks, but in general, these properties are for leisure travelers with minimal demands beyond comfort and an appealing decor. A separate concierge desk is not always available, but the front desk staff is usually willing to make reservations and book tours. Parking is sometimes valet, but more often it's self-parking at lots up to three blocks away. Room service is usually nonexistent. Make sure to inquire about extras such as bathrobes and modem lines if these things are important to you. Often the more expensive suites are well-equipped, but the low-end rooms won't have that all-important hair dryer unless you ask for it.

✔ **$$$ ($175–$300):** At this price, expect attentive service — usually including valet parking and porters — and larger rooms with finer fabrics and decor. Many properties in this range also have on-site Stairmasters, and at least one has a pool. Although at the low end of this scale you may not find hand-milled soaps in the bathroom, at the high end, you will feel pretty pampered.

When you're willing to pay this kind of money for a hotel, you probably have certain expectations. Make them known when you make your reservation. Don't wait until check-in to ask if you can receive faxes or if valet parking actually means a bellhop is going to fetch your car for you at 6 a.m.

✔ **$$$$ ($300+):** Your big bucks buy views, personal service, and tasteful decor. Be prepared to be royally pampered by the well-trained staff. Large rooms usually feature fancy products and thick terry robes in the mirrored bathroom, an iron in the closet, art on the walls, and in some cases, umbrellas and flowers. Honor bars and baskets of overpriced goodies are also standard. For this much money, it would be a shame if you didn't spend some quality time in the hotel, fingering the drapes and calling down to the concierge desk for a weather report. Again, room rates are tied to location, with Nob Hill and the Embarcadero charging whatever the market will bear.

Chapter 7

Booking Your Room

● ●

● ●

This chapter covers a few strategies for obtaining a better room for your money. Frankly, you can get all the service and style you want if price is no object. But when it is, as is usually the case, a little advice for chatting up the reservations desk is always handy. Charm is useful; being completely clear about your expectations is just as important.

Uncovering the Truth about Rack Rates

The *rack rate* is the maximum rate that a hotel charges for a room. If you walked in off the street and asked for a room, the rack rate is the amount you would be billed. The hotel usually posts the rate on the back of your door, along with the fire/emergency exit diagrams.

Hotels will be delighted to charge you the rack rate, but you often don't have to pay it, especially if the hotel isn't full. The best way to avoid this is surprisingly simple: Just ask for a cheaper or discounted rate when you book. Things like special weekend rates or AAA and AARP discounts can add up to big savings, so don't be afraid to ask. If your timing is right and business is slow, you may be pleasantly surprised.

Getting the Best Room Rate

Make sure you cover all the bases. Sometimes you can get the best rate through the hotel's toll-free central reservations number, but sometimes the local manager will run a discount or promotion that central reservations doesn't know about, and it's better to call the hotel directly. Your best bet is to call both and see which one offers a better deal.

A travel agent may be able to negotiate a better price with certain hotels than you can yourself. (This is because the hotel often gives the agent a discount in exchange for steering his or her business toward that hotel.) And don't forget to do some searching on the Internet — sometimes hotels offer special discounts if you book online.

When budgeting for hotel rates, watch out for hidden fees and extra costs. Knowing things up front is better than getting stuck later. The following sections discuss expenses to look out for.

Dealing with taxes

A hotel room that costs $99 a night actually will end up closer to $114 because of the 14% hotel tax tacked onto the bill. It's steep, but it's unavoidable. Room service charges can also inflate your final room tab. Local phone calls, minibars in your room, enticing baskets of goodies on an end table — none of these are gratis. If you like to snack in bed, buy your favorite goodies at a nearby market or convenience store and bring them up to your room.

Don't forget that most hotels tack on a fee for merely dialing out on the phone in your room. This starts at 75¢ and increases depending on what the market will bear. This is, of course, in addition to long-distance charges. For dinner reservations or event tickets, let your hotel concierge do the talking.

Selecting the right season

Officially, the low season in San Francisco is from November to March, but one highly experienced downtown concierge joked that the low season was the weekends (when business travelers leave town). Although more tourists do visit between spring and early fall, your actual concerns should center around business travelers. The San Francisco Convention and Visitors Bureau keeps a calendar of major conventions, and I recommend checking with them before you finalize your plans (see Chapter 10). Hotels and restaurants around Union Square and SoMa are always packed when Moscone Center is booked.

Generally, you'll get your best rate on a room in the winter, on weekends when the suits go home, and around holidays when you're actually supposed to be at Cousin Seymour's and not gallivanting around San Francisco. Don't let that discourage you from arriving whenever it's convenient for you, however. Just make your reservations far in advance.

As room rates change with the season (and the economy), occupancy rates rise and fall. A hotel is less likely to extend discount rates if it is close to full, but it absolutely will negotiate if it's close to empty. Tourist-oriented hotels usually offer discounted rates for midweek stays because they're usually most crowded on weekends. The reverse is true for business hotels in downtown locations. Wine Country hotels tend to charge the most in the fall, around harvesttime, and on weekends during the summer. Rates listed in this book may be different than the actual rate you're quoted when you make your reservation, because room prices are subject to change without notice. In addition, discounts for membership in AAA, AARP, frequent-flier programs, and other corporate rewards programs can change room rates significantly regardless of the season.

Getting the Room You Deserve

After you've made your reservation, asking one or two pointed questions can go a long way toward making sure you have the best room in the house.

- ✔ **Is there a corner on the market?** Ask for a corner room. They're usually larger, quieter, closer to the elevator, and have more windows and light than standard rooms, and they don't always cost any more.

- ✔ **What's that noise?** Inquire about the location of the restaurants, bars, and discos in the hotel — these could all be a source of irritating noise. The quietest rooms tend to be on the highest floors, facing away from the street.

- ✔ **Are you renovating?** If the hotel is renovating, request a room away from the jackhammers. And try to get a room on the most recently renovated floor — the furnishings and decor are likely to be newer and nicer.

- ✔ **Does this room come in another color?** If you aren't happy with your room when you arrive, talk to the front desk. If they have another vacancy, they should be happy to accommodate you, within reason.

- ✔ **What kind of beds do you have?** If having a queen or king bed is important to you, be sure to ask for it when booking.

- ✔ **Mind if I smoke?** You can smoke outside in San Francisco to your heart's content, but be aware that the city has stringent anti-smoking laws inside public buildings, restaurants, and even bars. A sizable number of hotels, especially the smaller ones, are completely smoke-free. Other hotels only have smoking rooms on designated floors. Common courtesy in the Golden Gate city is to ask before getting ready to light a cigarette; you'd be surprised at the number of people who are allergic to smoke. If a smoking (or non-smoking) room is important to you, let the reservations desk know when you call.

Surfing the Web for Hotel Deals

The Web can be a good resource for hotel deals, but in my humble opinion, you usually get the best rate and the most accurate information by calling the hotel directly. No matter what assurances you receive from online agencies, hotel agency Web sites *cannot* guarantee specific rooms (unless, perhaps, you asked for the bridal or presidential suite), and they really know very little about the hotel they're selling. In many cases, the "reviews" you read online are provided and paid for by the hotels and, therefore, are likely to be promotional rather than critical. Another problem recently brought to my attention is the difficulty in getting a refund from some of these reservation services if you have to cancel your stay. It's the service, not the hotel, that has your money until they settle with the hotel sometime after you've checked out. Finally, there may be a difference between the amount of dough you pay the agency for your room and the amount the agency pays the hotel (that's the profit motive for you). If you don't like the place, again, you're stuck negotiating for a refund from the online agency rather than the hotel itself.

Having said all that, you can sometimes get a good deal by booking through a lodging agency Web site. Although the major travel Web sites (such as Travelocity, Expedia, Yahoo! Travel, and Cheap Tickets) offer hotel booking, you're often better off using a site devoted primarily to lodging, because you may find properties that aren't listed with more general online travel agencies. Some lodging sites specialize in a particular type of accommodation, such as bed-and-breakfasts, which you won't find on the more mainstream booking services. Others, such as TravelWeb (see the following list), offer weekend deals on major chain properties, which cater to business travelers and have more empty rooms on weekends. But don't assume that the hotels offered on the sites are all in handy, safe neighborhoods or offer the amenities you want. These sites merely list the properties; they don't judge them.

Check out these hotel-lodging sites on the Web:

- ✔ The name **All Hotels on the Web** (www.all-hotels.com) is something of a misnomer, but the site *does* have tens of thousands of listings throughout the world. Bear in mind that each hotel has paid a small fee (of $25 and up) to be listed, so it's less an objective list and more like a book of online brochures.

- ✔ **Hoteldiscount!com** (www.180096hotel.com) lists bargain room rates at hotels in more than 50 U.S. and international cities. The cool thing is that hoteldiscount!com pre-books blocks of rooms in advance, so sometimes it has rooms — at discount rates — at hotels that are "sold out." Select a city, input your dates, and you get a list of best prices for a selection of hotels. This site is notable for delivering deep discounts in cities where hotel rooms are expensive. The toll-free number (☎ **800-364-0801**) is printed all over this site; call it if you want more options than are listed online.

✔ **InnSite** (www.innsite.com) has B&B listings in all 50 U.S. states and more than 50 countries around the globe. You can find an inn at your destination, see pictures of the rooms, and check prices and availability. This extensive directory of bed-and-breakfasts only includes listings if the proprietor submitted one (getting an inn listed is free). The descriptions are written by the innkeepers, and many listings link to the inn's own Web sites. Try also the **Bed and Breakfast Channel** (www.bedandbreakfast.com).

✔ **Places to Stay** (www.placestostay.com) lists one-of-a-kind places in the U.S. and abroad that you may not find in other directories, with a focus on resort accommodations. Again, listing is selective — this isn't a comprehensive directory, but it can give you a sense of what's available at different destinations.

✔ **TravelWeb** (www.travelweb.com) lists more than 26,000 hotels in 170 countries, focusing on major chains, and you can book almost 90 percent of these online. TravelWeb's Click-It Weekends, updated each Monday, offers weekend deals at many leading hotel chains.

Finally, always examine the hotel's own Web pages. I found a terrific deal on the site of one of my favorite hotels, and the price was $40 a night less than what the reservations clerk offered me over the phone.

Traveling without Reservations

I am constantly amazed at how many travelers come to San Francisco without hotel reservations, believing that a fabulous $30-a-night room is awaiting them in a fancy hotel. They usually end up sleeping in the "No-Tell Motel" in a dicey neighborhood because that's all that was available. Or they spend the better part of a day looking for accommodations, wasting valuable vacation time searching for a bargain, or finally, just a room, when there are none to be had. Don't be one of them. Plan your vacation lodgings ahead of time.

But if you disregard my advice about making advance reservations, you can try the following suggestions if you get stuck:

✔ Call a free reservation service such as **SF Reservations** (☎ **888-782-9673** or 415-974-4499 outside of North America) or **California Reservations** (☎ **415-252-1107**).

✔ Make your way to a full-service boutique hotel and hope the desk clerk takes pity on you. Most of the boutique properties in town are part of small, independent chains, and a good-hearted staff person may be willing to make some calls to sister hotels to help you secure a room.

✔ Find a friendly concierge you can leave your luggage with so you can look for a room in the neighborhood unencumbered. If the town appears to be booked solid (ask the desk clerk's opinion), don't be picky or cheap if you find a room you don't love or that's over your budget. You can always move the next day if something better opens up.

Chapter 8

Your Home Away from Home

In This Chapter
▶ Locating the perfect San Francisco hotel
▶ Finding a room when there's no room anywhere else

So, you're ready to make San Francisco your home, for a short period of time at least. You probably have an idea of how much money you want to spend (if not, check out Chapter 3), and you may have an idea what neighborhood suits your fancy (see Chapter 6 for descriptions). Other features and amenities may be important to you, too. Take a look at the following reviews to discover which hotel is the one for you.

The hotel selections in this chapter are, in my opinion, among the best accommodations in San Francisco — balancing comfort, location, character, and price. With few exceptions, each has a distinct, only-in–San Francisco style I believe you'll find memorable and pleasing. For those traveling on frequent-flier miles, you won't find a lot of the big chain hotels listed here, but there are plenty located throughout the city; turn to the appendix for toll-free numbers and Web sites. I've also left out the majority of hotels on less desirable blocks, many of the priciest palaces, as well as those a bit too far from the action. Finally, three well-known hotels are listed that I actually don't love, but I include them for reasons mentioned in the write-ups. (For a more complete rundown of places to stay, see *Frommer's San Francisco*.)

The rack rates I give do not include the 14% hotel tax. And those outrageous valet garage prices are per day. Many of these hotels offer weekend discounts and other packages. Before you book, always ask if there are any specials, packages, or promotions going on that may get you a better rate.

See the indexes at the end of this chapter for lists of recommended hotels organized by neighborhood and price.

Unlike in resort destinations, few hotels in San Francisco offer special kids' programs or amenities. The hotels that I've designated as Kid Friendly are the ones that are a good choice for families because of room size, location, or their willingness, in my experience, to accommodate my family's needs and make us feel welcome.

San Francisco Accommodations

The Andrews Hotel **24**
The Argent Hotel **36**
Campton Place **35**
The Cartwright Hotel **20**
Chancellor Hotel **19**
Clift **30**
Commodore Hotel **25**
Edward II Inn **2**
Embarcadero Hyatt Regency **41**
Galleria Park Hotel **38**
Golden Gate Hotel **14**
Handlery Union Square Hotel **31**
Harbor Court Hotel **43**
Hotel Bijou **32**
Hotel Bohème **9**
Hotel Del Sol **4**
Hotel Griffon **42**
Hotel Juliana **39**
Hotel Milano **33**
Hotel Monaco **29**
Hotel Palomar **34**
Hotel Rex **15**
Hotel Triton **40**
Hotel Vintage Court **16**
The Huntington Hotel **12**
Inn at Union Square **21**
Kensington Park Hotel **22**
The Marina Inn **5**
The Marina Motel **1**
The Maxwell **27**
Nob Hill Lambourne **11**
The Orchard Hotel **17**
Petite Auberge **13**
Ritz-Carlton **10**
San Reno Hotel **7**
The Sheehan Hotel **23**
Sir Francis Drake Hotel **18**
Tuscan Inn **6**
Union Street Inn **3**
W **37**
Warwick Regis **26**
Washington Square Inn **8**
Westin St. Francis **28**
White Swan Inn **13**

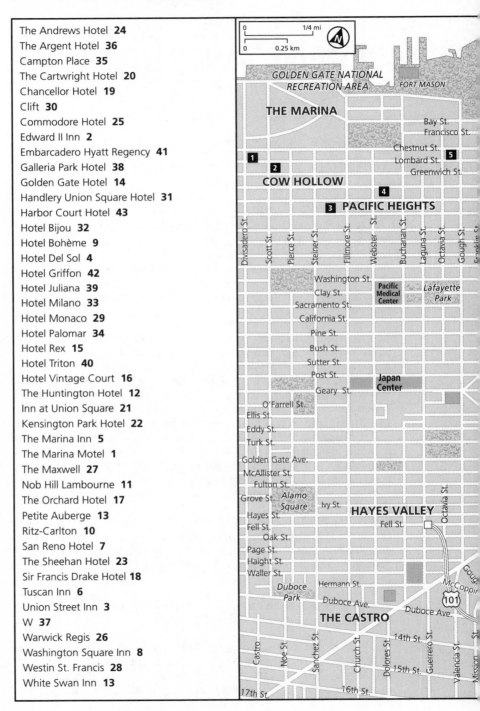

Hotel Highlights: From Uptown to Downtown and All Points in Between

Andrews Hotel

$–$$ **Union Square**

The services and location make this 48-room, 1905 Victorian hotel a deal for couples on a budget, although the rooms and baths are pretty small. You get continental breakfast and evening wine gratis, and an attractive, homey, wood-trimmed decor. Amiable receptionists serve double duty as concierge staff. You won't have movie channels, air-conditioning, or many other amenities, but you can open the windows. Consider spending the extra $20 per night on a sunny Bay King room like #403. Avoid the dark, tiny rooms ending in 08.

624 Post St., between Taylor and Jones streets, two blocks west of Union Square. ☎ *800-926-3739 or 415-563-6877. Fax: 415-928-6919. Internet:* www.andrews hotel.com. *Self-parking: $20. Rack rates: $105–$155. Ask about AARP and extended-stay discounts. AE, DC, MC, V.*

The Argent Hotel

$$$–$$$$ **SoMa**

This is a big, run-of-the-mill convention hotel with larger-than-average rooms and all the extras you'd better receive for the price — irons, hair dryers, quality bath products, and so on. What really earns it a place in this chapter, besides its location, are the nearly floor-to-ceiling windows with great views in rooms above the 14th floor. A fitness center, sauna, and pretty garden also help raise The Argent beyond the ordinary. Off-season rates can be exceptionally low.

50 Third St., near Market Street. ☎ *877-222-6699 or 415-974-6400. Fax: 415-543-8268. Internet:* www.argenthotel.com. *Parking: $38. Rack rates: $265–$305. Check Web site for deals. AE, DC, DISC, JCB, MC, V.*

Campton Place

$$$$ **Union Square**

The harpsichord music piped into Campton Place's classically decorated lobby tells you right away that this is one genteel hotel. The atmosphere is intimate, clubby, and reserved — you'll want to use your company manners as the valet unpacks your bags and shows off the many luxury amenities (a Bose sound system, for one). You can even bring your dog (if he's well-behaved). The restaurant has been the recipient of many awards and kudos — you may want to eat here even if you stay elsewhere.

340 Stockton St., at Post Street. ☎ *800-235-4300 or 415-781-5555. Fax: 415-955-5536. Internet:* www.camptonplace.com. *Parking: $28. Rack rates: $335–$460. AE, DC, DISC, JCB, MC, V.*

Chancellor Hotel
$$ Union Square

This 137-room hotel has been owned and managed by the same family since 1917 and offers a level of intimacy and value you just won't find in many other comparable inns. It's also right on the Powell Street cable car line, a handbag's throw from Saks Fifth Avenue. The little bathrooms are well-stocked; the petite bedrooms are brightly decorated and comfortably furnished; and you get a choice of pillows. For views, request front rooms ending in 00 to 05. Amenities include ceiling fans (instead of air-conditioning) and cookies at the front desk. Smoking is not allowed.

433 Powell St., between Post and Sutter streets. ☎ *800-428-4748 or 415-362-2004. Fax: 415-362-1403. Internet:* www.chancellorhotel.com. *Parking: $25. Rack rates: $163. AAA, AARP discounts available. AE, DC, DISC, MC, V.*

Clift
$$$$ Union Square

This is not your father's Clift Hotel, and if you loved the old girl, you're in for a shock. An Ian Schrager/Phillippe Starck renovation in 2000 may have kicked the venerated Clift into the 21st century, but thanks for nothing, fellas. Once known for fabulous service and a classy, San Francisco aura, the new Clift exhibits neither. The post-modern guest rooms lack warmth (and at these prices deserve roomier baths) and, strangely enough, the focal points of the white interiors are orange Lucite nightstands. There are a few amusing details in the lobby and bar, but the Redwood Room is a pale imitation, with sulky 20-somethings crowding the bar. I thought you ought to know.

495 Geary St., at Taylor Street. ☎ *800-652-5438 or 415-775-4700. Fax: 415-441-4621. Internet:* www.ianschragerhotels.com. *Parking: $30. Rack rates: $325–$530; suites $455 and up. AE, CB, DC, MC, V.*

Commodore Hotel
$–$$ Union Square

Colorful but diminutive rooms and bathrooms give a boost to an older building that shows some signs of wear. And this section of Sutter Street is just close enough to the Tenderloin to put me on alert for drug dealers and prostitutes. Still, the location doesn't discourage European tourists, who appreciate the excellent value and relaxed vibe. It's just three flat blocks from Union Square, so food and entertainment are near at hand. The Titanic Cafe is on one side of the building, and the fun, trendy Red Room bar is on the other. No air-conditioning.

Accommodations Near Union Square, SoMa & Nob Hill

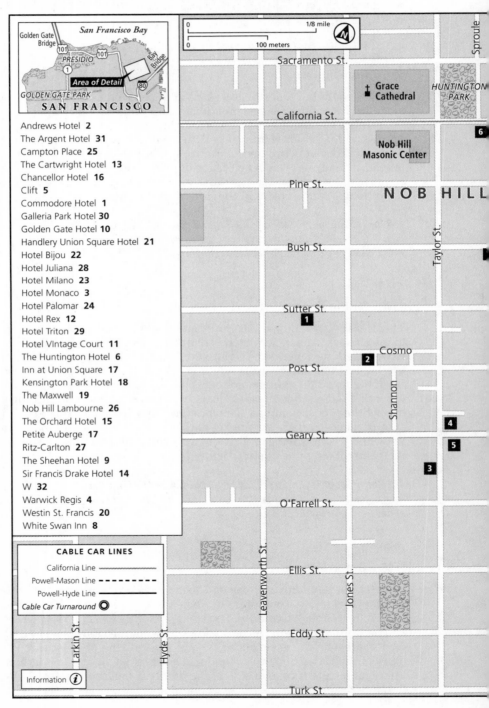

San Francisco Bay

Golden Gate Bridge

PRESIDIO

Area of Detail

GOLDEN GATE PARK

SAN FRANCISCO

Andrews Hotel **2**
The Argent Hotel **31**
Campton Place **25**
The Cartwright Hotel **13**
Chancellor Hotel **16**
Clift **5**
Commodore Hotel **1**
Galleria Park Hotel **30**
Golden Gate Hotel **10**
Handlery Union Square Hotel **21**
Hotel Bijou **22**
Hotel Juliana **28**
Hotel Milano **23**
Hotel Monaco **3**
Hotel Palomar **24**
Hotel Rex **12**
Hotel Triton **29**
Hotel Vintage Court **11**
The Huntington Hotel **6**
Inn at Union Square **17**
Kensington Park Hotel **18**
The Maxwell **19**
Nob Hill Lambourne **26**
The Orchard Hotel **15**
Petite Auberge **17**
Ritz-Carlton **27**
The Sheehan Hotel **9**
Sir Francis Drake Hotel **14**
W **32**
Warwick Regis **4**
Westin St. Francis **20**
White Swan Inn **8**

CABLE CAR LINES

California Line ————
Powell-Mason Line - - - - - - -
Powell-Hyde Line ————
Cable Car Turnaround ⊙

Information ⓘ

1/8 mile
0
100 meters

Sacramento St.

† Grace Cathedral

HUNTINGTON PARK

California St.

Nob Hill Masonic Center

Pine St.

NOB HILL

Bush St.

Taylor St.

Sutter St.

Cosmo

Post St.

Shannon

Geary St.

O'Farrell St.

Leavenworth St.

Ellis St.

Jones St.

Eddy St.

Larkin St.

Hyde St.

Turk St.

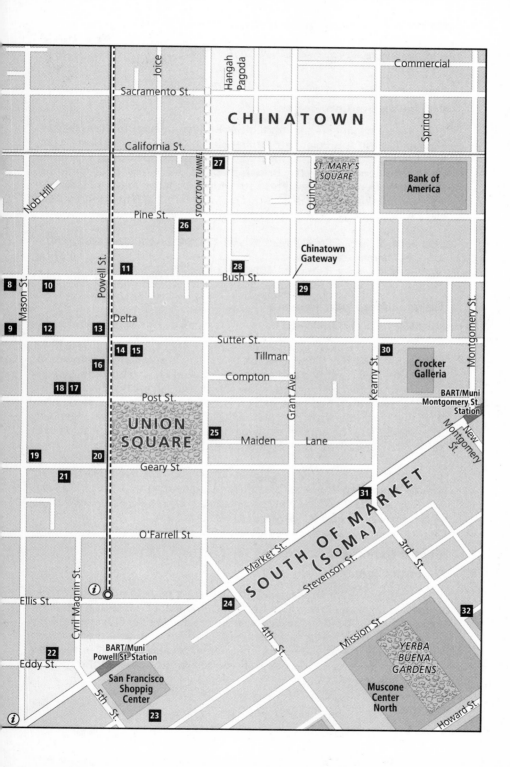

825 Sutter St., near Jones Street. ☎ *800-338-6848 or 415-923-6800. Fax: 415-923-6804. Internet:* www.sftrips.com. *Parking: $22. Rack rates: $99–$149. AAA, AARP discounts available. AE, CB, DC, DISC, MC, V.*

Edward II Inn
$ The Marina/Cow Hollow

This place is a giant step up from other budget lodgings in the area. B&B aficionados will appreciate the intimate feel of this 1914 English-style inn, but due to its busy corner location, be prepared for noise. The small rooms are done in a pretty, British-inspired decor. A second building, across the street, features suites with whirlpool baths. Rates include continental breakfast. No air-conditioning, no smoking. The friendly desk clerk will handle your tour arrangements.

3155 Scott St., at Lombard Street. ☎ *800-473-2846 or 415-922-3000. Fax: 415-931-5784. Internet:* www.edwardiiinn.citysearch.com. *Self-parking: $15 at limited offsite spaces. Rack rates: $83–$115; suite $195–$235. AE, MC, V.*

Embarcadero Hyatt Regency
$$$–$$$$ The Embarcadero

This huge (you're likely to get lost looking for your room) corporate hotel at the foot of Market Street gets the thumbs up for its tempting location. Rooms are well-equipped and spacious (some also have beautiful views), plus there are two restaurants, a few shops, and an on-site fitness center. This is probably your best bet for a hotel in the Embarcadero area if you're traveling with kids, who will find the indoor glass elevators irresistible. And the hotel's revolving Equinox Bar and Restaurant is irresistible to out-of-towners, who line up at the lifts for a ride to the view.

5 Embarcadero Center, at Market Street. ☎ *800-233-1234 or 415-788-1234. Fax: 415-398-2567. Internet:* www.sanfrancisco.regency.hyatt.com. *Parking: $30. Rack rates: $179–$320. Corporate discounts available. AE, CB, DC, DISC, MC, V; personal checks from U.S. banks. Dogs welcome.*

Golden Gate Hotel
$ Union Square

If you're flexible (or broke) enough to share a bathroom, this cheerful, charming, 23-room Edwardian hotel with the feel of a B&B is a fabulous deal, in a great location for cable-car lovers and walkers. Traveling with older children? Take two of the small, pretty rooms, and buy yourself some privacy. A complimentary continental breakfast and afternoon tea are served. There's a hotel cat, so if you're allergic, this isn't the spot for you. No air-conditioning.

775 Bush St., between Powell and Mason streets, two blocks from the Chinatown gate. ☎ *800-835-1118 or 415-392-3702. Fax: 415-392-6202. Internet:* www.golden gatehotel.com. *Self-parking: A relative bargain at $15. Rates: $85 (shared bath) or $130 (private bath) double. DC, MC, V.*

Handlery Union Square Hotel
$$$ **Union Square**

This favorite with tour packagers happens to be one of the better family hotels downtown because it features a heated outdoor pool — a rarity in San Francisco — as well as Nintendo, if you consider that a positive. (And kids under 15 stay free!) The regular doubles with smallish bathrooms will have been renovated by the time you read this, but if you like a dressing area, cozy robes, the morning paper, and extra space, splurge on one of the larger Club Rooms located in an adjacent building, a slightly longer walk to the lobby. The hotel's two-bedroom suites are also good value, and refrigerators are provided on request.

351 Geary St., between Powell and Mason streets, ½ block from Union Square. ☎ *800-843-4343 or 415-781-7800. Fax: 415-781-0269. Internet:* www.handlery. com. *Parking: $21. Rack rates: $189–$240. Ask about AAA discount; corporate, federal government, and senior citizen rates; and Internet specials. AE, CB, DC, JCB, MC, V.*

Harbor Court Hotel
$$$ **The Embarcadero**

Located just steps from the bay, this is an especially romantic and sophisticated hotel, and my first choice of the Embarcadero hotels reviewed in this chapter. Rooms are handsomely designed if small, featuring half-canopy beds, and many have spot-on views of the water. Guests have free access to the state-of-the-art Embarcadero YMCA pool and health club right next door. A complimentary wine reception is held each evening, and after a glass you can step into trendy Ozumo (see review in Chapter 14), which is accessible from the lobby.

165 Steuart St., between Mission and Howard streets. ☎ *800-346-0555 or 415-882-1300. Fax: 415-882-1313. Internet:* www.harborcourthotel.com. *Parking: $26. Rack rates: $210–$265. AE, CB, DC, DISC, MC, V.*

Hotel Bijou
$–$$ **Union Square**

Film buffs will get a kick out of this cinema-themed inn. In the evening, it shows San Francisco-based videos in a ten-seat screening room off the lobby, and there's even a candy counter. Freshly decorated rooms and baths (some with shower only) are tight and amenities few, but the staff is professional and service-oriented. Continental breakfast is included in the rates. A warning: This hotel shares the block with a sleazy strip club; if you think that will bother you, book elsewhere.

111 Mason St., at Eddy Street, around the corner from Hallidie Plaza. ☎ *800-771-1022 or 415-771-1200. Fax: 415-346-3196. Internet:* www.hotelbijou.com. *Parking: Shockingly reasonable at $21. Rack rates: $109–$159. AE, DC, MC, V.*

Hotel Bohème

$$ North Beach/Fisherman's Wharf

Set in the heart of North Beach, this charming, intimate hotel echos the old Bohemian feel of the area. Fifteen small but beautiful rooms are vividly painted and arrayed with iron beds and generous in-room amenities, but the teensy bathrooms have showers only, no tubs. The accommodating staff is happy to assist with tours, rental cars, and restaurant reservations; you'll have to schlep your own luggage up the narrow stairs, though. No air-conditioning, but the windows open. You're likely to find a younger, less conservative crowd staying here than at the Washington Square Inn, another small hotel in this neighborhood and price range.

444 Columbus Ave., between Vallejo and Green streets. ☎ *415-433-9111. Fax: 415-362-6292. Internet:* www.hotelboheme.com. *Self-parking: $25 in a garage 1½ blocks away. Rack rates: $164–$184. AE, CB, DC, DISC, JCB, MC, V.*

Hotel Del Sol

$$ Marina/Cow Hollow

Paint, mosaic tiles, and a lively imagination can do a lot to reinvent a motel, and there's no better example of this than the Del Sol. You'll think you're in Southern California (after the fog lifts), but it's lots better here, because you can walk around without getting startled looks from drivers. The heated pool and a hammock suspended between palm trees complete the hallucination. Multi-colored, way-fun, reasonably-sized guest rooms and suites could have stepped out of a '90s Habitat catalog, and one is configured especially for families, with games and bunk beds. The best part: Parking is free.

3100 Webster St., at Filbert Street. ☎ *877-433-5765 or 415-921-5520. Fax: 415-931-4137. Internet:* www.thehoteldelsol.com. *Free parking. Rack rates: $145–$165. AE, DC, DISC, MC, V.*

Hotel Griffon

$$$–$$$$ The Embarcadero

One of the few Embarcadero hotels, the Griffon has top-notch concierge services, while six end rooms and three suites offer unsurpassed bay views. Sadly, the small rooms don't sing style — vintage white brick walls and a lack of artwork equal a drab appearance. In some, sink/vanity combos sit just a few feet from the bed — a juxtaposition I find unsettling. Still, it has more personality than the Embarcadero Hyatt, and I like the location — very close to the water. A well-equipped YMCA (free for guests) is next door, and a good restaurant is off the lobby. Continental breakfast is included in the rates.

155 Steuart St., between Mission and Howard streets. ☎ ***800-321-2201*** *or 415-495-2100. Fax: 415-495-3522. Internet:* www.hotelgriffon.com. *Self-parking: $24. Rack rates: $245–$285; suites $395–$435. AE, DC, DISC, MC, V.*

Hotel Juliana

$$$ **Union Square**

Perched between Nob Hill and Union Square, this hotel appeals to couples who desire the benefits of both neighborhoods and like a cozy atmosphere. It's also a reasonable choice for small families, with suites available for around $269. Among the Union Square hotels in this price range, this is where I'd stay if I had young children with me (I'd probably take my teens to the Drake.) The rooms are gaily decorated, complete with coffeepots, irons, and hair dryers. An evening wine reception is gratis; continental breakfast is available for an extra charge. Guests can also use the Fairmont Hotel's health club, two blocks away, for a fee of $12 per day.

590 Bush St., at Stockton Street. ☎ ***800-328-3880*** *or 415-392-2540. Fax: 415-391-8447. Internet:* www.julianahotel.com. *Parking: $30. Rack rates: $239–$269. AE, DC, DISC, JCB, MC, V.*

Hotel Milano

$$$ **SoMa**

This well-designed and maintained modern Italian-themed boutique hotel isn't flashy or cool, but you won't find a better value in SoMa. Amenities include one of the more spacious on-site fitness rooms, a restaurant, and fine room amenities. The multi-story San Francisco Shopping Centre is a few feet away, and Yerba Buena Gardens is just around the corner, so you won't lack for things to do. Personally, I prefer this hotel to The Argent (also in this neighborhood and price range), but if you're looking for a room with a view, The Argent is a better bet.

55 Fifth St., between Market and Mission streets. ☎ ***800-398-7555*** *or 415-543-8555. Fax: 415-543-5885. Internet:* www.hotelmilano.citysearch.com. *Parking: $24. Rack rates: $199–$299. AE, DC, MC, V.*

Hotel Monaco

$$$ **Union Square**

You'll wish you'd brought your fox-tail–trimmed scarf and vintage Vuitton steamer trunk when you sashay into the Art Deco–inspired Monaco. The medium-sized rooms are lushly decorated with patterned wallpaper, floral prints, and canopied beds. All the amenities — like room service and a fitness center — are available, plus it's a pet-friendly hotel with doggie treats. The aptly named Grand Cafe restaurant (reviewed in Chapter 14) is next door. And if you're feeling lonely, they'll deliver a bowl of goldfish to your room.

501 Geary St., at Taylor Street. ☎ *800-214-4220 or 415-292-0100. Fax: 415-292-0111. Internet:* www.hotelmonaco.com. *Parking: $30. Rack rates: $219–$309. AE, CB, DC, DISC, MC, V.*

Hotel Palomar

$$$$ SoMa

This new, extremely grown-up hotel sits above a busy corner close to Union Square and the attractions south of Market. The hotel was designed for sophisticated business and leisure travelers; you can expect a high-quality experience (at high-quality prices) in luxuriously sedate surroundings. The ample guest rooms are fitted for work and play with multiline phones, fax, CD player, spa tubs, and Aveda products. There's room service, a fitness center, and The Fifth Floor, one of the most glamorous restaurants in town. Palomar guests, of course, don't have to wait four weeks for a table. Hotel Palomar compares in price to its neighbor, the W. So what's the difference between the two hotels? The Palomar is what the W will be when it's all grown up. But the W is convinced it's having more fun.

12 Fourth St., at Market Street. ☎ *877-294-9711 or 415-348-1111. Fax: 415-348-0302. Parking: $30. Rack rates: $379–$429; suites $559–$959. Rates include morning paper and shoeshine. AE, DC, DISC, MC, V.*

Hotel Rex

$$$ Union Square

Dorothy Parker fans will appreciate this sophisticated 94-room delight, which, despite its artsy leanings, is thankfully unpretentious. Listen to the cable cars clank by or peruse a book from the lobby library while drinking complimentary wine. The rooms are all smartly designed and colorfully decorated; sizes vary from smallish doubles on up. Enjoy full service here, too, including thoughtful amenities such as CD players.

562 Sutter St., between Powell and Mason streets. ☎ *800-433-4434 or 415-433-4434. Fax: 415-433-3695. Parking: $30. Rack rates: $215–$245. Rates include evening wine. AE, DC, DISC, MC, V.*

Hotel Triton

$$$ Union Square

The music of the Grateful Dead and/or their close personal friends blares from lobby speakers in this hip 'n happening ode to rock 'n' roll. Doubles are small here, but, oh baby, are they sweet. This wacky place is heavy on style, but also substance, with plenty of amenities, including Nintendo. To pay homage to the ab gods, there's a small on-site fitness room. The fabulous location, across from Chinatown's Dragon Gate, makes standing outside on the sidewalk an exotic experience. Rooms ending in 07 are especially compact.

342 Grant Ave., at Sutter Street, across from the Dragon Gate. ☎ *888-364-2622 or 415-394-0500. Fax: 415-394-0555. Internet:* www.hotel-tritonsf.com. *Parking: $35. Rack rates: $219–$279; suites $329–$389. AE, CB, DC, DISC, MC, V. Well-behaved dogs welcome.*

The Huntington Hotel
$$$$ Nob Hill

The Boston Brahmin in you will adore this refined, quiet oasis with its subtle elegance, impeccable service, and the most gorgeous spa around. The 1924 building originally housed apartments, so guest rooms and baths are larger than average; most are labeled suites. Rooms above the eighth floor have views; the ones below are extra spacious. Children are welcome in the hotel but not in the spa. The staff, concierge included, will anticipate your every need. Manicured Huntington Park, complete with a playground, is across the street. If you can afford to lay down the cash for a room here, you could also choose to stay at the Ritz-Carlton, the Huntington's Nob Hill neighbor. Personally, I prefer the old-fashioned, old–San Franciscan feel of the Huntington. If you want the total San Francisco experience, this is it. You'll certainly get pampered here, but if you're looking for really over-the-top, no-holds-barred coddling and luxury, go with the Ritz.

1075 California St., at Taylor Street. ☎ *800-227-4683 or 415-474-5400. Fax: 415-474-6227. Internet:* www.huntingtonhotel.com. *Parking: $30. Rack rates: $310–$455; suites $485–$750. AE, DC, DISC, MC, V.*

Inn at Union Square
$$$ Union Square

This very discreet, small hotel is just the ticket if you desire luxury but don't care to make a scene. You get those little extras — continental breakfast, newspapers, fresh flowers, wine in the early evening, nice linens, 24-hour concierge, health club access — combined with a no-tipping policy that makes it a pleasure to part with some, but not too much, money. Tasteful rooms range from small to very large, and all are beautiful. No air-conditioning.

440 Post St., near Powell Street. ☎ *800-288-4346 or 415-397-3510. Fax: 415-989-0529. Internet:* www.unionsquare.com. *Parking: $23. Rack rates: $195–$245. AE, CB, DC, DISC, MC, V.*

Kensington Park Hotel

$$$ Union Square

This 88-room property, with a theater on the second floor and a well-known restaurant next door (which I don't recommend due to the snotty service), is a find among Union Square hotels. The larger-than-average rooms were renovated in 1998; the bathrooms were already among the handsomest in the area. If you like a great view (who doesn't?), request a room above the seventh floor, either on the Nob Hill side or on a corner. Rates include continental breakfast and afternoon tea. Workout facilities are available and the staff is delightful.

450 Post St., between Mason and Powell streets. ☎ *800-553-1900 or 415-788-6400. Fax: 415-399-9484. Internet:* www.kensingtonparkhotel.com. *Parking $22. Rack rates: $185–$249. AE, CB, DC, DISC, JCB, MC, V.*

The Marina Inn

$ The Marina/Cow Hollow

Anyone looking for value, and a terrific location near Chestnut Street shops, is in luck. A two-story arched entrance gives this budget 40-room Victorian inn an air of quiet grandeur. The furnishings are simple: armoires, pine beds and tables. If you seek the light, the street-side rooms are bright but noisy; inside rooms are quieter, but natural light comes from a light well. A continental breakfast is included in the room rates; prices vary with room sizes. The desk staff will make restaurant, tour, and airport shuttle reservations on request.

3110 Octavia, at Lombard Street. ☎ *800-274-1420 or 415-928-1000. Fax: 415-928-5909. Internet:* www.marinainn.com. *Self-parking: $12 at the nearest public garage. Rack rates: $65–$135. AAA, AARP discounts. AE, MC, V.*

The Marina Motel

$ The Marina/Cow Hollow

Because this was originally an apartment building, 15 of the rentals in this funky, flower-bedecked, courtyard-style budget motel feature fully equipped kitchens. A granddaughter of the original owner recently redecorated the medium-sized studios with Italian bathroom tiles, Mission-style furniture, and pretty quilts, making this one of the few places on Lombard Street with even a hint of charm. Families can reserve two connecting rooms with a shared bath. Surprisingly, considering the location, rooms off the street are remarkably quiet. The front desk clerk will arrange tours or rental cars at your request.

2576 Lombard St., near Divisadero Street. ☎ *800-346-6118 or 415-921-9406. Fax: 415-921-0364. Internet:* www.marinamotel.com. *Parking: Free in little garages on the premises. Rack rates: $85–$149; family room $99–$199. AE, MC, V. Dogs welcome.*

The Maxwell

$$ Union Square

If you're a serious shopper, you'll like this attractive hotel's supportive resources, such as its *Shopologist* newsletter. The guest rooms, which are either spacious and Art Deco–chic or dark and small (depending on your pocketbook or the kindness of the desk clerk), lie off an intimate, theatrical lobby. During the last remodel, designers thoughtfully didn't alter the original bathroom tile or the deep bathtubs. Max's on the Square provides room service; on my last visit the hotel staff was unimpressive, so this is a better choice for independent travelers.

386 Geary St., at Mason Street. ☎ *888-734-6299 or 415-986-2000. Fax: 415-397-2447. Internet:* www.maxwellhotel.com. *Parking: $18 at a nearby garage. Rack rates: $155–$215. Ask about corporate discounts and special packages. AE, DC, DISC, MC, V.*

Nob Hill Lambourne

$$$–$$$$ Nob Hill

An intimate 20-room hotel, the relaxed and soothing Lambourne has spacious rooms with compact kitchenettes and many amenities. Suites are available for vacationing families — and they're beauties. Massages and other on-site spa treatments can be scheduled by the front-desk staff, and nightly turndown service substitutes vitamins for chocolates on your buckwheat hull–filled pillow. Continental breakfast is included in the rates, and a fresh fruit basket is in the hallway for your pleasure. You won't find a better deal on Nob Hill, and you'll feel like management has your best interests at heart. No smoking.

725 Pine St., at Stockton Street. ☎ *800-274-8466 or 415-433-2287. Fax: 415-433-0975. Internet:* www.nobhilllambourne.com. *Parking: $24. Rack rates: $180–$325 including continental breakfast and evening wine reception. AE, CB, DC, DISC, MC, V.*

The Orchard Hotel

$$$ Union Square

Opened in 2001, the 105-room Orchard was built from scratch and can boast some of the largest bedrooms and most luxurious baths in the neighborhood. However, this also means it has less personality than older, true boutique hotels such as Hotel Rex and Hotel Juliana. Still, for sheer comfort, this is probably your best bet in this neighborhood and price range. The conservatively decorated guest rooms will gratify business as well as vacation travelers, and include CD/DVD players, high-speed Internet access, and top amenities, including room service, provided by the well-mannered and professional staff. Cable cars stop just around the corner.

665 Bush St., between Stockton and Powell. ☎ ***888-717-2881*** *or 415-362-8878. Fax: 415-362-8088. Internet:* www.theorchardhotel.com. *Parking: $30. Rack rates: $229–$299; suites $419–$499. Rates include continental breakfast. AE, DC, MC, V.*

Petite Auberge
$$–$$$ Union Square

Romantics will find happiness here among the florals and French country effects. The high-end rooms are enormous, the less expensive rooms are cozy and have showers only — but all are equally comfortable. Along with a full breakfast served downstairs in the homey dining room, complimentary tea, wine, and hors d'oeuvres are served in the afternoon. Petite Auberge is well known and exceedingly popular, so if you want to experience the charms of a Provençal inn in the city, book well in advance.

863 Bush St., between Mason and Taylor streets. ☎ ***800-365-3004*** *or 415-928-6000. Fax: 415-775-5717. Internet:* www.foursisters.com. *Parking: $30. Rack rates: $150–$245. AE, DC, MC, V.*

Ritz-Carlton
$$$$ Nob Hill

Okay, big spenders, here's your hotel. The Ritz takes posh to the extreme, and those who want to be treated like landed gentry will feel their money was well spent. After you settle into your beautiful, spacious nest, you can swim in the indoor pool, exercise in the fitness center, shop for antiques, and eat in a nationally-renowned restaurant, all without ever leaving the cushy confines. And how can you not love a hotel where the mantra is "Instant guest pacification will be ensured by all"?

600 Stockton St., between Pine and California streets. ☎ ***800-241-3333*** *or 415-296-7465. Fax: 415-291-0288. Internet:* www.ritzcarlton.com. *Parking: $30. Rack rates: Well, if you have to ask . . . $425–$4,800. Special occasion packages available. AE, DC, DISC, MC, V.*

San Remo Hotel
$ North Beach/Fisherman's Wharf

Think of staying in this 1906 building as bunking at a pal's home, because you're going to have to share the bathrooms. Rooms are small but adorable, and all the hotel guests are relaxed and friendly, thrilled to have found such a bargain close to the bay. The penthouse, with a private bath, is prized for its views. However, ambience from the low-income housing project on the next block may not be the sort you crave. Laundry facilities are available. No air-conditioning.

2237 Mason St., near Chestnut Street, two blocks from the Cannery. ☎ ***800-352-7366*** *or 415-776-8688. Fax: 415-776-2811. Parking: $12 at a garage two blocks north. Rack rates: $60–$80. AE, DC, MC, V.*

The Sheehan Hotel
$–$$ Union Square

No one would confuse this one-time YMCA for the Ritz, but if you aren't usually mistaken for Daddy Warbucks, we may have a match. The selling points here, besides low rates and a central location, are the indoor lap pool and sizable exercise room. There are even personal trainers and massage therapists available (for a fee), so if you have an active imagination, you can pretend you're at a spa. Rooms are serviceable if plain (to put it gently), some are spacious enough to accommodate a large family, and they're clean. A complimentary continental breakfast is included. No air-conditioning.

620 Sutter St., near Mason Street, about two blocks west of Union Square. ☎ **800-848-1529** *or 415-775-6500. Fax: 415-775-3271. Internet:* www.sheehanhotel.com. *Self-parking: $18. Rack rates: $99–$189. AE, MC, V.*

Sir Francis Drake Hotel
$$$ Union Square

A sigh of pleasure will escape your lips as you walk past uniformed valets into the elegant lobby of this historic hotel. The small-to-medium-sized, well-appointed and decorated rooms won't overwhelm you like the public space, but if you can secure a corner room above the tenth floor, the view will. Most of the rooms are in good shape, but a few of the older ones are starting to show their age. If a new-looking room is important to you, The Orchard (which charges similar rates) is probably a safer bet. But you'll definitely be sacrificing character, and the Drake has the best location of any Union Square hotel in this price range. An excellent restaurant (Scala's Bistro, reviewed in Chapter 14), cafe, small workout facility, and popular nightclub are on-site. Service is superlative.

450 Powell St., at Sutter, one block north of Union Square. ☎ **800-227-5480** *or 415-392-7755. Fax: 415-391-8719. Internet:* www.sirfrancisdrake.com. *Parking: $32. Rack rates: $179–$269. AAA and AARP discounts. AE, CB, DC, DISC, MC, V.*

Tuscan Inn
$$–$$$ North Beach/Fisherman's Wharf

The Tuscan is a welcome change compared to the rest of the chain hotels on Fisherman's Wharf. Personality doesn't abound, but the rooms are fairly large by local standards, and kids like the location. The concierge is enthusiastic and friendly, and all the amenities you expect are available. In warm weather, enjoy dining al fresco at the hotel restaurant.

425 North Point, between Mason and Taylor streets. ☎ **800-648-4626** *or 415-561-1100. Fax: 415-561-1199. Internet:* www.tuscaninn.com. *Parking: $18. Rack rates: $148–$300. Ask about AAA, corporate, and senior discounts. AE, CB, DC, DISC, MC, V.*

Union Street Inn

$$–$$$ The Marina/Cow Hollow

This B&B has six richly appointed rooms and a choice location on a prime shopping street. If you want a bit less urban color, this is a fantastic retreat. The charming managers serve as concierge and cook a full breakfast as part of the deal. Rooms are large, but beware of the steep stairs to the front door, which make this an impractical choice for anyone who has difficulty walking.

2229 Union St., between Fillmore and Steiner streets. ☎ **415-346-0424.** *Fax: 415-922-8046. Internet:* www.unionstreetinn.com. *Parking: $15 at a lot 1½ blocks away. Rack rates: $159–$269. AE, MC, V.*

W

$$$$ SoMa

Ultra-modern and light on the frou-frou, W precisely aims its glossy high style and service at hip business travelers. Of course, they generally head for the airport on Fridays, leaving the vaguely masculine, moderate-sized rooms available to the rest of us. Marvel at the handsome chrome-and-frosted-glass bathroom, the deluxe amenities, the CD player, and the dataports. A lap pool, fitness room, restaurant, cafe, bar, room service, and well-trained staff add heft to an already solid package.

181 Third St., at Howard St. ☎ **877-946-8357** *or 415-777-5300. Fax: 415-817-7860. Internet:* www.whotels.com. *Parking: $38. Rack rates: $319–$509. AE, DC, DISC, JCB, MC, V. Dogs welcome.*

The Warwick Regis

$$–$$$ Union Square

This is the closest you can get to a French chateau downtown. If circa–Louis XVI armoires, brocade fabrics, crown-canopied beds, and marble-tiled bathrooms get your heart racing, you're going to adore this hotel. Guests are privy to big hotel services — twice-daily housekeeping, fresh flowers, great amenities, a restaurant/bar, 24-hour room service — in an intimate, urbane atmosphere, and for an unbelievably reasonable price. Twelve of the beautiful suites contain two bathrooms; all the rooms, ranging from tiny to generous, are blissfully quiet.

490 Geary St., at Taylor Street. ☎ **800-827-3447** *or 415-928-7900. Fax: 415-441-8788. Internet:* www.warwickhotels.com. *Parking: $25. Rack rates: $149–$309. AE, DC, DISC, JCB, MC, V.*

Washington Square Inn

$$ **North Beach/Fisherman's Wharf**

The European atmosphere in North Beach makes this hotel a wonderful choice, and if you plan to walk the neighborhoods, you won't find a better location. The rooms in the lower price bracket are small, but amenities such as fresh flowers, continental breakfast, afternoon tea, and evening wine and hors d'oeuvres in the antiques-filled lobby make them a terrific deal. The staff will help you with your bags, but otherwise, the front-desk service isn't so impressive. There is a two-night minimum on weekends.

1660 Stockton St., at Filbert Street, across from Washington Square Park. ☎ *800-388-0220 or 415-981-4220. Fax: 415-397-7242. Internet:* www.washington squareinnsf.com. *Parking: $25. Rack rates: $125–$215; suites $195–$245. AE, DC, DISC, JCB, MC, V.*

Westin St. Francis

$$$–$$$$ **Union Square**

It's all about location. That and the glittering, bustling lobby are what give the historic St. Francis its air of excitement. But this is a really big, impersonal hotel — albeit one with 24-hour room service, concierges, shops, and dining opportunities. In any case, stick to the original (main) building. Its moderate-sized standard doubles are furnished with gorgeous reproductions and romantic antique chandeliers, although bathrooms are on the small side.

335 Powell St., across from Union Square. ☎ ***800-937-8461*** *or 415-397-7000. Fax: 415-774-0124. Parking: $30. Rack rates: $259–$390. AE, DC, DISC, JCB, MC, V.*

White Swan Inn

$$$ **Union Square**

The 26 guest rooms in this Englishy B&B are designed to be lingered in. You'll certainly want to take every advantage of the four-poster beds and fireplaces in the spacious rooms. A full breakfast is included in the rates, as is afternoon tea and sherry served downstairs in the parlor. You'll think you're visiting a well-to-do British aunt. Back rooms are sunnier; the queen rooms have showers only. Just as in the White Swan's sister inn, Petite Auberge, advance reservations are imperative here.

845 Bush St., between Mason and Taylor streets. ☎ ***800-999-9570*** *or 415-775-1755. Fax: 415-775-5717. Internet:* www.foursisters.com. *Parking: $30. Rack rates: $180–$285. AE, DC, MC, V.*

If You Need a Room When There Are No Rooms Available . . .

Having trouble finding a bed? If the hotels listed earlier in this chapter are filled up, try booking in one of the following accommodations. They may have saved you some room.

The Cartwright Hotel
$$ **Union Square**

Quiet and elegantly appointed with antiques in most rooms, families will be delighted with any of the two-bedroom suites. Guests here get health-club privileges at the Monaco.

524 Sutter St., at Powell Street. ☎ *800-227-3844 or 415-421-2865. Fax: 415-983-6244. Internet:* www.cartwrighthotel.com. *Parking: $30. Rack rates: $109–$259; suites $179–$369. AAA, AARP discounts. AE, CB, DC, DISC, MC, V.*

Galleria Park Hotel
$$$ **Union Square**

This is a terrific, small hotel in a clever location close to Chinatown, the Financial District, and Union Square. Unlike most downtown properties, this one has on-site parking, handy for travelers who need quick access to their automobile. The hotel's experienced concierge is a gold mine of information and assistance. There's a work-out room on-site.

191 Sutter St., at Kearny Street. ☎ *800-792-9639 or 415-781-3060. Fax: 415-433-4409. Internet:* www.galleriapark.com. *Parking: $30. Rack rates: $179–$299. AE, CB, DC, DISC, MC, V.*

Hotel Vintage Court
$$$ **Union Square**

This is a low-key, non-smoking, Wine Country–themed boutique hotel with good room amenities (including high-speed Internet access) and complimentary wine in the evening. Guests have preferred access to reservations at Masa's, a destination for gourmets.

650 Bush St., between Powell and Stockton streets. ☎ *800-853-1750 or 415-392-4666. Fax: 415-433-4065. Internet:* www.vintagecourt.com. *Parking: $28. Rack rates: $249–$375. AE, CB, DC, DISC, MC, V.*

Index of accommodations by neighborhood

Union Square
Andrews Hotel ($–$$)
Campton Place ($$$$)
The Cartwright Hotel ($$)
Chancellor Hotel ($$)
Clift ($$$$)
Commodore Hotel ($–$$)
Galleria Park Hotel ($$$)
Golden Gate Hotel ($)
Handlery Union Square Hotel ($$$)
Hotel Bijou ($–$$)
Hotel Juliana ($$$)
Hotel Monaco ($$$)
Hotel Rex ($$$)
Hotel Triton ($$$)
Hotel Vintage Court ($$$)
Inn at Union Square ($$$)
Kensington Park Hotel ($$$)
The Maxwell ($$)
The Orchard Hotel ($$$)
Petite Auberge ($$–$$$)
The Sheehan ($–$$)
Sir Francis Drake Hotel ($$$)
The Warwick Regis ($$–$$$)
Westin St. Francis ($$$–$$$$)
White Swan Inn ($$$)

Nob Hill
The Huntington Hotel ($$$$)
Nob Hill Lambourne ($$$–$$$$)
Ritz-Carlton ($$$$)

SoMa
The Argent ($$$–$$$$)
Hotel Milano ($$$)
Hotel Palomar ($$$$)
W ($$$$)

The Embarcadero
Embarcadero Hyatt Regency ($$$–$$$$)
Harbor Court Hotel ($$$)
Hotel Griffon ($$$–$$$$)

North Beach/Fisherman's Wharf
Hotel Bohème ($$)
San Remo Hotel ($)
Tuscan Inn ($$–$$$)
Washington Square Inn ($$)

The Marina/Cow Hollow
Edward II Inn ($)
Hotel Del Sol ($$)
The Marina Inn ($)
The Marina Motel ($)
Union Street Inn ($$–$$$)

Index of accommodations by price

$
Andrews Hotel (Union Square)
Commodore Hotel (Union Square)
Edward II Inn (The Marina/Cow Hollow)
Golden Gate Hotel (Union Square)
Hotel Bijou (Union Square)
The Marina Inn (The Marina/Cow Hollow)
The Marina Motel (The Marina/Cow Hollow)
San Remo Hotel (North Beach/Fisherman's Wharf)
The Sheehan (Union Square)

$$
Andrews Hotel (Union Square)
The Cartwright Hotel (Union Square)
Chancellor Hotel (Union Square)
Commodore Hotel (Union Square)
Hotel Bijou (Union Square)
Hotel Bohème (North Beach/Fisherman's Wharf)

Hotel Del Sol (The Marina/Cow Hollow)
The Maxwell (Union Square)
Petite Auberge (Union Square)
The Sheehan (Union Square)
Tuscan Inn (North Beach/Fisherman's Wharf)
Union Street Inn (The Marina/Cow Hollow)
The Warwick Regis (Union Square)
Washington Square Inn (North Beach/Fisherman's Wharf)

$$$

The Argent (SoMa)
Embarcadero Hyatt Regency (The Embarcadero)
Galleria Park Hotel (Union Square)
Handlery Union Square Hotel (Union Square)
Harbor Court Hotel (The Embarcadero)
Hotel Griffon (The Embarcadero)
Hotel Juliana (Union Square)
Hotel Milano (SoMa)
Hotel Monaco (Union Square)
Hotel Rex (Union Square)
Hotel Triton (Union Square)

Hotel Vintage Court (Union Square)
Inn at Union Square (Union Square)
Kensington Park Hotel (Union Square)
Nob Hill Lambourne (Nob Hill)
The Orchard Hotel (Union Square)
Petite Auberge (Union Square)
Sir Francis Drake Hotel (Union Square)
Tuscan Inn (North Beach/Fisherman's Wharf)
Union Street Inn (The Marina/Cow Hollow)
The Warwick Regis (Union Square)
Westin St. Francis (Union Square)
White Swan Inn (Union Square)

$$$$

The Argent (SoMa)
Campton Place (Union Square)
Clift (Union Square)
Embarcadero Hyatt Regency (The Embarcadero)
Hotel Griffon (The Embarcadero)
Hotel Palomar (SoMa)
The Huntington Hotel (Nob Hill)
Nob Hill Lambourne (Nob Hill)
Ritz-Carlton (Nob Hill)
W (SoMa)
Westin St. Francis (Union Square)

Chapter 9

Little Things Mean a Lot: Last-Minute Details to Keep in Mind

. . . .

In This Chapter

▶ Buying travel insurance — or not

▶ Dealing with illness away from home

▶ Deciding whether to drive

▶ Finding out what's going on in the city before you get here

▶ Getting your hands on tickets

. . . .

A fter you know how to get to San Francisco and know where you can stay, it's time to take care of details such as transportation and entertainment. In this chapter, I discuss these and a few other issues.

Buying Travel and Medical Insurance

The three primary kinds of travel insurance are trip cancellation, medical, and lost luggage.

There are a few types of trip-cancellation insurance — one, in the event that you prepay for a cruise or tour that gets cancelled, and you can't get your money back; a second for when you or someone in your family gets sick or dies, and you can't travel; and a third, for when bad weather makes travel impossible. Some insurers provide coverage for events like jury duty, natural disasters close to home, and even the loss of a job. A few have added provisions for cancellations due to terrorist activities. Always check the fine print before signing on, and don't buy trip-cancellation insurance from the tour operator that may be responsible for the cancellation; buy it only from a reputable travel insurance agency.

Your existing health insurance should cover you if you get sick while on vacation (double-check that your HMO fully covers you in this instance). If you require additional insurance, try one of the following companies:

- **MEDEX International**, 9515 Deereco Rd., Timonium, MD 21093-5375 (☎ **888-MEDEX-00** or 410-453-6300; fax: 410-453-6301; Internet: www.medexassist.com)

- **Travel Assistance International,** 9200 Keystone Crossing, Suite 300, Indianapolis, IN 46240 (☎ **800-821-2828;** Internet: www.travelassistance.com)

If your luggage gets lost or stolen, your homeowner's policy should cover it. Double-checking your existing policies before buying additional coverage can save you a lot of money. The airlines are responsible for $2,500 on domestic flights (and $9.07 per pound, up to $640, on international flights) if they lose your luggage. If your valuables are worth more than that, keep them in your carry-on bag. You may also purchase excess-valuation coverage from the airline, up to $5,000.

If you file a lost luggage claim, be prepared to answer detailed questions about the contents of your baggage, and be sure to file a claim immediately; most airlines enforce a 21-day deadline. After you've filed a complaint, persist in securing your reimbursement; there are no laws governing the length of time it takes for a carrier to reimburse you. If you arrive at a destination without your bags, ask the airline to forward them to your hotel or to your next destination; they will usually comply. If your bag is delayed or lost, the airline may reimburse you for reasonable expenses, such as a toothbrush or a set of clothes, but the airline is under no legal obligation to do so.

Automatic flight insurance against death or dismemberment in case of an airplane crash is offered by many credit cards, including American Express and some gold and platinum Visas and MasterCards. If you still feel you need more insurance, try one of the following reputable companies:

- **Access America**, 6600 W. Broad St., Richmond, VA 23230 (☎ **800-284-8300;** fax: 800-346-9265; Internet: www.accessamerica.com)

- **Travel Guard International,** 1145 Clark St., Stevens Point, WI 54481 (☎ **800-826-1300;** Internet: www.travel-guard.com)

- **Travel Insured International, Inc.,** P.O. Box 280568, 52-S Oakland Ave., East Hartford, CT 06128-0568 (☎ **800-243-3174;** Internet: www.travelinsured.com)

- **Travelex Insurance Services,** 11717 Burt St., Suite 202, Omaha, NE 68154 (☎ **800-228-9792;** Internet: www.travelex-insurance.com)

You should pay no more than 6% to 8% of the total value of your vacation for trip-cancellation insurance.

Getting Sick Away from Home

Getting sick away from home is no fun, so make sure you pack all your medications, as well as a prescription for more in case you run out or lose a bottle. Packing an extra pair of contact lenses or glasses is a good idea, too. And bring along some over-the-counter medications for common travelers' ailments like upset stomach or diarrhea.

If you have health insurance, check with your provider to find out the extent of your coverage outside of your home area. Be sure to carry your identification card in your wallet. And if you worry that your existing policy won't be sufficient, purchase medical insurance (see "Buying Travel and Medical Insurance" earlier in this chapter) for more comprehensive coverage.

If you suffer from a chronic illness, talk to your doctor before taking the trip. For such conditions as epilepsy, diabetes, or a heart condition, wearing a Medic Alert identification tag will immediately alert any doctor to your condition and give him access to your medical records through Medic Alert's 24-hour hotline. Membership is $35, with a $15 renewal fee. Contact the **Medic Alert Foundation**, 2323 Colorado Ave., Turlock, CA 95382 (☎ **800-432-5378;** Internet: www.medicalert.org).

Your hotel concierge can probably recommend a local doctor if you get sick. If you can't get a doctor to see you promptly, see whether the local hospital ER has a walk-in clinic for non–life-threatening emergencies. You may have to wait a while, but it'll be cheaper than a typical emergency room visit, which usually runs about $300, not including treatment or medications.

Renting a Car (Or Six Reasons Why You Shouldn't)

If lots of traffic, steep hills, no parking spaces, one-way streets, crazy bike messengers, and the occasional threat of a tow are your idea of fun, then by all means, get yourself a car. If you'd rather not deal with those sorts of hassles (and did I mention overly enthusiastic meter maids?), plenty of professionals are available to cart you all over the city.

Unfortunately, San Francisco doesn't have one of those enviable public transportation systems found in other cities; a bus can take you just about anywhere, but San Francisco's municipal railway system (Muni

Metro) is fairly limited. The Muni streetcars can get you close to where you want to go, but often you'll still need to catch a bus or cab or walk to get to many places. However, because San Francisco neighborhoods are small and distinct, and because you'll find beautiful or bizarre happenings around every corner, walking around is delightful.

Day-tripping: The one reason why you should rent a car

If you plan on any out-of-city excursions, perhaps to go wine tasting (if you don't like escorted tours, that is), you'll probably want to rent a car. To avoid exorbitant parking fees, wait until the day of your trip to pick up your car. Most rental car companies, including Enterprise Rent-A-Car (☎ 800-325-8007 or 415-441-2100) can pick you up and drop you off right at your hotel.

Getting the best rate

As much as airline fares vary, car-rental rates vary even more. How much you pay is determined by the car size, how long you keep it, where you drive it, and tons of other factors.

One tip that could save you some cold hard cash is to ask a few key questions, including the following:

- ✔ **Are weekend rates lower than weekday rates?** For example, ask whether picking up the car Friday morning is cheaper than picking it up Thursday night.

- ✔ **Can I get the weekly rate if I'm keeping the car five or more days?**

- ✔ **Will I be charged a fee for not returning the car to the same renting location?** Some companies assess a drop-off charge in this instance; others, such as National, do not.

- ✔ **Is it cheaper to pick up the car at the airport or at a location in town?** Remember to include garage charges if you must park at your hotel.

- ✔ **Are any specials running right now?** If you see an advertised price in your local newspaper, be sure to ask for that specific rate; otherwise, you may be charged the standard rate.

When making your rental reservations, don't forget to mention membership in AAA, AARP, frequent-flier programs, and trade unions. These usually entitle you to discounts ranging from 5% to 30%. Ask your travel agent to check any and all of these rates. And check to see whether your rental earns you points on your frequent-flier account — most rentals are worth at least 500 miles.

Comparing rates on the Web

As with other aspects of planning your trip, using the Internet can make comparison shopping for a car rental much easier. All the major booking sites — Travelocity (www.travelocity.com), Expedia (www.expedia.com), Yahoo! Travel (www.travel.yahoo.com), and Cheap Tickets (www.cheaptickets.com), for example — have search engines that can dig up discounted car-rental rates. Just enter the size of the car you want, the pickup and return dates, and the city where you want to rent, and the server returns a price. You can even make the reservation through these sites.

Taking care of insurance, gas, and other charges

In addition to the standard rental prices, other optional charges can raise the cost of your car-rentals. For example, if you choose to add the Collision Damage Waiver (CDW), you may pay an added fee of as much as $10 per day! Many credit-card companies already offer this insurance option when you charge the car rental to that credit card, so call your credit-card company to inquire about this before you leave home.

Another optional charge is additional liability insurance (which covers you if you're in an accident where others are injured), personal accident insurance (if you or your passengers are injured), and personal effects insurance (if someone steals your luggage from your car). The insurance on your car at home probably covers you for most of these unlikely events. If your own insurance doesn't cover you for rentals, or if you don't have auto insurance, consider getting the additional coverage on your rental. Car-rental companies are liable for certain base amounts, varying from state to state.

As for putting gas in your car, you have the option of paying for a full tank of gas up front. In this package, the gas price is average compared with local prices, but you don't get reimbursed for gas you leave in the tank after your trip. Your other option is to pay only for the gas you use, but you have to return the car with a full tank of gas, or the company will charge you $3 to $4 a gallon for the deficiency. If you don't want to bother filling up the tank at the last minute, then go with the package deal. If you know you won't be rushed, then don't bother.

Getting the Jump on Dinner Reservations and Tickets for Events and Attractions

Finding out what interesting events will be going on in San Francisco during your stay is easy. Check out the quality entertainment listings in the local publications and Web sites listed in the next section. If you hear about a concert scheduled during your stay that excites you, you can easily find out the details in time to get tickets.

You can also buy tickets ahead of time for special events, theatre performances, or even a baseball game at Pacific Bell Park. Many Web sites, including those for the ballet, the opera, and the Giants baseball team, enable you to purchase tickets online. Or you can call **BASS Ticketmaster** (☎ 800-225-2277 outside California or 510-762-2277) or check out the local Ticketron.

The concierge at the hotel where you'll be staying (or the desk staff if the hotel doesn't have a separate concierge desk) can usually help you acquire tickets to events and shows after you make your hotel reservations. Take advantage of their services.

For **Alcatraz tours,** reserve tickets at least two weeks in advance during the summer. Call ☎ 415-705-5555 to charge tickets by phone with a credit card. A $2.25 service charge will be added to each ticket. Your tickets will be mailed to you, or you can pick them up at the pier.

Finding events via publications and the Web

Check out the following local publications for the latest happenings around town:

- ✔ *The Bay Guardian:* This weekly is a favorite of locals because of its up-to-date entertainment listings and yearly "Best Of" awards. Issues cost $3 by mail; call ☎ 415-255-3100 to order a copy.

- ✔ *The San Francisco Chronicle:* Check out the "Datebook" section for information about the arts. To save on the high cost of postage, don't order a copy by mail; buy the paper from your local newsstand instead.

- ✔ *San Francisco:* Our very own monthly magazine is chock-full of arts and entertainment information. You can find it on newsstands in all major cities, or you can order a single copy for $2.95 by calling ☎ 415-398-2800.

> ✔ *SF Weekly:* This alternative paper contains entertainment listings and investigative reporting. Call ☎ **415-541-0700** to request a copy.

If you prefer to surf for entertainment information and current event listings, check out the following Web sites:

- ✔ `www.bayarea.citysearch.com`: Citysearch not only lets you search on specific places, but it also directs you to restaurants and points of interest close to wherever you plan to be.
- ✔ `www.sfbay.yahoo.com`: Yahoo!, the Web search engine, publishes this guide to San Francisco.
- ✔ `www.sfbg.com`: You can find *The Bay Guardian*'s complete entertainment listings online. Try this one first.
- ✔ `www.sfgate.com/eguide`: This is the *San Francisco Chronicle*'s entertainment Web site.
- ✔ `www.sfweekly.com`: This is the Web site for *SF Weekly,* another great lefty weekly with provocative features, lots of local info, and reviews.

Checking out sports on the Web

In addition to the following specific sites, where (in most cases) you can purchase tickets online, swing by the Bay Area's general sports site at `www.bayinsider.com`.

- ✔ **Golden State Warriors:** `www.nba.com/warriors`
- ✔ **Oakland A's:** `www.oaklandas.com`
- ✔ **Oakland Raiders:** `www.raiders.com`
- ✔ **San Francisco 49ers:** `www.sf49ers.com`
- ✔ **San Francisco Giants:** `www.sfgiants.com`

Surfing for performing arts information

Check out the following sites for all your performing arts needs:

- ✔ **American Conservatory Theater:** `www.act-sfbay.org`
- ✔ **Best of Broadway theater info:** `www.bestofbroadway-sf.com`
- ✔ **Lamplighters light opera company:** `www.lamplighters.org`
- ✔ **San Francisco Ballet:** `www.sfballet.org`
- ✔ **San Francisco Opera:** `www.sfopera.org`
- ✔ **San Francisco Symphony:** `www.sfsymphony.org`
- ✔ **Theatre on the Square:** `www.theatreonthesquare.com`

Finding museums on the Web

Find out what San Francisco's museums have to offer at the following Web sites:

- **Asian Art Museum:** www.asianart.org
- **California Academy of Sciences:** www.calacademy.org
- **The Exploratorium:** www.exploratorium.edu
- **M.H. de Young Memorial Museum and California Palace of the Legion of Honor:** www.thinker.org
- **Museum of the City of San Francisco:** www.sfmuseum.org
- **San Francisco Museum of Modern Art:** www.sfmoma.org

Getting a table at 8:00

San Francisco has thousands of restaurants, but if you don't make dinner reservations — sometimes way in advance — you may not get to eat where you want. For dinner seating (7 to 9 p.m.) at some of the award-winning restaurants, such as Charles Nob Hill, Gary Danko, Hawthorne Lane, Boulevard, Masa's, and Jardinière, you will need to make reservations several weeks in advance. Even some of the slightly lower profile, but equally fabulous restaurants that attract more locals and fewer tourists, such as Slanted Door and Delfina, get booked up quickly. Make your reservations as much as four weeks in advance if you have a particular restaurant in mind.

You can also ask your hotel to make dinner reservations for you. Restaurants like to stay on good terms with hotel concierges — which means you may have better luck obtaining that hard-to-get res for 8 at the ten-table bistro-of-the-moment if the concierge calls for you. It doesn't always work, but it's worth a try.

You can also make reservations over the Web. A number of excellent local restaurants now belong to OpenTable (www.opentable.com), a Web site that will book your table for two at dozens of places around the Bay Area. The service is free and instant. I've used them three times thus far with no trouble and excellent results. If you decide to try this site but it says a table isn't available at the time you want, go ahead and phone the restaurant directly. The restaurants offer OpenTable a limited number of tables each night — they don't open their entire reservations book to the company.

Packing like a Pro

My cousin Irene, an inveterate traveler, actually spent two weeks in South Africa, partly on safari, with only two short-sleeved seersucker suits, a couple of sweaters, and a coordinating jacket. She arrived with room in her suitcase, which was fortunate, because she returned with 2 tons of gifts and a 5-foot-tall carved walking stick, and she had to borrow an extra bag. Maybe you don't need to be as extreme as Irene was, but I recommend you approach your packing by taking everything you think you'll need and laying it out on the bed. Then get rid of half of it.

I recommend this strategy not because I expect you to fill the crevices of your luggage with your vacation purchases, but because you don't want to hurt yourself by toting half your earthly belongings around with you. I promise, you won't wear all that stuff anyway.

No matter what time of year you visit San Francisco, don't forget to bring along a coat or warm jacket; the weather can change almost instantly from sunny and warm to windy and cold. Also, don't forget the following:

- ✔ Good walking shoes
- ✔ A camera
- ✔ A versatile sweater and/or blazer
- ✔ A belt
- ✔ Toiletries and medications (pack these in your carry-on bag so you'll have them if the airline loses your luggage)
- ✔ Pajamas

Unless you'll be attending a board meeting, a wedding, or one of the city's posh restaurants, you probably won't need a suit or a fancy dress. A pair of jeans or khakis and a comfortable sweater will be more useful to you. (See the packing list in the next section for other packing wisdom.)

Call your airline to find out how many pieces of carry-on luggage you can bring. (At press time, passengers were limited to just one, plus one personal item like a purse or briefcase.) In your carry-on, pack a book or other entertainment for the flight, any breakable items you don't want to put in your suitcase, a snack in case you don't want what the airline is serving that day, any vital documents you don't want to lose in your luggage (like your return tickets, passport, wallet, and so on), and space to put your sweater or jacket if you get warm in an over-heated terminal.

Checking off items on your packing list

Here's a list of essentials to help you make sure you don't forget anything:

- ✔ Bathing suit (if your hotel has a pool or spa)
- ✔ Belt

✔ Camera (don't forget the film — it can be very expensive when you're traveling)

✔ Coat and tie or a dress (only if you plan to go someplace fancy)

✔ Medications (pack these in a carry-on bag so you'll have them even if you lose your luggage)

✔ Pants and/or skirts

✔ Shirts or blouses

✔ Shoes (only bring two or three pairs, including a good pair of walking shoes)

✔ Shorts (only if you'll be in warmer climes)

✔ Socks

✔ Sweaters and/or jackets

✔ Toiletries (a razor, toothbrush, comb, deodorant, makeup, contact lens solutions, hair dryer, extra pair of glasses, sewing kit)

✔ Umbrella (you never know when you'll need one)

✔ Underwear

Dressing like the locals

It's a tradition to scoff at tourists in cargo shorts wandering around Union Square in the dead of summer (when temperatures rarely top 70 degrees and a chilling fog rolls in most mornings and evenings). Avoid the guffaws (and catching cold) by dressing in layers — a T-shirt under a sweater under a jacket. Sure, you'll end up tying the jacket and the sweater around your waist in the mid-afternoon, but at least we'll think you're one of us.

The city is known for informality, but it still has style. Men who don't want to be considered rubes ought to pack a sports coat for an evening at the theatre, symphony, opera, or a really nice restaurant. For women, a good pair of lightweight wool slacks and a sweater set will take you anywhere. Anyone planning on heading to dance clubs will want to dress on the trendy side, which around here means wearing black and having something other than your ears pierced.

Part III
Settling Into San Francisco

The 5th Wave   By Rich Tennant

SAN FRANCISCO'S AMAZING CABLE CARS

Travelers can ride from Market Street to the Financial District, through the Rocky Mountains and on to Denver all for the price of one Muni Passport.

©RICHTENNANT

In this part . . .

This part gets you from the airport to the city, introduces you to the neighborhoods, and explains how to use San Francisco's handy public transportation system. If you're driving, you can flip directly to the tips for upping your parking karma quotient — you'll need it around San Francisco.

Chapter 10

Orienting Yourself in San Francisco

*Y*ou can't really glean much about a place from its airports and highways. But as you head toward San Francisco, the industrial sites and parking lots you pass gradually become the neighborhoods and landmarks you may have seen in films and magazines or heard about from fellow travelers. That's when you realize that you're starting an adventure in an exciting, new place. Welcome to San Francisco.

Getting around San Francisco International Airport

San Francisco International Airport (SFO) consists of four main terminals: North (Terminal 3), South (Terminal 1), Central (Terminal 2, currently closed for remodeling), and International. The baggage level of each terminal also houses information booths. Bank of America operates a branch on the mezzanine level of the North terminal, and you can find ATMs on the upper level of all terminals.

You can call the airport (☎ **650-875-8575**) for recorded information, or try ☎ 650-817-1717 for transit information. The traveler's information desk in each of the three main terminals can also give you information on options to reach your destination. Or go to the Web site at www.flysfo.com for more about the airport and ground transportation.

To reach your destination by taxi or shuttle, here are the specifics:

- ✔ Taxis line up for passengers at the center island outside the lower level of the airport. The 14-mile trip to Union Square takes 20 to 30 minutes or so depending on traffic and should cost around $35 plus tip.

- ✔ If you're patient enough to wait 10 to 20 minutes for the one heading to your neighborhood, shuttle vans offer door-to-door service from the airport. However, the shuttle may make up to three stops before it's your turn to exit. You can find the shuttles by leaving the airport from the upper level and heading to the center island outside the ticket counter nearest you. A guide will direct you. Look for exact shuttle fares posted throughout the terminals; most charge between $10 and $12. **Super Shuttle** (☎ **415-558-8500;** Internet: www.supershuttle.com) is my personal favorite. You don't need to make advance reservations.

- ✔ Also traversing the terminals is a free minibus marked **CalTrain SFO Shuttle,** which takes passengers to the Millbrae Cal Train Station, a few miles from the airport. From there, you can board Cal Train to the depot at Fourth and King streets in San Francisco. The fare is a bargain at $2, and the ride takes under 30 minutes. For the train schedule, go to www.transitinfo.org or call ☎ **650-817-1717.**

- ✔ If you're renting a car, a free bus will transport you to the vast building where all the counters and cars are located. Catch the bus from the upper-level center islands outside the terminals.

To drive yourself into town, follow the airport signs to Highway 101 north and Highway 280. Stay toward the left, so you don't end up on 280. If you want to go to Union Square, exit 101 north at Fourth Street. Traffic is manageable until rush hour, from 3 to 7 p.m.

Getting around Oakland International Airport

At **Oakland International** (☎ **510-577-4000**), all ground transportation is on one level. A shuttle service called **Bayporter Express** (☎ **800-287-6783**) picks up passengers from Terminal 1 at the center island, and from Terminal 2 around the corner from baggage claim. The fare to San Francisco is $26 for one person, $36 for two people in the same party, and $5 for kids under 12. You'll have an easier time if you make reservations for the 45– to 90-minute ride. To take a cab downtown, expect to pay around $40; the trip takes 30 to 40 minutes, depending on traffic. You can find ATMs in the airport.

Bay Area Rapid Transit, known as BART (☎ **510-464-6000;** Internet: www.bart.org), also runs from Oakland into the city. You can catch the **AirBART** shuttle (☎ **510-430-9440**), which runs every 15 minutes, in front of Terminal 1 or 2. The fare is $2 for the 15-minute ride to the Oakland Coliseum BART station. From there, transfer to a BART train into San Francisco; the fare is about $2.45. Purchase your ticket from well-marked kiosks inside the airport or at the BART station. If you're staying around Union Square, the city's commercial hub, exit BART on Powell Street; the ride takes about 25 minutes.

All the major rental-car company counters are inside the terminals. If you're driving into San Francisco, exit the airport on Hegenberger Road. Follow it north to Highway 880 toward San Francisco. From there, follow the signs to Highway 80 to San Francisco. When you reach the Bay Bridge, you'll have to pay $2 at the tollbooths to cross. On the other side, exit on Fifth Street to reach Union Square.

Arriving Some Other Way

The following sections explain what to do if you're arriving by train or automobile.

By train

Amtrak trains arrive in Emeryville, just south of Berkeley. From there, an Amtrak bus will take you the rest of the way to downtown San Francisco. The buses stop at the CalTrain station, where there's a new Muni streetcar line to the Embarcadero (and thus, into downtown) and at the Ferry Building. The Ferry Building is more convenient to the hotels recommended in this book, and from there you can take a taxi to Union Square or wherever.

By automobile

Drivers arriving from east of town will cross the Bay Bridge into downtown. Cars coming from the south on Highway 101 will discover the same view a few miles past 3-Com (or Candlestick) Park. Anyone making the journey along Highway 101 coming from the north will enter San Francisco from the Golden Gate Bridge. After you pass the toll booth (it's $3 coming into the city), exit along the bay to Van Ness Avenue.

Figuring Out the Neighborhoods

San Francisco is perfectly situated at the end of a 32-mile-long peninsula between the Pacific Ocean and the San Francisco Bay. The city
itself covers just 7 square miles. Streets are laid out in a traditional grid
pattern, except for two major diagonal arteries, Market Street and
Columbus Avenue. Market cuts through town from the Embarcadero up
toward Twin Peaks. Columbus runs at an angle through North Beach,
beginning near the Transamerica Pyramid in the Financial District and
ending near the Hyde Street Pier. You'll find numbered *streets* downtown, and numbered *avenues* in the Richmond and Sunset districts
southwest of downtown.

San Francisco neighborhoods are as diverse and interesting as their
inhabitants. Of course, you'll have no trouble distinguishing Union
Square from Chinatown. But even if you amble through largely residential neighborhoods, you'll notice distinct differences in the makeup of
the locals and the commercial establishments. The best way to
immerse yourself in the local culture is to pick a neighborhood and
take a stroll. The following sections tell you where to start.

The Castro

An historic and active gay community is the Castro's claim to fame.
Visitors can admire the beautifully restored Victorian homes, visit the
Castro Theater, and try out a new image in the superb men's clothing
stores. For shopping and people-watching, head to Castro Street,
between Market and 18th streets.

China Basin

This neighborhood is quite old, but B.S. (before the PacBell baseball
stadium), visitors had no reason to come here. Boy, have things
changed. King Street from Third Street to the Embarcadero is the main
drag; that's where you can find restaurants, bars, and the boys of
summer.

Chinatown

The borders of Chinatown are always in a state of flux, but you can generally wander this densely packed area roughly between Broadway,
Taylor, Bush, and Montgomery streets. It is every bit as vivid and fascinating as advertised. The **Dragon Gate** entrance on Grant Avenue leads
to touristy shops, but you'll swear you're in another country after you
wander up Stockton and through the abundant alleyways.

The Civic Center and Hayes Valley

If you're seeking the New Main Library; the brand-new Asian Art Museum; the Ballet, Symphony, and Opera buildings; or City Hall, then the Civic Center, bordered by Van Ness and Golden Gate avenues, and Franklin, Hyde, and Market streets, is where you want to be. This neighborhood also attracts a large homeless population and is dicey after dark. If you have plans in the area at night, I recommend taking a cab.

Hayes Valley, west of Civic Center, is surrounded by Franklin Street to the east, Webster Street to the west, Grove Street to the north, and Page Street to the south. Here you'll find places to shop and a few quality restaurants.

Cow Hollow

Between Van Ness Avenue, Broadway, and Lyon and Lombard streets is Cow Hollow, a residential utopia. You can find the famous Union Street here, popular for its trendy cloister of shops, restaurants, and however many young, urban professionals are left after the last economic downturn. Architecture and history fans can get a close look at the **Octagon House** (circa 1861) at 2645 Gough St. (at Union).

The Embarcadero

Liberated from the pylons and cement of the Embarcadero Freeway, which was damaged by the 1989 Loma Prieta earthquake and subsequently torn down, this area runs along the bay from the eastern edge of Fisherman's Wharf to the beginning of China Basin. **Embarcadero Center,** a collection of five multi-use buildings connected by bridges and walkways at the end of Market Street from Drumm to Sansome, houses upscale chain stores, restaurants, and movie theaters.

Financial District

The Financial District encompasses prime bay real estate roughly between Montgomery Street and the Embarcadero, on either side of Market Street. The **Transamerica Pyramid,** at Montgomery and Clay streets, is a skyline landmark. Seek out **Belden Place,** an alley between Kearny, Bush, and Pine streets, for outdoor dining opportunities. Antiques hounds will like the hunting grounds around Jackson Square.

San Francisco Neighborhoods

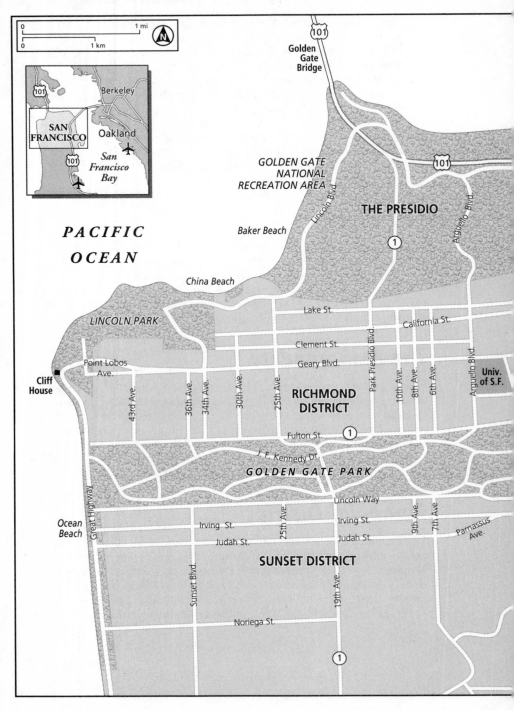

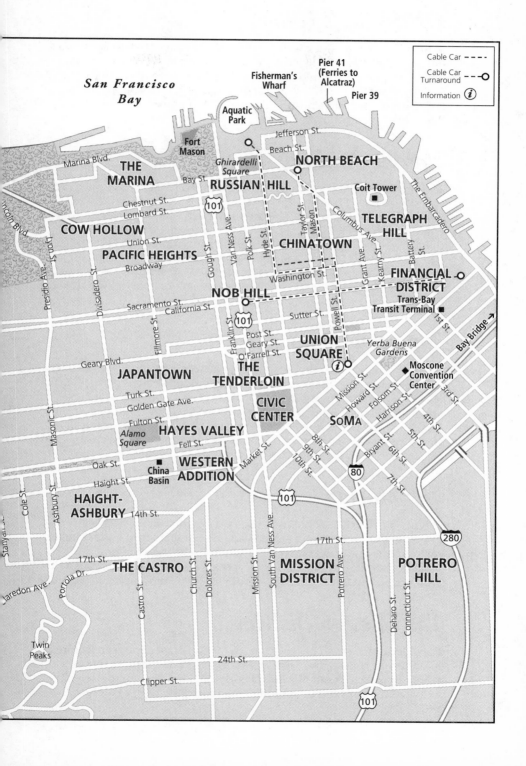

San Francisco Bay

Fisherman's Wharf

Pier 41 (Ferries to Alcatraz)

Pier 39

Aquatic Park

Jefferson St.

Fort Mason

Beach St.

NORTH BEACH

THE MARINA

Ghirardelli Square

Bay St.

RUSSIAN HILL

Coit Tower

Marina Blvd.

Chestnut St.

Lombard St.

101

TELEGRAPH HILL

Columbus Ave.

COW HOLLOW

Union St.

CHINATOWN

PACIFIC HEIGHTS

Broadway

Van Ness Ave.

Polk St.

Hyde St.

Taylor St.

Mason

Grant Ave.

Kearny St.

Battery

The Embarcadero

FINANCIAL DISTRICT

Washington St.

Gough St.

Lincoln Blvd.

Presidio Ave.

Lyon St.

Divisadero St.

Fillmore St.

NOB HILL

Sacramento St.

California St.

Trans-Bay Transit Terminal

101

Sutter St.

Powell St.

Geary Blvd.

Franklin St.

Post St.

Geary St.

O'Farrell St.

UNION SQUARE

Yerba Buena Gardens

Bay Bridge

1st St.

JAPANTOWN

THE TENDERLOIN

Moscone Convention Center

Masonic St.

Turk St.

Golden Gate Ave.

Fulton St.

CIVIC CENTER

SoMa

Mission St.

Howard St.

Folsom St.

Harrison St.

3rd St.

Alamo Square

HAYES VALLEY

Fell St.

Oak St.

WESTERN ADDITION

China Basin

8th St.

9th St.

10th St.

Bryant St.

4th St.

5th St.

6th St.

7th St.

80

Cole St.

Ashbury St.

Haight St.

HAIGHT-ASHBURY

14th St.

Market St.

South Van Ness Ave.

101

17th St.

280

Stanyan St.

17th St.

Portola Dr.

THE CASTRO

Castro St.

Church St.

Dolores St.

Mission St.

MISSION DISTRICT

Potrero Ave.

POTRERO HILL

Deharo St.

Connecticut St.

Claredon Ave.

Twin Peaks

24th St.

Clipper St.

101

Cable Car

Cable Car Turnaround

Information *i*

Fisherman's Wharf

Millions of tourists flock to Fisherman's Wharf, located on Bay Street between Powell and Polk streets, but the former working piers have been stripped of their glory and are now filled with the sounds of cash registers. Pass by Pier 39 and the plethora of schlock shops to the Hyde Street Pier and Ghirardelli Square. Don't forget to visit Aquatic Park and the Maritime Museum.

Haight-Ashbury

The Haight, or Haight-Ashbury, is surrounded by Stanyan Street to the east, Divisadero Street to the west, Fulton Street to the north, and Waller Street to the south. The area still hasn't fully recovered from what must have been a real bummer to some of its residents — the demise of the '60s. You can find most of the action on Haight Street, which continues to hold a magical appeal over scruffy groups of youngsters campaigning for handouts. Used-clothing stores compete for space with all kinds of commercial endeavors, most of which are perfectly legit.

Japantown

Off Geary, between Webster and Laguna streets, is Japantown, which at first glance appears to consist of ugly indoor shopping centers. However, you can find some good, inexpensive noodle restaurants and some interesting shops housed in these dismal gray buildings. Check out the AMC-Kabuki movie theaters here, or have a soak at the Kabuki Hot Springs. Across Sutter Street (between Fillmore and Webster), look for Cottage Row, the last bit of the real Japantown left.

The Marina

On the Marina's commercial blocks — Chestnut Street between Franklin and Lyon streets — you can find a full array of coffeehouses, restaurants, and shops targeting the sleek and the slender. This is the neighborhood of choice for newly arrived singles. Tourists stop by to see Fort Mason Center, the Palace of Fine Arts, and the Exploratorium.

The Mission District

Located from Cesar Chavez Street to Market Street between Dolores and Potrero streets, the Mission District is a busy, largely Hispanic community. Check out Mission Dolores, Dolores Park, and 24th Street, along with a plethora of affordable restaurants and eye-catching outdoor murals. You can find a multitude of restaurants on Valencia and Guererro streets between 16th and 23rd streets.

Nob Hill

One of the oldest and most fashionable addresses, Nob Hill envelops California Street from Leavenworth to Stockton and overlooks the Financial District. Grace Cathedral and a selection of expensive apartments and hotels leave quite an impression.

North Beach

North Beach isn't an actual beach — it's the old Italian neighborhood next to Chinatown. Head here to sit in cafes, to browse bookstores and other shops, and to sample the selections at the various delis and pastry shops. Columbus Avenue is the main street, but you can find family-style restaurants and crowded bars from Washington to Grant. The XXX-rated clubs stick together on Broadway. **Telegraph Hill** is just to the east of North Beach, behind Coit Tower and the Filbert steps.

Pacific Heights

Pacific Heights, which is bordered by Broadway, Pine, Divisadero, and Franklin Streets, is where the wealthy lounge around their extravagant but tasteful homes. You can visit the **Haas-Lilienthal House,** an 1886 Queen Anne Victorian at 2007 Franklin St., at Washington, and stare at Mrs. Doubtfire's fictional digs on the corner of Broadway and Steiner.

The Presidio

These 1,500 acres on the westernmost point of the city are part of the **Golden Gate National Recreation Area.** If you love to hike, go to the visitor's center for maps and suggestions. The views and landscape are sensational. If you'd rather play ten pins, a great little bowling alley is also located here. A patch of Presidio land along the bay, named **Crissy Fields,** is the newest park in the city and features wetlands, picnic areas, bay views, and a drop-in center with weekend activities.

The Richmond District

The Richmond District stretches from **Golden Gate Park** (see Chapter 16) at one edge to the Pacific Ocean at the other. **Lincoln Park, Land's End,** the **California Palace of the Legion of Honor museum,** and the **Cliff House** are all located in this large neighborhood. Clement Street is akin to Chinatown, and you can find authentic Russian food on Geary.

Russian Hill

Polk Street from Broadway up to around Greenwich Street suddenly has become *trés chic*. This is a delightful area for shopping and snacking with some terrific little restaurants, bakeries, antiques shops, and boutiques. Just to the northwest, you'll find the wiggly part of Lombard Street and Macondry Lane, immortalized in Armistead Maupin's *Tales of the City.*

South of Market

Although the dot-com bust tempered the building frenzy, South of Market Street (or SoMa for short) between Tenth, King, and Steuart streets has exploded in the past 12 years, particularly along Mission Street between Second and Fifth. Attractions include the **San Francisco Museum of Modern Art,** the **Cartoon Art Museum, Yerba Buena Gardens,** and the kid-magnet **Sony Metreon** (see Chapter 16). Clubs have multiplied around Folsom Street; restaurants and bars are thick from Howard Street down to the tiny South Park neighborhood. Avoid Sixth and Seventh streets below Market; these blocks are rife with unsavory characters.

The Tenderloin

The blocks bounded by Sutter and Mason streets and Van Ness and Golden Gate avenues are a section of town currently home to immigrant families attempting to live their lives alongside flop houses, bars, massage parlors, and people subsiding on the fringes of society. A slim rectangle of space from roughly O'Farrell to Market streets between Larkin and Polk is dangerous at night and rough during the day. The only place worth visiting here is **Glide Memorial Church** for Sunday services.

Union Square

The center of tourist activity, Union Square is tucked inside Sutter, Grant, Market, and Mason streets. Big department stores, expensive boutiques, theaters, restaurants, and the greatest concentration of hotels in the city surround the actual square, which is undergoing a facelift.

The Western Addition

I mention this old neighborhood between Geary, Haight, Gough, and Divisidero streets because people studying their maps often believe it's an easy walk from Civic Center to Golden Gate Park by way of Oak or Fell streets. That's not entirely accurate. First, it's hilly. Second, it's not the safest section of town.

Getting Information After You Arrive

If I've left something important out, ask your hotel concierge or desk clerk, or stop by the **Convention and Visitors Bureau Information Center** on the lower level of Hallidie Plaza, 900 Market St. (at Powell), or call ☎ **800-220-5747** or 415-391-2000. The office is open Monday through Friday from 9 a.m. to 5:30 p.m., Saturday from 9 a.m. to 3 p.m., and Sunday from 10 a.m. to 2 p.m. It's closed Thanksgiving Day, Christmas Day, and New Year's Day.

Look for a free *Bay Guardian* or *SF Weekly* from sidewalk kiosks or coffee-houses for listings of city events and entertainment. The Convention and Visitors Bureau also operates a 24-hour events line at ☎ **415-391-2000.**

Chapter 11

Getting Around San Francisco

● ●

In This Chapter

▶ Strolling through the city

▶ Using Muni and BART

▶ Riding the cable cars

▶ Getting driving and parking tips

● ●

As you may have gleaned from earlier chapters, having a car in the city isn't highly advised and isn't necessary most of the time. San Francisco really caters to walkers, with benches appearing just when you need one and cafes at hand for a shot of caffeine when energy flags. Getting around on a bus or Muni metro streetcar is cheap if not perfect. In the rare instance that you do need a car, renting one from downtown is easy.

This chapter contains everything you need to know about cruising around the city sans car. It even includes some inside tips on parking should you decide to throw caution to the wind and join the legendary drivers — and I don't mean that in a good way — gracing our city's roads and highways. (See Chapter 9 to read about car-rental companies in San Francisco.)

The one-stop shopping number for local traffic or public transit information is ☎ **415-817-1717**. This number connects you to whatever you need, be it BART and Muni routes or traffic conditions.

Heading Out on Foot

Walking is the best way to travel if you aren't in a rush, and it's also the only way to really see and enjoy the neighborhoods. I recommend some walking tours in Chapter 18, and I can't urge you enough to take one or more. Walking is the only means of seeing the neighborhoods in the way they deserve to be seen.

Use caution when walking, because San Francisco has seen a rash of vehicle/pedestrian accidents lately. Be alert at all times. Watch for drivers running red lights (a common occurrence here) or turning right on a red light; make sure bus drivers see you entering the crosswalk; and be especially wary of bike messengers, who show no mercy.

Among the best neighborhoods for walkers are **Chinatown, North Beach, Russian Hill,** and **The Embarcadero.** If you're in good shape and don't mind a little wind, a walk across the **Golden Gate Bridge** is much more satisfying than a drive, especially if you're the one who has to keep your eyes on the road.

Traveling by Streetcar

Walking probably won't take you everywhere you want to go. But getting around by public transportation is easy when you know a few basics. The **San Francisco Municipal Railway,** known as Muni (☎ **415-673-6864**), is much maligned by locals for inefficiency, but tens of thousands of commuters rely daily on its buses and electric streetcars for a lift to the office. The fare is $1 for an adult and 35¢ for seniors and children to ride a bus or streetcar anywhere in the system; exact change is required. Muni Passports, accepted on buses, streetcars, and even cable cars, are a bargain for visitors planning to take public transportation extensively. A one-day passport is $6, a three-day pass is $10, and a seven-day pass is $15. You can purchase them at the Convention and Visitors Bureau Information Center at Hallidie Plaza, at the Powell and Market or Beach and Hyde streets Cable Car Turnaround police booth, or online at www.sfmuni.com. You may also purchase single-day passes on board the cable cars.

Citypass, a booklet of discounted tickets to five major attractions, including the **Museum of Modern Art, Palace of the Legion of Honor, California Academy of Sciences**, **Exploratorium,** and a Blue & Gold Bay Cruise or Alcatraz tour, now includes a seven-day Muni Passport, making it quite a bargain for those who are ambitious enough to use all the coupons. It's $33.75 for adults and you can purchase it at the participating attractions or at Hallidie Plaza, or you can order it in advance from Blue & Gold Fleet Cruise (☎ **415-705-5555;** Internet: www.citypass.net).

You can also save two dollars by purchasing a roll of ten Muni tokens for $8. Tokens are available at the cable car booth at Powell and Market and at the ticket booths inside the Montgomery and Embarcadero stations. Don't buy tokens from anyone hawking them on the street. For a complete listing of token vendors, check the Muni Web site (www.sfmuni.com).

At the underground Muni stops from Civic Center to the Embarcadero, the fare boxes (which are located at the entry point prior to reaching the escalators) only accept coins or tokens, an important point to remember if you're in a hurry and have only dollar bills in hand. There are change machines on the walls next to the BART ticket dispensers.

Muni streetcars run underground downtown and above ground in the outlying neighborhoods from 6 a.m. until 1 a.m. (although I did attempt to take Muni home late in the evening once, only to discover that the station entrance was gated shut). The five Muni Metro streetcar lines — the J, K, L, M, and N — make the same stops as BART (see the discussion later) along Market Street, including Embarcadero Station, Montgomery and Powell streets (both near Union Square), Civic Center, and Van Ness Avenue. Past Van Ness Avenue, the routes go off in different directions. The N-Judah line services Haight-Ashbury and parallels Golden Gate Park on its way down Judah Street to the ocean. The J-Church line passes close to Mission Dolores and the Castro. The L-Taraval line travels through the Sunset District within walking distance of the San Francisco Zoo.

The newest and most picturesque line, the F-Market, is made up of a collection of vintage streetcars from around the world. It runs along Market Street to the Castro Street station and back. The F line was extended in 2000, allowing these rejuvenated antiques to continue from Market Street over to Mission Street and down the Embarcadero to Fisherman's Wharf. Muni cars marked Mission Bay end their journey at the CalTrain Station on King Street, just past the new Giants baseball park.

Spend the $3 to get the Official San Francisco Street and Transit Muni Map. It is invaluable for public transportation users. It shows all bus, streetcar, cable car, and BART routes and stations. You can buy the maps at the Convention and Visitors Bureau Information Center. You can also call ☎ 415-673-MUNI for route information.

Trekking by Bus

The Muni buses are clearly numbered on the front and run through the city from 6 a.m. to midnight (however, I don't recommend taking them too late at night). Street-corner signs and painted yellow bands on utility poles and on curbs mark bus stops. Buses come by every 5 to 20 minutes, depending on where you want to go and the time of day. Rapid transit — in the truest sense of the adjective — they are not, but with 80 transit lines, they are the most complete. Muni metro streetcars are faster, but the buses cover a wider area. Expect most buses to be extremely crowded during rush hours (from 7 to 9 a.m. and 4 to 6 p.m.).

Exact change is required on the buses, as it is on the streetcars (for information on fares, see the previous section, "Traveling by Streetcar"). The driver will likely hand you a paper transfer, which is good for a second ride within two hours. If you plan on riding another bus or streetcar within the time limit, make sure to get a transfer.

Befriending BART

BART (☎ 650-992-2278), which stands for Bay Area Rapid Transit, is not Muni. Tourists often get the two systems mixed up because they share the same underground stations downtown. You won't get into too much trouble if you get the systems confused within the city limits. BART, however, runs all over the Bay Area, and if you are inattentive, you may end up in a place far different from where you expected to go. More than one unsuspecting traveler has ended up in Fremont when he intended to exit at the Embarcadero. If BART is what you want, check the signs carefully in the stations and pay attention to the cars themselves. The sleek silver and blue BART trains do not resemble Muni's orange-trimmed electric streetcars in the least. You purchase tickets for BART from machines at the station. Fares to and from any point in the city are $1.10 each way; outside the city, fares vary depending on how far down the line you go. You can't use Muni transfers, tokens, or passes on BART.

Getting Around by Cable Car

There's no law that says you have to ride the cable cars, but no self-respecting tourist would leave San Francisco without the experience. Three lines cross the downtown area. If you're in the mood for some scenery, take the **Powell-Hyde line,** which begins at Powell Street and ends at the turnaround across from Ghirardelli Square. The **Powell-Mason line** goes through North Beach and ends near Fisherman's Wharf. The **California Street line,** the least scenic, crests at Nob Hill and then makes its way to Van Ness Avenue. (The lines for the California Street cable cars are usually much shorter because the route isn't as twisty.) Rides are $2 one way, so buy a Muni Passport and take all three as often as you like. The pass is worth every penny. You may only board a cable car at specific, clearly marked stops.

Cable cars operate from 6:30 a.m. to 12:30 a.m., but I suggest taking one early in the day if you want to have a little elbow room as you ride; as the day goes on, tourists jam-pack the cars.

Cable Car Routes

Catching a Taxi

You can easily get a taxi downtown, especially in front of hotels, but you have to call a cab to retrieve you almost anywhere else. Unfortunately, reaching the taxi companies by phone can take a while. Keep these numbers handy:

- ✔ **Desoto Cab:** ☎ 415-970-1300
- ✔ **Luxor Cabs:** ☎ 415-282-4141
- ✔ **Pacific:** ☎ 415-986-7220
- ✔ **Veteran's Cab:** ☎ 415-552-1300
- ✔ **Yellow Cab:** ☎ 415-626-2345

Rates are about $2 for the first mile and $1.80 for each additional mile.

Motoring Around on Your Own

Drivers unfamiliar with the area often have a difficult time navigating the heavy downtown traffic and multitude of one-way streets. Add to these problems the lack of parking and heavy-handed meter maids, and leaving your car outside the city limits makes sense. However, if you plan to go over the Golden Gate or Bay bridges, or south to Monterey and Santa Cruz, a car will be essential.

Dealing with rush hour

During the week, traffic backs up on bridge approaches throughout the Financial District and downtown from 3 p.m. until about 7 p.m. North Beach is usually busy from the late afternoon into the evenings, and because the streets bump into Columbus Avenue, navigating the area can be confusing. On the weekends, Lombard Street and Van Ness Avenue take the brunt of all the cars inching their way toward the Golden Gate Bridge. Getting through Chinatown's narrow, crowded streets by car is basically impossible during waking hours. If you must cross town, I suggest taking California Street past the Financial District.

For sanity's sake, avoid traveling north on the Golden Gate or Bay bridges between 3 and 7 p.m. weekday afternoons. If you plan to drive to Point Reyes or the Wine Country (see Chapters 25 and 26), do not leave on a Friday after 2 p.m., if at all possible. Traffic across the Golden Gate Bridge is generally awful on weekends, especially if the weather is nice. Leave before 10 a.m. if you must leave at all.

Driving by the rules

California law requires that both drivers and passengers wear seat belts. You may turn right at a red light (unless otherwise indicated) after yielding to traffic and pedestrians, and after making a complete stop. Cable cars and streetcars always have the right-of-way, as do pedestrians, especially if they use intersections and crosswalks. On Market Street, one lane is exclusively for buses unless you're making a right turn. Heed the signs.

Being cautious with red lights

San Francisco drivers have a wretched tendency to run red lights, so pause to check oncoming traffic carefully before entering an intersection just after the light turns green.

Parking the car

I'm not going to take up space discussing the many parking regulations; just take my advice: Park in a garage. They are expensive, but they could save you some money in the long run because parking tickets start at $30.

Legal street parking spaces are next to unpainted curbs. Yellow, white, green, and red painted curbs are all off limits in general — the only exception being commercial zones (yellow curbs), which are okay to park in after delivery hours. Pay attention to the signs liberally posted on the streets. Be very aware of tow-away zones. You can't park on most streets downtown between 4 and 6 p.m. without running the risk of having your car towed. Never park in front of a driveway. Otherwise, you'll find your rental at the **City Tow Lot** at 375 Seventh St., between Harrison and Folsom streets (☎ **415-621-8605**), faster than you can blink. If your car isn't where you thought you left it, call ☎ **415-553-1235** to find out whether your vehicle has been towed or stolen. If your car has been towed to the city tow lot, you need to go there in person to pay the ticket and the storage charges (which vary depending on how long the car has been there). This misadventure will cost you at least $130, cash or credit card only.

Legal parking spots are hard to come by. If you're driving, park in a public garage or use the services of a valet — don't keep circling your prey hoping someone will drive off, unless you have a lot of time to spare. And if you do happen to find a legal space within walking distance of your destination, grab it immediately. By my calculations, walking distance is about four blocks, not two doors down.

Improving your parking karma

So, you want a parking space, huh? You'll have to be one step ahead of the crowd. Following these suggestions will be a big help:

- ✔ **Carry quarters.** Most parking meters accept nothing else.
- ✔ **Watch the clock.** Many crosstown downtown streets do not allow parking during rush hour, from 4 to 6 p.m. Get to the Financial District, Union Square, SoMa, or Nob Hill a few minutes before 6 p.m. to grab the great street parking space of your choice.
- ✔ **Spring for valet parking.** The extra money now may be worth avoiding the headache of finding a parking spot later.
- ✔ **Check out public parking garages.** Public parking garages are cheaper than privately owned ones. In North Beach, park in the garage on Vallejo Street (between Kearny and Green). In Chinatown, park at the Portsmouth Square garage on Kearny Street.

✓ **Make note of street sweeping times.** If you find street parking galore in some outlying neighborhood, check posted signs for sweeping hours and days: That's generally the real reason for your good luck. Don't park without carefully checking the signs, unless you want to give the Department of Traffic a $30 donation. If your timing is right however, you'll pull up after the sweeper trucks have made their rounds, when it's okay to park.

✓ **Stop "runaway" car syndrome.** To keep your car from rolling away while you're parked on a hill, follow these easy steps: Put the car in gear, apply the hand brake, and *curb your wheels* — turn your wheels toward the curb when facing downhill and away from the curb when facing uphill. Curbing your wheels is the law! (This won't actually contribute to your finding a parking place, but it will help you keep the one you found.)

Chapter 12

Keeping Track of Your Cash

● ●

In This Chapter

▶ Getting cash in San Francisco

▶ Knowing what to do if your wallet is stolen

▶ Adding up the taxes

● ●

*B*ring money. Vacationing in San Francisco costs a lot. Recent Convention and Visitors Bureau statistics show that the average daily per capita spending for all visitors, including those who stay with relatives or friends, is a substantial $130.40. The major cost is for lodging, while food takes the next largest bite out of your pocketbook.

You can always find ways to keep costs down. By using public transportation rather than renting a car, you can save a small fortune, even if you splurge on cabs now and then. As for food, San Francisco has such a wide variety of low-cost ethnic restaurants and inexpensive cafes that you can save some dough and still eat like a frugal gourmet. Two can spend as little as $85 per night for a pleasant hotel room, depending on the level of comfort and privacy you require.

Finding Cash in San Francisco

You're never far from an ATM on most commercial streets, and most machines accept cards from any network. Withdraw only as much money as you need every couple of days, so that you don't have to carry a large amount of cash. Note, however, that a fee ranging from $1 to $3 is imposed by just about every bank every time you use the ATM, if you don't have an account with that bank. Your own bank may also charge you a fee for using ATMs at other banks.

In San Francisco, Bank of America, Wells Fargo Bank, and California Federal Bank have the largest ATM networks. They all charge fees — $1.50 seems to be the going rate. Watch out for privately owned ATMs at convenience stores, in shopping centers, or in non-bank businesses. These machines usually charge a few dollars on top of bank fees.

Some people like to carry traveler's checks because they can be replaced if lost or stolen, and they offer a sound alternative to carrying a lot of cash at the beginning of the trip. ATMs have made traveler's checks unnecessary, but if you prefer the security of traveler's checks, you can get them at almost any bank. You pay a service charge ranging from 1 to 4% for most checks. **American Express** checks are available through banks as well as at most AAA offices. You can also get American Express traveler's checks over the phone by calling ☎ 800-221-7282. **VISA** (☎ 800-227-6811) also offers traveler's checks, available at Citibank locations across the country and at several other banks. For **MasterCard** traveler's checks; call ☎ 800-223-9920 for a location near you.

A safe way to carry money and provide a convenient record of all your travel expenses is with credit cards. You can even get cash advances with your credit card at any bank. And if you don't like waiting for a teller, you can get a cash advance at the ATM if you know your PIN. If you need your PIN (or didn't even know you had one), call the phone number on the back of your credit card and ask the bank to send it to you. It usually takes five to seven business days. Some banks will do it over the phone if you can answer some security questions to verify that you're the owner of the credit card.

Another hidden expense to contend with: Interest rates for cash advances are often significantly higher than rates for credit-card purchases. More importantly, you'll start paying interest on the advance *the moment you receive the cash.* On an airline-affiliated credit card, a cash advance does not earn frequent-flier miles.

Dealing with the Nightmare of a Stolen Wallet

Although it's pretty unlikely that you'll be the victim of a crime while on vacation, there are some talented pickpockets roaming the streets of San Francisco. And I can tell you from sorrowful personal experience that discovering that your wallet has magically disappeared, leaving you with only the change that's fallen to the bottom of your purse, is not thrilling. So here's a reminder: If you must carry a handbag, hold it in front of you, not dangling from your shoulder. Never leave your pocketbook or backpack unattended. Don't carry your wallet in a back pocket. Carry only as much cash as you need in a day and consider keeping your ATM card, credit cards, and driver's license in an inside pocket.

If the worst does happen and your wallet or purse is stolen, call the credit card company's emergency toll-free number. In many cities, the company can get you an emergency credit card within a day or two. Some may also be able to wire you a cash advance off your credit card right away. The issuing bank's toll-free number is usually on the back of the card, but that doesn't help much if the card was stolen. Write down the phone and credit-card numbers before you leave, and keep them in a safe place just in case. **Citicorp Visa's** U.S. emergency number is ☎ **800-645-6556. American Express** cardholders and traveler's check holders should call ☎ **800-221-7282** for all money emergencies. **MasterCard** holders should call ☎ **800-307-7309.**

If your wallet is stolen, chances are excellent that you won't be seeing it again, and the police are unlikely to recover it. Be sure to inform the police anyway, though, because you may need the police report number for credit-card or insurance purposes later.

Taxing Your Wallet

Along with the more obvious expenses, such as souvenir bridges and *Escape from Alcatraz* T-shirts, you have those little extras called taxes that add up. In our fair city, a sales tax of 8.5% is added to just about everything but snacks and take-out food. Additionally, a hotel tax of 14% is added to the cost of your room. The good news is that most of it goes to fund local arts organizations, which makes it a bit more palatable, I hope.

Part IV
Dining in San Francisco

The 5th Wave   **By Rich Tennant**

"OK Cookie-your venison in lingdonberry sauce is good, as are your eggplant soufflé and the risotto with foie gras. But whoever taught you how to make a croquembouche should be shot!"

In this part . . .

An entire section devoted to food? You betcha. If not in a book devoted to the culinary center of the universe — or at least a good three-quarters of the U.S. — then where? Read these chapters and you'll soon be able to discuss the intricacies of the local food scene as if you had spent all your weekends dining in these parts. And if you prefer to eat and run, you'll get a head start with a chapter on food to go — and I don't mean fast food.

Chapter 13

Making the Scene: The Ins and Outs of Dining in San Francisco

• •

In This Chapter

▶ Experiencing the latest dining trends

▶ Getting the local flavor

▶ Reserving your table

▶ Dressing the part

• •

*W*hether you're a genuine gourmet or a fledgling foodie, San Francisco has more culinary options than you can shake a credit card at. But no matter where you rank yourself on the scale of adventuresome eating, there's no excuse to waste a meal in this city. Fast-food counters, chain restaurants, marketing enterprises masquerading as dining establishments — you'll find them here, but do yourself a favor and pass 'em by. Instead, take advantage of the fresh food and skilled chefs that keep San Francisco in the culinary spotlight, and I guarantee you'll dine to your heart's content.

Turning Up the Heat

Restaurants debut in this town with great hoopla, but what's hot today may be out of business by the time you turn this page. At the moment, the newest trend is sharing. I don't mean spilling your life story — I mean sharing plates of food with your tablemates. Although this isn't unusual in your average Chinese restaurant, it is unexpected in most other eateries, so if you sup at Rose Pistola or Asia de Cuba, for example, be advised those hefty portions are meant for the entire table. On the other end of the spectrum, small plates, or *tapas,* are all the rage, and they, too, are meant to be shared. See Chapter 14 for more restaurant suggestions.

Finding the trendiest tables

San Francisco has no lack of sizzling white-tablecloth restaurants. It's still tough to get last-minute reservations at **Jardinère** (call ☎ 415-861-5555 if you want to try) or at two of the city's even more sophisticated purveyors of fine dining, **Fifth Floor** (☎ 415-348-1555) and **Gary Danko** (see Chapter 14). Call ahead, way, way ahead, if you have your heart set on supping at either of these bastions of chic. Wrangling a table at the always sublime **Masa's** (☎ 415-989-7154), where Ron Siegel (the kitchen god who bested Japanese television phenom "Iron Chef") now rules the stoves, can be equally challenging.

Cooking up San Francisco cuisine

When it comes to cuisine, international influences are making themselves at home on Bay City menus. This is not odd considering the ethnic makeup of the city's population, but it may throw you for a loop when your menu runs the gamut from East to West with a little southern comfort thrown in for good measure. Those restaurants serving tapas (alluded to in the previous section) are the most keen to take advantage of various culinary styles, and it's a clever way for a young chef to show his or her stuff. Tapas are also a pleasing way to order a meal. You don't have to choose between dishes that sound equally appealing, because the prices are low enough, and the portions small enough, to sample them all.

California cuisine continues to have a presence here as well, although it's being usurped by Modern American or New American cuisine. California cuisine features fresh seasonal ingredients prepared in simple and light ways. New American cuisine, on the other hand, also uses seasonal, American ingredients, but the preparations are influenced by whatever foreign cuisines interest the chef. Although the subtleties may be lost on you if you don't deconstruct your meals, I mention this because many new restaurants describe their cooking in these terms.

Another welcome dining trend has to do with accommodating those who are organizationally challenged. Many excellent restaurants in town, including **Boulevard, Charles Nob Hill,** and **Gary Danko** (see Chapter 14), accommodate walk-ins with counter seats or service in their bar areas. This is your best chance to eat at these top spots if you don't have reservations.

Making Reservations

If you really want to be able to experience some of the great restaurants while you're in town, make sure you reserve a table before you get here. It's not that the hostess takes pleasure in turning you away on a Friday night at 7 p.m. — did you notice all the other people drinking in the bar who also thought they could just amble in and get a table?

Besides picking up the phone, you can contact a number of restaurants through the Web site `www.opentable.com`. I've used this Web site a number of times, always with excellent results (see Chapter 9 for more information). You may also put your hotel to work by requesting that they assist you with dinner reservations. If you're really desperate, you can show a little *chutzpah* like my old friend Josephine, who has been known to march up to the host, look him or her in the eye, and announce she has reservations, even when that's not entirely accurate. The caveat here is to make sure your dining partners don't buckle under pressure.

Exploring the dining zones

Cafes and restaurants often congregate on certain blocks, making it easy to stroll down the street until an enticing odor or open table calls out to you. One of my absolute favorite dining blocks is **Belden Place** in the Financial District, a one-block alley closed to traffic off Bush and Pine streets between Kearny and Montgomery. Two standouts on multi-cultural Belden are **Plouf,** a delightful French restaurant specializing in fish and shellfish, and **B-44,** a Spanish newcomer specializing in paella and Catalan dishes (see Chapter 14 for a review). All the establishments on Belden close on Sundays.

North Beach is awash in Italian cafes, Italian restaurants of all persuasions, and some inexpensive little cafes. The family-style **La Felce** (1570 Stockton at Union) and **Capps Corner** (1600 Powell at Green) are among the last of the breed, where complete meals are no understatement. You order a bottle of Chianti and watch as your table fills with an antipasti, then a tureen of minestrone, followed by huge platters of spaghetti, chicken cacciatore, and spumoni for dessert.

The **Mission District** gourmet zone is booming, especially 16th Street between Valencia and Dolores, where you'll find the highly popular creperie **Ti Couz,** and a moderately priced Italian trattoria, **Il Cantuccio** among others. Mexican-food lovers should try **Pancho Villa,** which draws a crowd with its inexpensive and fresh burritos, tacos, and specialty platters. The mood in this neighborhood is casual and urban; it's populated by students, techies, a large Hispanic community, and a fair number of street people. Parking isn't easy, but there's a BART stop at 16th and Mission — a rather dicey station, so you may want to take a cab on the way home.

You can take the N-Judah streetcar to Irving Street and Ninth Avenue near Golden Gate Park to find another great couple of blocks of moderately priced and high-quality restaurants. **Chow** (see Chapter 14) has a location here, and you can't go wrong at **P.J.'s Oyster Bed** on Irving

Street at Ninth. There are also some great Japanese and Thai restaurants nearby, including **Hana Sushi,** 408 Irving St., between Fifth and Sixth avenues.

Discovering off-the-beaten-track restaurants

Restaurants are mining new territory as well, as evidenced by the dozens of places opening in neighborhoods most visitors would have shunned once upon a time. The blocks around **Dolores, Valencia,** and **Guerrero streets** in the **Mission District** from 16th to 23rd streets are just one example. Storefronts and former corner markets have become the domain of chefs hoping to create the next big thing food-wise. The popular **Slanted Door** (see Chapter 14) is one of the area's stars, while **Delfina** (see Chapter 14), a poorly-kept secret, had to quickly expand into the building next door in order to keep up with the multitudes who were begging for a taste from the Tuscan-Italian menu.

A section of **SoMa** that edges **Potrero Hill** is also drawing lots of interest from professional eaters and cooks. Mosey around **Florida and Mariposa streets** for a taste of high-style American cooking at **Gordon's House of Fine Eats** (see Chapter 14), but call for reservations first and take a cab; the parking is either valet or impossible.

Sampling San Francisco's Ethnic Eats

Certain neighborhoods in San Francisco are hubs for particular regional cuisines, as is the case in other big cities. You can find several ethnic enclaves, although **Chinatown** is the most obvious example. Head to **North Beach,** full of trattorias and bakeries, for authentic Italian. Not to be outdone, the **Mission District** serves up terrific, inexpensive taquerias and you can see Central American cafes alongside new gourmet restaurants. The tasty, authentic fare is worth the trip beyond downtown.

Head over to the **Richmond District** (see Chapter 10) where you'll notice a clutch of Russian bakeries, delicatessens, and restaurants, most notably **Katia, A Russian Tea Room,** 600 Fifth Ave., at Balboa Street (☎ 415-668-9292), open Tuesday through Sunday for lunch and dinner. You can also find many more Asian and Chinese eateries in the Richmond District. Another excellent local Asian favorite is the **Mayflower,** 6255 Geary Blvd., near 27th Avenue (☎ 415-387-8338), open daily for excellent dim sum, lunch, and dinner. Call for evening reservations.

Japantown (see Chapter 10) is bargain-town when it comes to dining. Inside the **Japan Center** on Post Street (at Webster Street) are a number of noodle houses and sushi bars with more across the way. **Mifune** (☎ 415-922-0337), upstairs in the Japan Center, is a perennial favorite for big bowls of udon noodles in broth with slices of beef or chicken and vegetables. It's open until 10 p.m. every day. **Isuzu,** at 1581 Webster (☎ 415-922-2290), is a great spot for sushi or tempura.

All Dressed Up and Everywhere to Go

Most restaurants do not enforce a dress code nowadays, but if they do, they usually keep a small stock of ties on hand for gentlemen. For most places in town, casual wear is the norm. But among those who pay attention to such things, diners tend to dress up for venues with specific types of delicacies, such as any place that has a cheese course or a wine steward. Actually, there seem to be lots of hipster types who, when out on the town, look down on jeans in favor of a ventless sports coat or a vintage little black dress. Although I doubt you will encounter attitude even in rooms once known for attitude (and I do my best to keep 'em out of this book), dressing the part never hurts. In general, however, wearing trousers and a handsome sweater or jacket will do for any culinary spot your taste buds want to go.

Saving Money

Do not head to the nearest fast-food joint, even if your travel budget doesn't allow for a $100 dinner for two every night. You can limit the stress on your credit card, and save your waistline, if you share an appetizer and dessert, or order beer instead of wine, or better yet, skip the alcohol entirely. (The markup on wine is usually outrageous!) If you read all about a certain restaurant you're dying to try that's way too expensive, have lunch there instead of dinner, if it's open; you'll get the same quality of food, but for less money. Or you can eat brunch or have an inexpensive picnic lunch and contribute your savings toward a really nice dinner. See Chapter 15 for places to get a quick but delicious meal or snack.

You can eat for under $10 per person at any of the ground-floor restaurants at the **Metreon** on Mission and Fourth streets. There are four informal cafes serving sushi, salads, grilled meats, and Asian noodle dishes for lunch and dinner. And, for dessert, $9.25 will get you into a movie upstairs. Another good choice for inexpensive, flavorful dishes is to try out one of the city's many ethnic restaurants. Head to the **Mission District** for cheap Mexican, Salvadoran, and Cambodian food; to Geary and Clement streets in the **Richmond District** for excellent Vietnamese, Chinese, and Thai; and to **Japantown** for tempura and noodles. Your wallet will thank you and your taste buds will still be satisfied.

Experiencing Dinner as Theater

Foreign Cinema in the Mission District (see Chapter 14) screens films on a wall in their patio, which is handy if you don't have much to say to your date. But for live entertainment to accompany your meal, stay tuned.

San Francisco has always had its fair share of fair maidens, many of whom shave twice daily, and there is no better or safer place to gawk at "gender illusionists" than at **AsiaSF,** a SoMa nightclub/restaurant, 201 Ninth St., at Howard (☎ **415-255-2742**). The "waitresses" do double duty, taking your order for small plates of fusion dishes (such as duck quesadillas), then lip-synching to your favorite tunes while strutting down the vinyl bar. You'd think that the gimmick would bury the food, but in fact, the place manages to do a great job in every area. There's even a disco in the basement so you can shake your thang afterwards, should you be so inclined.

Down at **Pier 29** on the Embarcadero, look for a stylized 1926 *Spiegelent* (a circular, tented pavilion), the home of **Teatro ZinZanni** (☎ **415-438-2668;** Internet: www.teatrozinzanni.org). Tickets are $99 to $125, and shows are Wednesday through Sunday. This is an immensely funny dinner show with a twist: The audience is part of the proceedings. Don't worry — you won't be asked to get up and recite. Along with an acceptable, if not stellar, five-course meal (it reminds me of hotel wedding suppers), diners are regaled by a talented group of performers, who combine cabaret, opera, acrobatics, comedy, and improv in most unusual ways. The cast changes periodically, and strangely enough, Joan Baez has appeared in the show off and on, so it's worth investigating who's in the lineup when you come to town. This isn't a cheap date, but it's something to consider if you're celebrating or looking for an evening out of the ordinary.

Dining and dancing

The **Top of the Mark** (☎ 415-616-6916), in the Mark Hopkins Intercontinental Hotel, 1 Nob Hill, at Mason and California streets, has it all — views, music from 9 p.m., dancing, and a convivial crowd of suits. The hotel serves a $49 prix-fixe dinner on Friday and Saturday nights; with 7:30 reservations, a night on the town is a done deal. **Harry Denton's Starlight Room,** in the Sir Francis Drake Hotel on Union Square, 450 Powell St. (☎ 415-395-8595), attracts tons of hotel guests and locals who appreciate the Starlight Orchestra, the drop-dead views, and the adult prom-night atmosphere. It's a glorious room for drinking expensive glasses of whatever, dancing, and having a little bite. A more youthful group congregates at **Cafe du Nord,** 2170 Market St., at Sanchez (☎ 415-861-5016; Internet: www.cafe dunord.com). This basement-level club serves dinner (sandwiches, salad, chicken, steak), but the draw is the live music. Check the Web site to see if the Monday Night Hoot is happening during your vacation; there isn't much to do in town on Monday evenings and this "anti-open mic" night (featuring eight to ten carefully selected up-and-coming bands and musicians) can be fun.

Chapter 14

San Francisco's Fine Food Fare

So, what are you in the mood for? Chinese? California-Mediterranean? Catalan tapas? There's no reason to go hungry seeking the right restaurant. The recommendations below only scratch the surface of my favorite places to dine in San Francisco. What you have here is a representative cross section of the best the city has to offer, in a variety of price ranges and neighborhoods. And unless the kitchen is having an off night, there's not a lemon in the bunch.

Restaurants that I've designated with the Kid Friendly icon all have items on the menu that most kids like, and they will treat your children with respect. If things like crayons at the tables and booster seats are important to your little ones, please call the restaurants directly for more information.

The dollar signs attached to the restaurant recommendations in this chapter give you an idea of how much you'll have to shell out for dinner for one person, including appetizer, main course, dessert, one drink, tax, and tip. If a place is marked with $, a meal there will run under $25. At $$ places, expect to spend between $25 and $40. Restaurants with $$$ will cost from $40 to $60. Feel like going for broke? You'll sup like royalty, then fork over lots more than $60 at places with $$$$. To locate a restaurant based on its cost, location, or cuisine, see the indexes at the end of this chapter.

San Francisco Dining

Andalu **33**
Asia de Cuba **28**
B-44 **24**
Bistro Aix **2**
Boulevard **20**
Cafe Kati **38**
Cafe Marimba **1**
Charles-Nob Hill **14**
Chow **34**
Enrico's Sidewalk Cafe **16**
Fringale **32**
Gary Danko **6**
Globe **17**
Gold Mountain **13**
Grand Cafe **27**
Green's **3**
Hawthorne Lane **30**
Hayes Street Grill **36**
Jardinière **37**
Kay Cheung **15**
Kokkari Estiatorio **18**
Lapis **7**
Le Charm **29**
Le Colonial **26**
Lichee Garden **12**
L'Osteria del Forno **11**
Merenda **4**
Moose's **8**
Ozumo **21**
Pazzia **31**
R&G Lounge **23**
Rose Pistola **9**
Scala's Bistro **25**
Spoon **5**
Tadich Grill **22**
U.S. Restaurant **10**
Yank Sing **19**
Zuni Cafe **35**

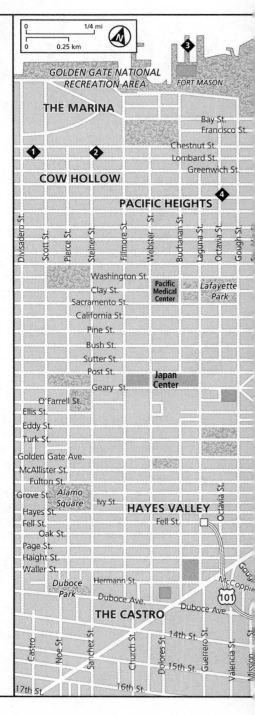

CABLE CAR LINES

California Line

Powell-Mason Line

Powell-Hyde Line

Cable Car Turnaround

San Francisco Bay

Eating to Your Heart's Content:
A Complete Listing of Restaurants

Andalu

$$ **Mission District**   **INTERNATIONAL**

Andalu is a prime example of the modern San Francisco restaurant. Chef-driven, with minimialist decor that doesn't upstage the hipster clientele, the eclectic menu of small plates speak to many cultures. But it's also about substance, with flavor and complexity, charming service, and value. Eat at Tadich Grill (later in this section) to get a feel for San Francisco's past; come here to get a sense of the city in the 21st century.

3198 16th St., at Guerrero Street. ☎ *415-621-2211. Reservations recommended, especially on weekends. To get there: BART to 16th Street and walk west two blocks. Main courses: $8–$13. AE, D, MC, V. Open: Mon–Wed 5:30–11:00 p.m.; Thurs–Fri 5:30 p.m.–1:00 a.m.; Sat brunch 11 a.m.–2 p.m. and dinner 5:30 p.m.–1:00 a.m.; Sun brunch 11 a.m.–2 p.m.*

Asia de Cuba

$$$$ **Union Square**   **ASIAN/LATIN FUSION**

Around us, the tables were turning, the waiters were running, and the music was so loud I practically fell to my knees begging for relief — to no avail — so why am I recommending this obscenely over-priced "it" restaurant in the Clift (see Chapter 8)? Well, the menu is interesting (you can't find oxtail springrolls or Cuban black bean soup dumplings just anywhere), the beef short ribs are tasty, and much of the clientele seems to think that someone is going to take their picture, which can be fun to observe at least once.

495 Geary St., at Taylor. ☎ *415-929-2300. Reservations recommended, especially on weekends. To get there: It's two blocks south of Union Square. Main courses: $20–$64. AE, DC, MC, V. Open: Daily 6–11 a.m., 11:30 a.m.–2:30 p.m., and 5:30 p.m.–1:00 a.m.*

B-44

$$$ **The Financial District**   **SPANISH**

You will not find such authentic and homey Spanish food of this ilk outside of Barcelona — the fish cheeks are a treat, a variety of paellas are suffused with treasures, and you can make a happy meal of tapas, starting with my favorite: sausage and white beans. There's not a lace fan or flamenco guitarist to be found within a mile of this thoroughly modern spot, so don't come expecting a Spanish-theme evening. But if you want to feel like you're eating something out of the ordinary, you'll be delighted.

44 Belden Place, off Bush Street. ☎ 415-986-6287. Reservations recommended. To get there: Walk on Stockton Street north from Union Square to Bush Street and turn east for two blocks. Main courses: $15–$19. AE, MC, V. Open: Mon–Fri 11:30 a.m.–2:30 p.m. and 5:30 p.m. to midnight; Sat 5:30 p.m. to midnight.

Bistro Aix

$ The Marina/Cow Hollow   BISTRO FRENCH

This casual French-style bistro caters to lucky neighborhood residents who don't have to look for parking. Dining alfresco is a delight during any season in the heated, covered patio out back — it's the perfect setting to enjoy a bottle of wine and plates of crispy-skinned chicken, fresh pasta, grilled sirloin, and perfectly dressed salads. The $14.95 prix-fixe menu, served from 6 to 8 p.m. Sunday through Thursday, would be a bargain even if the food were half as good.

3340 Steiner St., between Chestnut and Lombard streets. ☎ 415-202-0100. Reservations recommended. To get there: 22-Fillmore, 28-19th Avenue, 30-Stockton, and 43-Masonic buses. Main courses: $12–$14; prix-fixe menu $14.95. AE, DC, MC, V. Open: Mon–Thurs 6–10 p.m.; Fri–Sat 6–11 p.m.; Sun 5:30–9:30 p.m.

Boulevard

$$$$ The Embarcadero   AMERICAN

Housed in an elegant turn-of-the-century building with views of the Bay Bridge (from tables in the very back only), this deservedly popular restaurant serves consistently excellent and generous plates of seasonal comfort food, such as tender lamb shanks accompanied by a flavorful artichoke risotto. Noisy but comfortable, the place caters to an upscale, older crowd. Counter and bar seating is available for those without reservations, but call three or four weeks in advance for a prime-time table.

1 Mission St., at Steuart Street. ☎ 415-543-6084. Reservations advised three weeks in advance. To get there: Take any Muni streetcar to the Embarcadero Station and walk one block east to Mission Street. Main courses: $22–$35. AE, CB, DC, D, MC, V. Open: Mon–Fri lunch 11:30 a.m.–2:00 p.m. and bistro menu 2:30–5:15 p.m.; dinner Sun–Wed 5:30–10:00 p.m., Thurs–Sat 5:30–10:30 p.m.

Cafe Kati

$$$ Japantown   CALIFORNIA

As in all the best spots, the menu here changes depending on what's available locally, but it always reflects the unique influence of Chef Kirk Webber, who likes to include a little something eastern and a little something western. Thus, you may find seafood steamed in red Thai curry and a marinated skirt steak with onion rings sharing the table and giving patrons great pleasure. This husband-and-wife-run spot has been a popular neighborhood restaurant for years, so be prepared to wait on the weekends unless you have an early reservation.

1963 Sutter St., between Fillmore and Webster streets. ☎ *415-775-7313. Reservations advised two weeks in advance. To get there: 3-Jackson, 4-Sutter, 22-Fillmore, or 38-Geary buses. Main courses: $19–$28. AE, MC, V. Open: Tues–Sun 5:30–10:00 p.m.*

Cafe Marimba

$$ The Marina/Cow Hollow   MEXICAN

Disregard any preconceived notions of Mexican cuisine that those Tex-Mex chain restaurants have stamped on your brain. When you visit this colorful and generally packed restaurant, you're in for a treat. This is authentic Mexican food. The flavorful, fresh fish and grilled meats arrive at your table with exceptional salsas, and the guacamole puts Cafe Marimba in a class of its own. It's a great choice for a late lunch after touring the Presidio or the Palace of Fine Arts — dinner can be too crowded.

2317 Chestnut St., between Scott and Divisidero streets. ☎ *415-776-1506. Reservations recommended on weekends. To get there: 30-Stockton bus. Main courses: $8–$14. AE, MC, V. Open: Mon 5:30–10:00 p.m.; Tue–Thurs 11:30 a.m.– 10:00 p.m.; Fri–Sat 11:30 a.m.–11:00 p.m.*

Charles-Nob Hill

$$$$ Nob Hill   CALIFORNIA/FRENCH

Celebrating? Two small, elegantly appointed dining rooms tucked inside a swanky apartment building give Charles an extra-intimate feel. Dishes are exquisitely prepared and presented, from the tiny appetizers brought gratis by the mannerly waitstaff to the plate of miniature sweets that ends each meal. Living large? Consider the foie gras tasting, or just hand over your wallet and sink into the splendid six-course tasting menu. Don't skimp on the wines, either, because this will be a meal to remember. Walk-ins are served in the bar, so rejoice all ye who live in the moment.

1250 Jones St., at Clay Street. ☎ *415-771-5400. Reservations recommended four weeks in advance. To get there: California cable car line. Main courses: $26–$34; six-course tasting menu $70. AE, DC, MC, V. Open: Tues–Sun 5:30–9:45 p.m.*

Chow

$ The Castro   AMERICAN

If there weren't so many people eagerly waiting for a table at this noisy, casual, and friendly joint, it might qualify as a quick-bite place. But after you score a table, it's more fun to sit a while and savor the straightforward pasta dishes, brick-oven roasted chicken, thin-crusted pizzas, and yummy desserts (love that ginger cake). A great price performer, too. Their second location, Park Chow (1240 Ninth Ave., near Golden Gate Park) is just as great.

215 Church St., at Market Street. ☎ *415-552-2469. Reservations not accepted. To get there: J-Church or F-Market streetcars to Church Street. Main courses: $5.95–$12.95. MC, V. Open: Sun–Thurs 11 a.m.–11 p.m.; Fri–Sat 11 a.m. to midnight.*

Dining Near North Beach & Chinatown

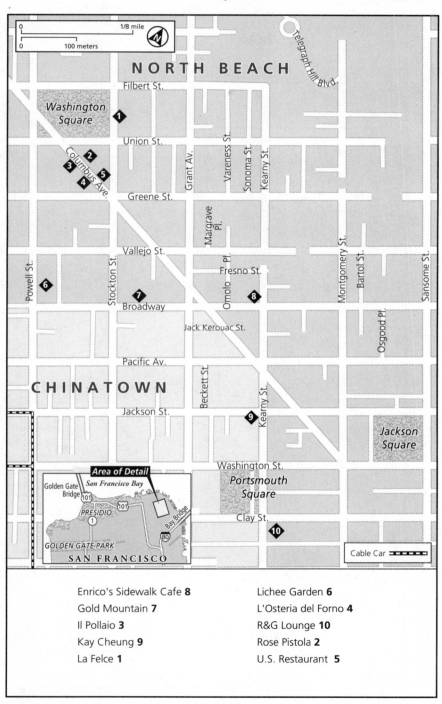

Enrico's Sidewalk Cafe **8**

Gold Mountain **7**

Il Pollaio **3**

Kay Cheung **9**

La Felce **1**

Lichee Garden **6**

L'Osteria del Forno **4**

R&G Lounge **10**

Rose Pistola **2**

U.S. Restaurant **5**

Dining Near Union Square, SoMa & Nob Hill

Asia de Cuba **4**
B-44 **7**
Charles Nob Hill **1**
Globe **10**
Grand Cafe **3**

Kokkari Estiatorio **9**
Le Colonial **2**
Pazzia **6**
Scala's Bistro **5**
Tadich Grill **8**

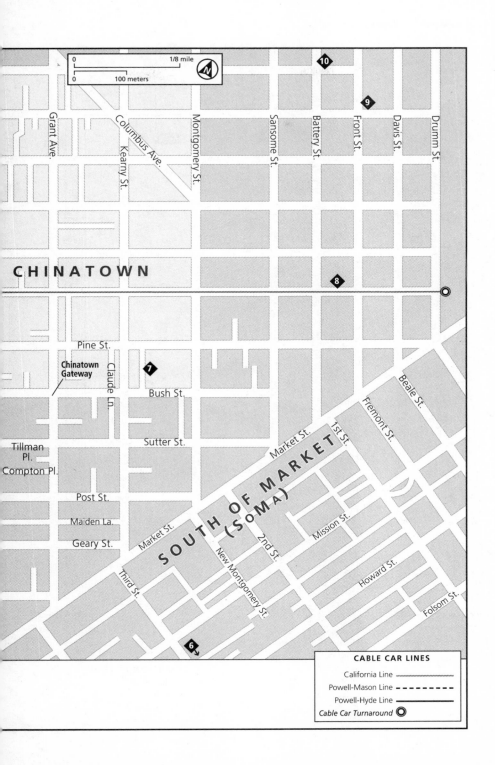

The Mission District

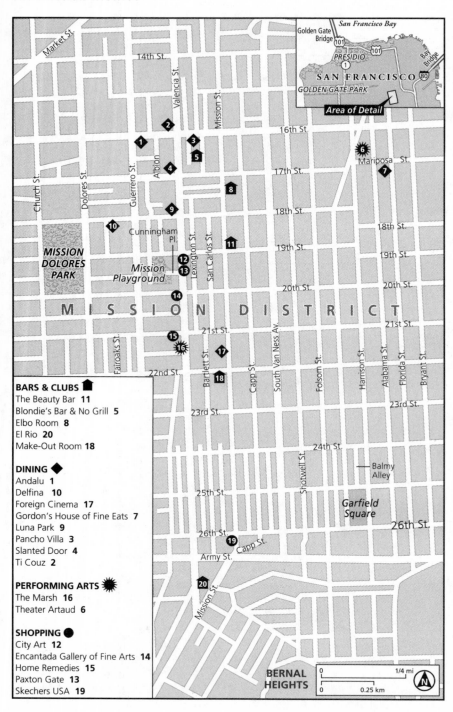

BARS & CLUBS 📍
The Beauty Bar **11**
Blondie's Bar & No Grill **5**
Elbo Room **8**
El Rio **20**
Make-Out Room **18**

DINING ◆
Andalu **1**
Delfina **10**
Foreign Cinema **17**
Gordon's House of Fine Eats **7**
Luna Park **9**
Pancho Villa **3**
Slanted Door **4**
Ti Couz **2**

PERFORMING ARTS ✴
The Marsh **16**
Theater Artaud **6**

SHOPPING ●
City Art **12**
Encantada Gallery of Fine Arts **14**
Home Remedies **15**
Paxton Gate **13**
Skechers USA **19**

Delfina

$$ Mission District TUSCAN ITALIAN

This wonderfully friendly and now-renowned restaurant defines what's incredible about the city's neighborhood eats. Dishes such as chianti-braised beef ravioli, quail with spring onion–chanterelle bread salad, or roasted beets with local goat cheese are full of flavor and feature the freshest ingredients, a smattering of herbs, and brilliant preparation. Leave Union Square and make the effort to eat here.

3621 18th St., between Dolores and Guerrero streets. ☎ 415-552-4055. Reservations advised three weeks in advance. To get there: J-Church Muni line to 18th Street, then walk east two blocks. Main courses: $12–$18. MC, V. Open: Sun–Thurs 5:30–10:00 p.m.; Fri–Sat 5:30–11:00 p.m.

Enrico's Sidewalk Cafe

$$ North Beach CALIFORNIA/ITALIAN

Dining on a patio with a view of the bawdy section of Broadway would liven up any evening, but at this cosmopolitan bar/restaurant you also get live jazz and a menu of solid seasonal fish and meat dishes. Casual and fun.

504 Broadway, at Kearny Street. ☎ 415-982-6223. Reservations recommended. To get there: Powell-Mason cable car line or 30-Stockton bus. Main courses: $12–$22. AE, DC, MC, V. Open: Sun–Thurs 11:30 a.m.–11:00 p.m.; Fri–Sat 11:30 a.m. to midnight.

Foreign Cinema

$$$ Mission District NEW AMERICAN/FRENCH

Mission District regulars nearly lost their *empanadas* when the shiny, chic Foreign Cinema opened in 1999. The expansive dining room — plus outdoor patio where foreign films are screened on a concrete wall — would throw anyone at first, but an elegant plate of endive and smoked trout or some oysters from the raw bar helps to lower resistance to the inevitable changes in the neighborhood.

2534 Mission St., between 21st and 22nd streets. ☎ 415-648-7600. Reservations highly recommended. To get there: BART to 24th Street. Main courses: $17–$22. AE, MC, V. Open: Dinner Tues–Sun 5:30–10:00 p.m. (until 11 p.m. Fri–Sat); late-night menu until 1 a.m.

Fringale

$$$ SoMa FRENCH BASQUE

Set a few blocks east of Yerba Buena Center, away from the madness of Union Square and North Beach, this small, *três* French bistro is especially warm and welcoming on a cold night. Plates of steamed mussels, pork tenderloin confit, and a superb rack of lamb, among other delights, are prepared with an eye toward simplicity and taste.

570 Fourth St., between Brannan and Bryant streets. ☎ 415-543-0573. Reservations necessary. To get there: 45-Union/Stockton or 30-Stockton buses. Main courses: $13–$21. AE, MC, V. Open: Mon–Fri 11:30 a.m.–3:00 p.m. and 5:30–10:30 p.m.; Sat 5:30–10:30 p.m.

Gary Danko

$$$$ Russian Hill NEW AMERICAN/FRENCH

The ovens were barely lit at this new fine-dining center before the food and wine cognoscenti were all over Danko's like a hollandaise, proclaiming it among the best restaurants not only in town, but in the country. You choose your own three-course (or more if you like) meal from the menu — perhaps a composed lobster salad followed by day boat scallops and ending with a mango Napoleon or selections from the cheese cart — then let the kitchen make magic. If you don't mind eating at the bar, you can actually walk in without reservations.

800 Northpoint, at Hyde Street. ☎ 415-749-2060. Reservations advised four weeks in advance. To get there: Powell-Hyde cable car line. Prix-fixe menu from $55. AE, MC, V. Open: Sun–Wed 5:30–9:30 p.m.; Thurs–Sat 5:30–10:00 p.m.

Globe

$$ Financial District RUSTIC AMERICAN

One of the few places open after the rest of the chefs fold their aprons for the evening, tiny Globe is generally buzzing until 1 a.m., should you get sudden cravings for a pretty bowl of pasta or a hefty pork chop. The idea here is comfort-food as art (in the most unpretentious sense), so it looks inviting and tastes even better. On my last visit, a crew from the television show *Bay Area Back Roads* was filming, so I guess this place is assumed to be off the beaten track, but everyone who likes to eat well and reasonably stops by eventually.

290 Pacific Ave., near Battery Street. ☎ 415-391-4132. Reservations recommended. To get there: 1-California, 30-Stockton buses. Main courses: $16–$22. AE, MC, V. Open: Mon–Fri 11:30 a.m.–1:00 a.m.; Sat 6 p.m.–1 a.m.; Sun 6:00–11:30 p.m.

Gordon's House of Fine Eats

$$–$$$ Mission District AMERICAN

So maybe your mom served corn flake–fried chicken, but trust me, it's nothing like the tender, moist, and savory basketful delivered at this industrial-chic trend center. The seasonal menu includes more sophisticated items, too — a perfectly executed asparagus eggroll, twice-cooked crab in black bean sauce, pork osso buco — and everything's delicious. You can sit at the counter and check out the line chefs if you arrive without reservations — a kid-pleasing view as well.

500 Florida St., at Mariposa Street. ☎ *415-861-8900. Reservations recommended. To get there: Take a cab. Main courses: $9–$30. CB, DISC, MC, V. Open: Lunch Mon–Fri 11:30 a.m.–4:30 p.m.; dinner Thurs 5:30–11:00 p.m.; Fri–Sat 5:30 p.m. to midnight; Sun 5:30–10:00 p.m.*

Grand Cafe
$$–$$$ Union Square   FRENCH

Living up to its name in every aspect, this vast, high-ceilinged, muraled bistro is abuzz with activity and energy. People gravitate to the Petit Cafe pre– and post-theater for brick-oven pizzas, sandwiches, and desserts; and to the larger dining room for a rib-eye steak or a lovely, fragrant bouillabaisse.

501 Geary St., at Taylor Street. ☎ *415-292-0101. Reservations accepted. To get there: Muni Metro to Powell Street; walk two blocks to Geary and two blocks south to Taylor. Main courses: $14–$25; Petit Café $7–$12. AE, CB, DC, DISC, MC, V. Open: Breakfast Mon–Sat 7:00–10:30 a.m.; brunch Sun 9:30 a.m.–2:30 p.m.; lunch Mon–Thurs 11:30 a.m.–2:30 p.m.; dinner Mon–Thurs 5:30–10:00 p.m., Fri–Sat 5:30–11:00 p.m., Sun 5–10 p.m.*

Green's
$$–$$$ The Marina/Cow Hollow   VEGETARIAN

If you haven't eaten in a gourmet vegetarian restaurant, or if your vegetarian dining has been limited to alfalfa sprouts, you're in for a marvelous new culinary experience. The Saturday evening prix-fixe menu is worth the price, especially when you see the gorgeous views that come with the meal. This attractive, bright room is a terrific destination for lunch if you're exploring the Marina.

Fort Mason, Building A, off Marina Boulevard at Buchanan Street. ☎ *415-771-6222. Reservations highly recommended at least two weeks in advance. To get there: Take the 30-Stockton bus to Laguna and transfer to the 28-19th Avenue into Fort Mason. Main courses: $15–$19; prix-fixe menu (Sat only) $46. DISC, MC, V. Open: Brunch Sun 10 a.m.–2 p.m.; lunch Tues–Sat 11:30 a.m.–2:00 p.m.; dinner Mon–Sat 5:30–9:30 p.m.; late evening desserts Mon–Sat 9:30–11:30 p.m.*

Hawthorne Lane
$$$$ SoMa   CALIFORNIA/ASIAN

This classy but relaxed, art-filled restaurant in a one-block alley near the Museum of Modern Art always delivers the goods. The Cal-Asian menu is beautifully executed (if you're lucky, the Chinese-style roasted duck with steamed green onion buns will be on the menu); the new young chef, Bridget Batson, is garnering terrific reviews; and the service is impeccable, a boast not many other restaurants can make. The bar attracts a grown-up crowd so if you're early for your reservation, take advantage and have a drink. (You may even see a local celeb like Boz Scaggs.) And dress up a little — it's a nice place.

22 Hawthorne Lane, off Howard Street between Second and Third streets. ☎ 415-777-9779; Internet: www.hawthornelane.com. *Reservations recommended two weeks in advance. To get there: Any Muni streetcar to Montgomery Street Station; 30-Stockton, 45-Union/Stockton buses. Main courses: $20–$29. CB, DC, DISC, JCB, MC, V. Open: Lunch Mon–Fri 11:30 a.m.–2:00 p.m.; dinner Sun–Thurs 5:30–10:00 p.m., Fri–Sat 5:30–10:30 p.m.*

Hayes Street Grill
$$ Civic Center/Hayes Valley   SEAFOOD

This 25-year veteran of the food biz remains one of the premier fish restaurants in the city. Whatever's been caught that morning will be prepared simply, carefully, and with integrity. The non-fish selections are equally delicious, and walk-ins can eat at the bar. The restaurant quiets down considerably around 8 p.m. when the opera/symphony/ballet-goers dash off to the show.

320 Hayes St., between Gough and Franklin streets. ☎ 415-863-5545. Reservations recommended. To get there: Take any Muni Metro to the Civic Center Station and walk north on Gough. Main courses: $13.50–$18.25. AE, DC, DISC, MC, V. Open: Lunch Mon–Fri 11:30 a.m.–2:00 p.m.; dinner Mon–Thurs 5:00–9:30 p.m., Fri–Sat 5:30–10:30 p.m., Sun 5:00–8:30 p.m.

Jardinière
$$$$ Civic Center   CALIFORNIA/FRENCH

This is where the upscale crowd sups before the opera, ballet, or symphony. Expect sophisticated surroundings, a lively bar, and highly touted, high-priced food. The risotto is heaven-sent. A jazz combo plays upstairs Sunday through Tuesday.

300 Grove St., at Franklin Street. ☎ 415-861-5555. Reservations required. To get there: Muni Metro to Civic Center; walk four blocks north on Franklin. Main courses: $23–$35. AE, DC, MC, V. Open: Sun–Wed 5:00–10:30 p.m.; Thurs–Sat 5:00–11:30 p.m.

Kay Cheung
$ Chinatown   CHINESE

For a fresh and interesting selection of dim sum or live seafood, this small, pleasant room can't be beat for quality or price. Most of the tables seat eight, so you'll probably end up sitting with Chinatown regulars — a terrific opportunity to chat up folks who really know their dumplings.

615 Jackson St., at Kearny Street. ☎ *415-989-6838. Reservations accepted. To get there: 15-Third bus. AE, MC, V. Main courses: $6–$11. Open: Dim sum and lunch daily 9:00 a.m.–2:30 p.m.; dinner daily 5:30–10:00 p.m.*

Kokkari Estiatorio

$$$ **Financial District** **GREEK**

Your average Mediterranean shipping tycoon would feel perfectly comfortable underneath the beamed ceilings of this richly appointed *taverna.* The California-meets-Greek menu does feature some familiar dishes, such as moussaka, but takes them to Mount Olympus–style heights. Order the *Yiaourti Graniti* (yogurt sorbet with tangerine ice) for dessert even if you're full.

200 Jackson St., at Front Street. ☎ *415-981-0983. Reservations required. To get there: 2, 3, or 4 bus; transfer to 42-Downtown loop; exit at Sansome and Jackson streets and walk two blocks west to Front. Main courses: $18–$33. AE, DC, MC, V. Open: Mon–Thurs 11:30 a.m.–10:00 p.m.; Fri 11:30 a.m.–11:00 p.m.; Sat 5–11 p.m.*

Lapis

$$$ **Embarcadero** **MEDITERRANEAN**

This is a very beautiful restaurant on the water, a comfortable, upscale place to take in the bay views before the sun sets completely. To make the most of the location, I'd come here for a late-afternoon meal (they open at 5:30), centered around the appetizers — spicy lamb and merguez kebobs, Mediterranean dipping sauces with warm pita bread, Moroccan spiced crab cakes — and a great bottle of wine. Dinner is absolutely fine, but when it's dark out, the view is wasted and trust me, you're paying for it.

Pier 33 on the Embarcadero. ☎ *415-982-0203. Reservations recommended. To get there: F-Market streetcar. Main courses: $17–$34. AE, DC, MC, V. Open: Lunch Mon–Fri 11:30 a.m.–2:30 p.m.; dinner Mon–Thurs 5:30–10:00 p.m., Fri–Sat 5:30–11:00 p.m.*

Le Charm

$$ **SoMa** **FRENCH**

Bargain-hunter alert! The Parisian-inspired three-course prix-fixe dinner for under $25 is the real deal at this popular little sponge-painted bistro. Diners choose from a menu that includes a lovely roasted quail served on salad greens, a fragrant leg of lamb with flageolet beans and, in season, a dessert soup of fresh apricots and cherries. Le Charm is also a winner for lunch, especially if the weather is decent and you can get a table outside in the garden.

315 Fifth St., between Folsom and Howard streets (near Yerba Buena Center). ☎ 415-546-6128. Reservations accepted. To get there: Powell Street muni; 27-Bryant or 30-Stockton buses. Main courses: $11–$14. MC, V. Open: Lunch Mon–Fri 11:30 a.m.–2:30 p.m.; dinner Mon–Thurs 6:00–9:30 p.m., Fri 6–10 p.m., Sat 5:30–10:00 p.m.

Le Colonial
$$$ Union Square   FRENCH-VIETNAMESE

Walking into this tall, whitewashed building sitting off by itself in an alley downtown, you immediately feel transported to another era. The pressed-tin ceiling, the fans, the potted palms, the rattan furniture — it could all easily feel contrived, but it doesn't. The look, the service, and the haute Vietnamese cuisine — starring a beautiful piece of sea bass steamed in a banana leaf — are all well executed. The enticing upstairs lounge is a great place to begin or end the evening. The clientele is unusually dressy, by the way.

20 Cosmo Place, off Taylor Street between Sutter and Post streets. ☎ 415-931-3600. Reservations advised. To get there: From Union Square, walk two blocks southwest on Post then north on Taylor. Cosmo Place is just off Taylor Street. Main courses: $16.50–$28. AE, DC, MC, V. Open: Sun–Wed 5:30–10:00 p.m.; Thurs–Sat 5:30–11:00 p.m.

Lichee Garden
$ Chinatown   CHINESE

This is a particularly great family-style Cantonese restaurant, popular with the locals, with a huge menu filled with familiar dishes (like Egg Foo Young), lots of seafood, and every Chinese dish you remember from childhood (unless you were raised in China). They also serve a good dim sum lunch. Prices are inexpensive (Peking duck being the biggest extravagance), service is fine, and the room is bright and lively.

1416 Powell St., near Broadway. ☎ 415-397-2290. Reservations accepted. To get there: Powell-Mason cable car. Main courses: $6.50–$24.50. MC, V. Open: Daily 7:00 a.m.–9:15 p.m.

L'Osteria del Forno
$ North Beach   ITALIAN

A tiny storefront with an equally tiny kitchen, L'Osteria manages to dish up fine thin-crusted pizzas, homey pasta dishes that change daily, and a great roast pork loin cooked in milk. It's equally satisfying to make a meal of antipasti. This is one North Beach restaurant that feels and tastes authentic.

519 Columbus Ave., between Green and Union streets. ☎ 415-982-1124. No reservations accepted. To get there: Powell-Mason cable car line; 30-Stockton bus.

Main courses: $7–$11. No credit cards. Open: Sun–Mon 11:30 a.m.–10:00 p.m., Wed–Thurs 11:30 a.m.–10:00 p.m.; Fri–Sat 11:30 a.m.–11:00 p.m.

Luna Park

$$ Mission District   NEW AMERICAN

The funky abstract art, rustic red walls, and gold velvet drapes announce that decor is in the eye of the decorator, but it's all part of the fun. The exceedingly well-priced menu attracts people from all parts of the city, making weekend nights especially loud, but that does make it comfortable for families with kids. Start with the tuna "poke" appetizer or one of the five beautiful green salads, then consider the lamb shank, beef brisket stew, or oven-roasted seabass. Attention campers: Make-your-own s'mores light up the dessert list!

694 Valencia St., at 18th Street. ☎ *415-553-8584. Reservations advised for dinner. To get there: BART to 16th Street and walk west to Valencia and south two blocks. Main courses: $9.25–$14. MC, V. Open: Lunch daily 11:30 a.m.–2:30 p.m.; dinner Mon–Thurs 5:30–11:30 p.m., Fri–Sat 5:30 p.m. to midnight, Sun 5:30–10:30 p.m.*

Merenda

$$$ The Marina/Cow Hollow   CALIFORNIA/FRENCH

This is the stirring sort of neighborhood restaurant that inspires fantasies about moving to the city. A nearly gift-priced prix-fixe menu allows you to order any combination of courses from the seasonal picks, and you just can't go wrong. There is always a fresh fish and vegetarian selection plus delicate soups, housemade pastas, and delectable starters such as frisee and chicken liver salad. The room is seductive and cozy; you get a big, delicious cookie along with the bill. I love this place.

1809 Union St., at Octavia Street. ☎ *415-346-7373. Reservations a must. To get there: 30-Stockton bus. Prix-fixe meals: $25–$42. AE, DC, MC, V. Open: Wed–Mon takeout counter 11 a.m.–9 p.m.; dinner 5:30 p.m.–9:00 p.m.*

Moose's

$$$ North Beach   CALIFORNIA/MEDITERRANEAN

Popular with politicos, socialites, and local luminaries, the great thing about Moose's, besides the food, is that even the little people have a great time eating here. Although a splendidly prepared appetizer of crab cakes followed by the filet of beef will definitely leave a draft whistling through your wallet, the smooth, professional staff and bright decor guarantee a memorable, very San Francisco meal.

1652 Stockton St., across from Washington Square. ☎ *415-989-7800. Reservations recommended. To get there: Powell-Mason cable car line; 30-Stockton bus. Main courses: $17–$30. AE, DC, JCB, MC, V. Open: Lunch Thurs–Sat 11:30 a.m.–2:30 p.m.; brunch Sun 10:00 a.m.–2:30 p.m.; dinner Mon–Thurs 5:30–10:00 p.m., Fri–Sat 5:30–11:00 p.m., Sun 5–10 p.m.*

Ozumo

$$$ Embarcadero   SUSHI/JAPANESE

High-quality sushi is available in a number of local restaurants, but the new, very contemporary Ozumo also offers a beautiful selection of Japanese dishes, featuring grilled meats and vegetables. Reserve a table in the back for views, and if you're coming for sushi, let the chef guide you. The sake tasting menu is an eye-opener and highly recommended.

161 Steuart St., near Mission Street. ☎ 415-882-1333. Reservations recommended. To get there: Any Muni streetcar to Embarcadero Station. Main courses: $11–$17. AE, DC, JCB, MC, V. Open: Lunch Mon–Fri 11:30 a.m.–2:30 p.m.; dinner Sun–Wed 5:30–10:00 p.m., Thurs–Sat 5:30 p.m. to midnight.

Pazzia

$ SoMa   NORTHERN ITALIAN

Have an authentic Northern Italian moment at this colorful, tiny place, a quick walk from Yerba Buena Center and the Museum of Modern Art. The tempting pizza, delicious pasta dishes, and heartier entrees provide something to please everyone. The staff is pleasant to kids and grown-ups alike; if you're in the area, there's no better pick for the price.

337 Third St. ☎ 415-512-1693. Reservations advised. To get there: Muni to Montgomery Street station; 15-Third, 30-Stockton, or 45-Union/Stockton buses. Main courses: $8.75–$16.95. AE, DISC, MC, V. Open: Lunch Mon–Fri 11:30 a.m.– 2:30 p.m.; dinner Mon–Thurs 6–10 p.m., Fri–Sat 6:00–10:30 p.m.

R&G Lounge

$ Chinatown   CHINESE

Downstairs, you get excellent Hong Kong Chinese dishes in a setting that reminds me of an airport lounge, with lackluster service. The small dining room upstairs is more attractive, so talk your way to a table up there. In either case, you'll have a chance to order live spot shrimp from the downstairs tank and fresh, crisp vegetables such as Chinese broccoli and *yin choy* (a leafy green vegetable with a red root, often boiled then braised with garlic).

631 Kearny St., between Sacramento and Clay streets. ☎ 415-982-7877. Reservations accepted. To get there: 15-Third bus. Main courses: $6.50–$8.50. AE, MC, V. Open: Daily 11:00 a.m.–9:30 p.m.

Rose Pistola

$$$ North Beach   ITALIAN

Walk by the sidewalk tables covered in gaily printed cloths, and you'll immediately feel the pull of this very "in" restaurant. From the couples praying for a few bar stools to free up, to the parties sipping wine in the more private dining areas in the back, the scene is intense, but the sophisticated Mediterrean food deserves the hype it gets. A former waiter suggests that you go for lunch or dinner during the week; on weekends, the kitchen is so crazed that your order may not get all the attention it deserves.

532 Columbus Ave., between Union and Green streets. ☎ 415-399-0499. Reservations recommended two weeks in advance. To get there: Powell-Mason cable car line; 30-Stockton bus. Main courses: $18.50–$36. AE, MC, V. Open: Sun–Thurs 11:30 a.m.–11:00 p.m.; Fri–Sat 11:30 a.m. to midnight.

Scala's Bistro
$$$ Union Square ITALIAN

Even on a Monday night, Scala's pulsates with laughter and conversation from a packed house of regulars and conventioneers (who either recognize a good thing when they see it or get lucky). The seductively masculine dining room complements the well-rounded menu of favorites, including an excellent Caesar salad and flavorful local bass.

432 Powell St., between Post and Sutter streets, next to the Sir Francis Drake Hotel. ☎ 415-395-8555. Reservations recommended. To get there: Powell-Hyde cable car line. Main courses: $12–$24. AE, DC, DISC, MC, V. Open: Breakfast Mon–Fri 7:00–10:30 a.m., Sat–Sun 8:00–10:30 a.m.; lunch daily 11:30 a.m.–4:00 p.m.; dinner daily 5:15 p.m. to midnight.

Slanted Door
$$ Mission District VIETNAMESE

Savvy travelers and locals come here to swoon over the buttery steamed sea bass, caramelized chicken, and plates of "shaking" beef. Even if dinner reservations are impossible to come by, show up around 6 p.m. (they hold a few tables for walk-ins) and you may get lucky. Or go for lunch.

584 Valencia St., at 17th Street. ☎ 415-861-8032. Reservations a must. To get there: BART to 16th and Mission. Main courses: $13–$27. MC, V. Open: Tue–Sun 11:30 a.m.– 3:00 p.m. and 5:30–10:00 p.m. Note: The restaurant has moved temporarily to 100 Brannan St. (Embarcadero) until Spring 2003, while the Valencia Street location is being remodeled.

Spoon
$$ Russian Hill AMERICAN

Ah, the duck confit salad with goat cheese–filled cherries, and the double pork chop served with an apple-raisin compote . . . every scrape eaten gratefully at the bar one night when cousin Ina and I arrived without reservations, but with great determination to eat. The food is so delicious at this small, sleek, and terribly popular new restaurant, that I'd grovel any day for a seat. Be forewarned: The host, if he's still at the front of the house, is charmless, but you don't have to eat with him.

2209 Polk St., at Vallejo Street. ☎ *415-268-0140. Reservations recommended. To get there: Powell-Hyde cable car to Vallejo, walk two blocks to Polk. Main courses: $15–$20. AE, MC, V. Open: Tues–Sun 5:30–11:00 p.m.*

Tadich Grill
$$ Financial District   SEAFOOD

If you're making the rounds of old San Francisco, lunch here is mandatory. This turn-of-the-century watering hole, with waiters to match, features a daily printed menu advertising dishes so old-fashioned (had Lobster Newburg lately?) that they're probably the next big thing (like martinis or bright colors). Order defensively: Stick with whatever fresh fish is available and the delicious creamed spinach.

240 California St., between Front and Battery streets. ☎ *415-391-1849. Reservations not accepted. To get there: Take any Muni streetcar to the Embarcadero Station. Main courses: $12–$18. MC, V. Open: Mon–Fri 11:00 a.m.–9:30 p.m.; Sat 11:30 a.m.– 9:30 p.m.*

U.S. Restaurant
$ North Beach   ITALIAN

In the old days (pre-1999), the stern waitresses at this North Beach mainstay never wrote down the orders or brought a bill. Instead, they memorized everything and met you at the cash register when you were ready to leave. Then someone got the stupid idea to modernize the place. That led to its closure, which was so upsetting to the already miserable regulars that the original owners found a new space a block away and, voila, we're back with veal parmigiana that flops over the plate, huge orders of fried calamari on Fridays, and sides of pasta with pesto. The waitresses use order pads now, but we can live with that.

515 Columbus Ave., between Union and Green streets. ☎ *415-397-5200. Reservations recommended. To get there: 30-Stockton bus. Main courses: $8.50–$16. AE, MC, V. Open: Tues–Thurs and Sun 11 a.m.–9 p.m.; Fri–Sat 11 a.m.– 10 p.m.*

Zuni Cafe
$$ Civic Center/Hayes Valley   CALIFORNIA

There's always a palpable buzz from the smartly dressed crowd hanging about Zuni's copper bar drinking vodka and snarfing oysters. Everything from the brick oven is terrific, but the roast chicken with bread salad for two is downright divine. Don't opt for an outside table; the view on this section of Market Street isn't all that pleasant.

1658 Market St., between Franklin and Gough streets. ☎ *415-552-2522. Reservations recommended. To get there: Muni Metro F-Market to Van Ness; walk two blocks southwest. Main courses: $11–$26. AE, MC, V. Open: Lunch and dinner Tues–Sat 11:30 a.m. to midnight; Sun 11 a.m.–11 p.m.*

Dim Sum 101

I wasn't sure what to expect the first time I tried dim sum. I'll admit — and only because you were kind enough to buy this book — that I was a little nervous. The idea of eating these little Chinese dumplings, filled with ingredients I couldn't identify, was a bit scary. I am delighted to report that I quickly overcame my initial wariness and now love dim sum. If you haven't tried it, I urge you to do so.

In many Chinese restaurants, dim sum is served from late morning until around 2 p.m., but not later. In fact, if you arrive much past 1 p.m., you run the risk of the kitchen losing interest in providing much of anything to eat. It's best to arrive around 11 a.m. Dim sum generally enters on carts wheeled about the room by waitresses. (Otherwise, you order from a menu.) Ask for a table near the kitchen in order to get first crack at whatever's on its way around the room. The ladies with their carts will stop by your table and show you what they have. If it looks appealing to you, nod or say yes; if not, just say, "No, thanks." It's okay to order slowly — finishing one plate, sipping tea, then ordering something else. By the way, if you run out of tea, open the teapot lid.

Here's a rundown of dim sum that first-timers will definitely enjoy:

- **Har Gau:** Shrimp dumplings encased in a translucent wrapper and steamed
- **Sui mai:** Rectangles of pork and shrimp in a sheer noodle wrapper
- **Gau choi gau:** Chives, alone or with shrimp or scallop
- **Jun jui kau:** Rice pearl balls with seasoned ground pork and rice
- **Law mai gai:** Sticky rice with bits of meat and mushrooms wrapped in a lotus leaf
- **Char siu bau:** Steamed pork buns — bits of barbecued meat in a doughy roll
- **Guk char siu ban:** Baked pork buns — bits of barbecued meat in a glazed roll
- **Chun guen:** Spring rolls — smaller, less crowded versions of egg roll
- **Gau ji:** Potstickers — a thick, crescent-shaped dough filled with ground pork

Where to go

Yank Sing, in the Embarcadero at Rincon Center, 101 Spear St. (☎ 415-957-9300), is considered by those in the know to be one of the premier dim sum houses in town.

In Chinatown, **Gold Mountain,** 644 Broadway, near Stockton Street (☎ 415-296-7733), is typical of the cavernous dim sum parlors that serve hundreds of families on the weekends.

Way out in the Richmond District at 6255 Geary at 27th Boulevard is one of my favorites, **The Mayflower** (☎ 415-387-8338). Dim sum is served every day, and the pleasant room caters to a mostly Chinese clientele.

Finding a Restaurant by Price, Location, and Cuisine

Need to find a place to eat in North Beach? Dead-set on French cuisine? Looking for budget-friendly spots only? Then check out the following indexes, which list all my dining recommendations according to location, price, and cuisine.

Index by price

$

Bistro Aix (French, The Marina/Cow Hollow)
Chow (American, The Castro)
Kay Cheung (Chinese, Chinatown)
Lichee Garden (Chinese, Chinatown)
L'Osteria del Forno (Rustic Italian, North Beach)
Pazzia (Northern Italian, SoMa)
R&G Lounge (Chinese, Chinatown)
U.S. Restaurant (Italian, North Beach)

$$

Andalu (International, Mission District)
Cafe Marimba (Mexican, The Marina/Cow Hollow)
Delfina (Tuscan Italian, Mission District)
Enrico's Sidewalk Cafe (California/Italian, North Beach)
Globe (Rustic American, Financial District)
Gordon's House of Fine Eats (American, Mission District)
Grand Cafe (California, Union Square)
Green's (Vegetarian, The Marina/Cow Hollow)
Hayes Street Grill (Seafood, Civic Center/Hayes Valley)
Le Charm (French, SoMa)
Luna Park (New American, Mission District)

Slanted Door (Vietnamese, Mission District)
Spoon (American, Russian Hill)
Tadich Grill (Seafood, Financial District)
Zuni Cafe (California, Civic Center/Hayes Valley)

$$$

B-44 (Spanish, Financial District)
Cafe Kati (California, Japantown)
Foreign Cinema (New American/French, Mission District)
Fringale (French, SoMa)
Kokkari Estiatorio (Greek, Financial District)
Lapis (Mediterranean, Embarcadero)
Le Colonial (French-Vietnamese, Union Square)
Merenda (California/French, The Marina/Cow Hollow)
Moose's (California/Mediterranean, North Beach)
Ozumo (Japanese/Sushi, Embarcadero)
Rose Pistola (Italian, North Beach)
Scala's Bistro (Italian, Union Square)

$$$$

Asia de Cuba (Asian/Latin Fusion, Union Square)
Boulevard (American, The Embarcadero)
Charles-Nob Hill (California/French, Nob Hill)

Gary Danko (New American/French, Russian Hill)
Hawthorne Lane (California/Asian, SoMa)

Jardinière (California/French, Civic Center/Hayes Valley)

Index by location

The Castro
Chow (American, $)

Chinatown
Kay Cheung (Chinese, $)
Lichee Garden (Chinese, $)
R&G Lounge (Chinese, $)

Civic Center/Hayes Valley
Hayes Street Grill (Seafood, $$)
Jardinière (California/French, $$$$)
Zuni Cafe (California, $$)

The Embarcadero
Boulevard (American, $$$$)
Lapis (Mediterranean, $$$)
Ozumo (Japanese/Sushi, $$$)

Financial District
B-44 (Spanish, $$$)
Globe (Rustic American, $$)
Kokkari Estiatorio (Greek, $$$)
Tadich Grill (Seafood, $$)

Japantown
Cafe Kati (California, $$$)

The Marina/Cow Hollow
Bistro Aix (French, $)
Cafe Marimba (Mexican, $$)
Green's (Vegetarian, $$–$$$)
Merenda (California/French, $$)

The Mission District
Andalu (International, $$)
Delfina (Tuscan Italian, $$)

Foreign Cinema (New American/French, $$$)
Gordon's House of Fine Eats (American, $$–$$$)
Luna Park (New American, $$)
Slanted Door (Vietnamese, $$)

Nob Hill
Charles-Nob Hill (California/French, $$$$)

North Beach
Enrico's Sidewalk Cafe (California/Italian, $$)
L'Osteria del Forno (Rustic Italian, $)
Moose's (California/Mediterranean, $$$)
Rose Pistola (Italian, $$$)
U.S. Restaurant (Italian, $)

South of Market (SoMa)
Fringale (French, $$$)
Hawthorne Lane (California/Asian, $$$$)
Le Charm (French, $$)
Pazzia (Northern Italian, $)

Russian Hill
Gary Danko (New American/French, $$$$)
Spoon (American, $$)

Union Square
Asia de Cuba (Asian/Latin Fusion, $$$$)
Grand Cafe (California, $$–$$$)
Le Colonial (French-Vietnamese, $$$)
Scala's Bistro (Italian, $$$)

Index by cuisine

American
Boulevard (The Embarcadero, $$$$)
Chow (The Castro, $)
Globe (RUSTIC, Financial District, $$)
Gordon's House of Fine Eats (Mission District, $$–$$$)
Spoon (Russian Hill, $$)

Asian/Latin
Asia de Cuba (Union Square, $$$$)

California
Cafe Kati (Japantown, $$$)
Grand Cafe (Union Square, $$–$$$)
Zuni Cafe (Civic Center/Hayes Valley, $$)

California/Asian
Hawthorne Lane (SoMa, $$$$)

California/French
Charles-Nob Hill (Nob Hill, $$$$)
Jardinière (Civic Center/Hayes Valley, $$$$)
Merenda (The Marina/Cow Hollow, $$)

California/Italian
Enrico's Sidewalk Cafe (North Beach, $$)

California/Mediterranean
Moose's (North Beach, $$$)

Chinese
Kay Cheung (Chinatown, $)
Lichee Garden (Chinatown, $)
R&G Lounge (Chinatown, $)

French
Bistro Aix (The Marina/Cow Hollow, $)
Fringale (SoMa, $$$)
Le Charm (SoMa, $$)

French-Vietnamese
Le Colonial (Union Square, $$$)

Greek
Kokkari Estiatorio (Financial District, $$$)

International
Andalu (Mission District, $$)

Italian
Delfina (Mission District, $$)
L'Osteria del Forno (North Beach, $)
Pazzia (SoMa, $)
Rose Pistola (North Beach, $$$)
Scala's Bistro (Union Square, $$$)
U.S. Restaurant (North Beach, $)

Mediterranean
Lapis (Embarcadero, $$$)

Mexican
Cafe Marimba (The Marina/Cow Hollow, $$)

New American
Foreign Cinema (Mission District, $$$)
Gary Danko (Russian Hill, $$$$)
Luna Park (Mission District, $$)

Seafood
Hayes Street Grill (Civic Center/Hayes Valley, $$)
Tadich Grill (Financial District, $$)

Spanish
B-44 (Financial District, $$$)

Sushi
Ozumo (Embarcadero, $$$)

Vegetarian
Green's (The Marina/Cow Hollow, $$–$$$)

Vietnamese
Slanted Door (Mission District, $$)

Chapter 15

On the Lighter Side: Top Picks for Snacks and Meals on the Go

In This Chapter

▶ Eating on the run

▶ Locating the best bakeries

▶ Tackling breakfast

▶ Savoring a slice of pizza or chowing down on a hamburger

With the exception of Fisherman's Wharf, where people attempt to walk while balancing bread bowls filled with questionable clam chowder, street food is practically nonexistent in San Francisco. (Although, in a very weak moment, and for research purposes only, I once bought a hot dog from a cart on Pier 39.) But that doesn't mean you should head to the closest fast-food chain for a meal on the go. Instead, head to one of the many sandwich counters, Asian bakeries, Italian delis, coffeehouses, or pastry shops that provide a grand variety of delicious foodstuffs quickly and for reasonable to downright cheap prices.

Whether you're feeling a bit peckish or positively peaked, you'll find something tempting to tide yourself over until the next big meal.

Have Food, Will Travel

Just two long blocks west of the Ferry Building on the Embarcadero, next to Pier 5, is a bench-lined, refurbished wooden wharf with fine views that practically begs for an impromptu picnic lunch. But there are plenty of other spots around the city to unpack a brown bag, too.

Serving up sandwiches on the go

You can generously fill your lunch pail at **Panelli Bros.**, a second-generation family-run Italian delicatessen with a fantastic assortment of cheeses; good, inexpensive Italian wines; and friendly people who make excellent sandwiches to go. It's located at 1419 Stockton St., near Vallejo Street in North Beach (☎ **415-421-2541**). Open daily.

Also in North Beach, on the corner of Columbus and Kearny, is a Parisian-inspired, Italian cafe owned by the director Francis Ford Coppola. Surprisingly, **Café Niebaum-Coppola** (☎ **415-291-1700**) — part wine bar, part kitchen store — serves the most delicious mufalatta (comprised of olive salad, mortadella, and provolone) outside of New Orleans, a sandwich that once made my husband so ecstatic he squirreled away half to eat the following day. The cafe is open daily until 11 p.m.

In the Financial District at **Palio Paninoteca,** 505 Montgomery St., near California Street (☎ **415-362-6900**), $7 gets you a panino large enough for two. Fillings range from grilled vegetables or meats to smoked prosciutto with gorgonzola, mascarpone, and arugula. Closed weekends.

Closer to Union Square, with another two locations in the Financial District, is **Specialty's Café & Bakery,** 1 Post St., at Market (☎ **415-896-9550**). This spot is popular for a vast array of fresh sandwiches served on made-from-scratch breads. Also open only on weekdays.

Down on the farm — Farmer's market, that is

Saturday mornings at the **Ferry Plaza Farmers' Market** at Green Street and Embarcadero (open from 8 a.m. to 1:30 p.m.) is a jumble of basket– and canvas sack–wielding couples picking over the heirloom tomatoes and grabbing the last of the wild strawberries while juggling coffee and a cell phone. The simple beauty of the organic vegetables and flowers makes a walk around the market an enormous pleasure, despite the crowds. The **Hayes Street Grill** and **Rose Pistola** restaurants cook gourmet breakfasts from their booths, and other vendors sell items such as bottles of olive oil, jars of local honey, and exotic orchid plants. This is also a great place to gather picnic food — fresh bread, artisan cheeses, and fruit — for later in the day. The F-Market streetcar makes a stop on Green Street.

Snacking at the Wharf

Let's be frank. **Pier 39/Fisherman's Wharf** is the most touristy part of town. The restaurants that crowd Jefferson Street exist for the people who are here today and gone tomorrow. I have learned to accept this, if not to embrace it, and I'm not going to sneer at anybody who spends part of a day here on the way to Alcatraz or simply to see what all the fuss is about. But let's say that this person is hungry. Let's say that this person has heard about all the crab vendors and the delicious sourdough bread, and thinks to himself, "That sounds like lunch to me." This is what I'd suggest: Buy a bottle of beer, buy a little round of sourdough bread, and ask one of the guys at a crab stand (try **Fisherman's Grotto No. 9**) to cook, clean, and crack a live crab for you. Then take these goodies and lots of napkins through the doors marked "Passageway to the Boats," walk down this relatively quiet area, sit on the dock, and have a good time. *Remember:* The local Dungeness crab season is from November through May. In the summer, the crabs are flown in from Alaska or parts east.

Unless you purchase a freshly cracked crab, rest assured that the $5.25 crab cocktail you ordered is made of canned crab — or even imitation crab.

Flour Power

You can have a swell time hunting and gathering among the bakeries in North Beach. For starters, drop by **Liguria Bakery** (☎ 415-421-3786) on the corner of Stockton and Filbert streets for a sheet of plain focaccia, or maybe one topped with green onions or tomato. They're all delicious and wrapped for portability. Liguria is open every day by 8 a.m. and closes when the last piece of focaccia is sold, usually by 2 p.m. I also love **Victoria Pastry Co.,** 1362 Stockton St., at Vallejo (☎ 415-781-2015), which sells a large selection of Italian sweets (the chewy almond cookies are good enough to give as a gift) and slices of its justly popular cakes.

Citizen Cake, 399 Grove St., in Hayes Valley (☎ 415-861-2228), creates the kind of homemade cookies, cakes, and desserts that ignites a love/hate relationship between your taste buds and your hips. The spacious cafe also serves lunch and dinner Tuesday through Friday and brunch and dinner on the weekends. Located near **Bellochio** (see Chapter 19) and the artist's home away from studio, **Flax,** you can get a little shopping in while visiting the neighborhood.

A small chain of Boulangerie Bay Bread bakery/cafes has popped up in the Haight-Ashbury, Cow Hollow, Fillmore, and Russian Hill neighborhoods, with my favorite being **Boulange de Polk,** 2310 Polk St., at Green Street (☎ 415-345-1107). Along with lovely French pastries (the cannelés de Bordeaux are swoon-worthy), you can order savory tarts, sandwiches, and salads to take away or eat at one of the coveted outdoor tables.

Chinese Bakeries

Chinese bakeries, which sell savory as well as sweet items, abound in **Chinatown,** in the **Sunset District** on Irving Street, and in the **Richmond District** on Clement Street. For snacking on the premises or on the go, delicious baked or steamed pork buns (baked buns are golden brown, and steamed buns are white) are ideal and a big hit with kids. If you want something on the sweet side, custard tarts and sesame seed–covered balls of rice surrounding a bit of sweet bean paste are standard issue. Look also for *bo lo bow,* slightly puffy and sweet bread with a crust that resembles the outside of a pineapple, or *chung yow bow,* green-onion bread. You may have to point to whatever looks appetizing, because the folks behind the counter don't necessarily speak English.

Coffee and Tea, If You Please

Places to sit and sip are as prevalent as pigeons in this caffeine-crazed piece of paradise. Coffeehouses — and I'm not even including the mega-chains — nestle in every neighborhood, seemingly on every block. I don't think drinking coffee as a lifestyle was invented in North Beach, but based on sheer numbers, it could have been. Regulars, of course, have their favorite blends and favorite tables, but no one will argue against hanging out at **Mario's Bohemian Cigar Store** on the corner of Columbus and Union Street (☎ **415-362-0536**). Along with excellent coffee (Graffeo), you can graze on a mouth-watering chicken parmigiana on focaccia. **Caffé Trieste,** on Vallejo and Grant streets (☎ **415-982-2605**), is a mob scene on Saturday afternoons, when the owners and friends take a turn at the microphone to sing. Coffee is served daily with or without opera.

Although that Seattle-based coffee Goliath continues to snap up real estate in a quest to make everyone drink frappuccinos, we have our own local chain to kick around. Actually, **Peet's Coffee and Tea** is worshipped by caffeine aficionados, and if you love really strong coffee, it's worth dropping by one of their many stores. The one closest to Union Square is in the Financial District at 22 Battery St., at Bush (☎ **415-981-4550**). You can also try the shop on Chestnut Street between Steiner and Pierce streets in the Marina. They're both open daily.

The peaceful **Imperial Tea Court,** 1411 Powell St., near Broadway (☎ **415-788-6080**), is a must-stop in which to rest your feet and take stock of your life — or maybe just the last half hour — over a pot of exotic leaves and blossoms that would make Celestial Seasonings blush. This is the place to sample the highest quality teas as they were meant to be brewed — and the staff will be happy to show you how it's done. Open daily.

Breakfast of Champions

Touring is hard work. You need a good breakfast. Around Union Square you can find lots of restaurants serving in the morning, including **The Grand Café** (see Chapter 14); **Sears Fine Food** on Powell across from Union Square (☎ 415-986-1160), open daily; and my favorite, **Dottie's True Blue Café,** 522 Jones St., between Geary Boulevard and O'Farrell Street (☎ 415-885-2767). Open Wednesday through Sunday only, Dottie's True Blue Café is a tiny diner that offers daily specials as well as the basics — eggs, pancakes, sausage — all prepared with great flair. The baked goods are so delicious, you may want to purchase some to go.

Bechelli's, in the Marina/Cow Hollow neighborhood at 2346 Chestnut St., between Divisadero and Scott streets (☎ 415-346-1801), serves a substantial breakfast until 3 p.m. during the week, and until 4 p.m. Saturday and Sunday. To my mind, the booths, scruffy leatherette chairs, and beat-up horseshoe-shaped wooden counter add to the charm of this neighborhood institution, but more importantly, the breakfast menu is nearly as huge as the portions. Buttermilk pancakes, French toast, homemade corned beef hash, and lots of omelets potentially will hold you for a good part of the day. Kids often enjoy bellying up to the counter, and the place has a very relaxed, family-friendly atmosphere. No reservations; credit cards are accepted.

Around the Embarcadero on Battery Street, **Il Fornaio** (☎ 415-986-0100) offers an excellent small breakfast menu daily, with egg dishes, oatmeal, and an array of homemade baked goods that are also sold from a takeaway counter just inside. If you don't mind traveling to Golden Gate Park to hunt down an early morning meal, take the N-Judah streetcar to Ninth Avenue, walk toward the park, and at the corner of Lincoln and Ninth avenues you'll find **The Canvas Café/Gallery** (☎ 415-504-0070), open daily. As the name implies, inside are paintings by local artists plus simple food for breakfast (oatmeal, bagels, frittatas); sandwiches, salads, pizza, and Mediterranean *mezza* (appetizer) or fondue platters to share for lunch; and afternoon pick-me-ups including wine and beer. It's exactly where you want to stop before or after a day in the park.

Pizza and Other Cheap Eats

Although I am known to criticize fast food, I consider pizza an exception. Good pizza can make a perfectly satisfying, easygoing, low-rent meal. And although San Francisco doesn't have the reputation of either New York or Chicago in the pizza department, you won't have any difficulty finding a ready slice in any neighborhood.

He doesn't deliver, but **Uncle Vito's Pizzadelli,** on the corner of Bush and Powell streets (☎ 415-391-5008), serves credible pie with a big selection of toppings, good salads, and enough pasta dishes to carbo-load for the next day's adventures. Uncle Vito's is inexpensive and convenient to Nob Hill and Union Square, so you'll see lots of foreign tourists here, attempting to put together just the right combination of pizza and beer. **Vicolo Pizzeria** is in Civic Center, at 201 Ivy, an alley off Gough Street between Hayes and Grove streets (☎ **415-863-2382**). It's perfect for a quick bite before the symphony or other cultural pursuits. Vicolo's offers a selection of more gourmet, cornmeal-crusted pizzas that are truly memorable, as well as inviting salads.

If too much exposure to coddled food makes you long for a touch of grease, you can find a couple places to deal with your craving for hamburgers, fries, and a shake. **Mo's Grill**, which makes many kinds of burgers, is south of Market at Folsom and Fourth streets, on the southwest side of Yerba Buena Gardens (☎ **415-957-3779**). You can also find a branch in North Beach on Grant Street, between Vallejo and Green. Because I have a soft spot for '50s-patterned Formica and bright colors, my favorite place to chew the fat is **Burger Joint** in the Mission on 807 Valencia St. (☎ **415-824-3494**). But to dine at a true San Francisco institution, head to **Clown Alley** at Columbus and Washington Street in North Beach (☎ **415-421-2540**). This old-fashioned dive is open until 3 a.m. Friday and Saturday nights. Late-night partygoers swear these are the best burgers in town.

North Beach also shelters at least two little eateries specializing in roasted chicken, the oldest being **Il Pollaio,** 555 Columbus Ave., between Union and Green streets (☎ **415-362-7727**). A very casual place to sit down for savory chicken and other meats and salads, this is where you go when the kids start rolling their eyes if you mention dim sum or sea bass. It's also a good choice when you're tired of spending too much money on dinner.

Adventure eaters in the mood for Indian food will barely feel a strain on the pocketbook at **Shalimar,** 532 Jones St., between Geary and O'Farrell (☎ **415-928-0333**), another Formica table hole-in-the-wall in the Tenderloin/Union Square area. Order at the counter, set your table, watch for your food to come up, and then enjoy delicious curries, savory naan bread, and tandoori. Open daily for lunch and dinner; cash only.

The Real Dill

Oh, happy day. A couple of enterprising and thoughtful chef guys with Jewish mothers saw fit to open a genuine delicatessen in the city. You don't know how we suffered until **East Coast West Delicatessen** started with the chicken soup and the matzoh balls, not to mention the pastrami, the pickled herring, and the brisket (every bit as good as mine, if not better). Located at 1725 Polk St. (☎ **415-563-3542**) and open daily, this is also a fine place to get sandwiches to take with you for the trip home — I wouldn't want you to go hungry.

Part V
Exploring San Francisco

The 5th Wave   By Rich Tennant

In this part . . .

Now you get to the main course. This part tells you about the landmarks and neighborhoods that define San Francisco to the world. And you know what? Most of them are worthy of their star billing.

How do you take in everything? That depends on how much time you have, of course. If you only have a day or two to spare, a guided tour may be the best way of at least seeing, if not savoring, the sites. Or you can pick and choose from a list of a few places to see, spend some quality time at each of those sites, and plan on coming back to the city another time to catch the rest. If you have three or more days to wander, take a look at my suggested itineraries at the end of this part for an idea of how to absorb as much of the city as possible.

Don't forget the shopping opportunities while the pleasure of browsing in one-of-a-kind stores is still possible. An entire shopping chapter awaits, and it's filled with suggestions of where to find interesting clothes, gifts, and foods that you won't find in your local shopping mall. Leave room in your suitcase — it'll be heavier on the trip home.

Chapter 16

San Francisco's Top Sights

Something is bringing you to San Francisco. Perhaps you've been overcome by recollections of old Rice-A-Roni commercials ("the San Francisco treat") that became synonymous with cable cars. Or maybe visions of the Golden Gate Bridge spanning the icy waters of the bay are pulling you to the left coast. Are the views from your window a bit too flat? Is the thrillseeker in you ready for the action our hills provide to drivers and passengers alike? Did you manage to schedule a week off from work and coming to San Francisco just seemed like a good idea? Whatever your reasons for choosing this city, I don't think you'll be bored, and I know you won't be disappointed.

You may be curious to understand firsthand why this city is different from any other urban center in the United States and why its residents are so fiercely passionate about where they live. After a few days making your way around, you may glean some of the reasons, the biggest of which is the sheer beauty of the setting. I think regarding this city and touring its attractions in context is most rewarding. Take those cable cars, for example: Sure, they're a fun ride in general, but as you climb aboard, observe the gripman (or gripwoman — there's one) and the other passengers, and note how the neighborhoods change as you head from Union Square through North Beach or past Nob Hill. Watching the passersby on the pavement is even an experience. I'll always remember how heads turned (and kept turning) to follow a particularly gorgeous girl in her black leather pants as she sashayed up Mason Street. It was certainly the first time I've ever been on a cable car that intentionally went backward!

The following index gives you a quick reference of the features that make San Francisco, well, San Francisco.

Index of Top Attractions by Neighborhood

Chinatown
Chinese Culture Center
Chinese Historical Society of America
Golden Gate Fortune Cookies
   Company
Portsmouth Square
Tin Hou Temple

Civic Center
Asian Art Museum

Fisherman's Wharf
Alcatraz Island
Cable cars
The Cannery
Ghirardelli Square
Hyde Street Pier
Maritime National Historical Park
Pier 39
USS *Pampinito*

North Beach/Telegraph Hill
Coit Tower
Lombard Street

Marina/Cow Hollow
The Exploratorium/Palace of Fine Arts
Golden Gate Bridge

The Richmond District
Golden Gate Park
California Academy of Sciences
Conservatory of Flowers
Japanese Tea Garden
Strybing Arboretum and Botanical
   Gardens

SoMa
Museum of Modern Art
Metreon
Yerba Buena Gardens
Zeum

Index by Type of Attraction

Museums and the Aquarium
Aquarium of the Bay
Asian Art Museum of San Francisco
California Academy of Sciences
Chinese Culture Center
The Chinese Historical Society of
   America
The Exploratorium
The San Francisco Maritime National
   Historical Park
San Francisco Museum of Modern Art
   (MOMA)
Zeum

Naval Exhibits
Hyde Street Pier
The San Francisco Maritime National
   Historical Park
USS *Pampanito*

Neighborhoods
Chinatown
Fisherman's Wharf

Parks, Gardens, and the Conservatory
Alcatraz Island
The Conservatory of Flowers

Golden Gate Park
Japanese Tea Garden
Palace of Fine Arts
Portsmouth Square
The Strybing Arboretum and Botanical
    Gardens
Yerba Buena Gardens and Center for
    the Arts

Historic Buildings and Attractions

Cable cars
The Cannery
Coit Tower
Ghirardelli Square

Golden Gate Bridge
Lombard Street
Palace of Fine Arts
Tin Hou Temple

Shops and Entertainment

The Cannery
Ghirardelli Square
Golden Gate Fortune Cookies
    Company
Pier 39
Sony Metreon
Yerba Buena Gardens and Center for
    the Arts

The Top Attractions from A to Z

Alcatraz Island
Fisherman's Wharf

Located in **San Francisco Bay,** "The Rock" — Alcatraz Island — has been transformed from a run-down prison remnant to a must-see attraction, thanks to Hollywood's dramatic depiction of the maximum-security prison. The self-guided tour of the grounds includes an orientation video, and for a few dollars extra you can rent a 35-minute audio tour of the cell block. National Park rangers also give intrepretive talks full of interesting anecdotes about Alcatraz's infamous residents. You'll be out in the middle of the perpetually-windy bay, so remember to bring a jacket, as well as comfortable shoes for the steep walk up to the **Cell House.** A wheelchair-accessible path leads up to the prison. The Alcatraz experience takes about 2½ hours, including the ferry ride.

To get the full effect of what being an inmate may have been like, try the **"Alcatraz After Hours"** tour. The prison becomes especially sinister when the sun goes down, so use discretion before deciding to bring kids along. The tour is offered Thursday through Sunday only; the ferry departs at 6:15 p.m. and 7 p.m. (4:20 p.m. during the winter).

During the summer, you must reserve tickets far in advance for the ferry ride to the island. Call ☎ **415-705-5555** to purchase tickets over the phone. There is a $2.25-per-ticket service charge for phone orders.

Pier 41, at Fisherman's Wharf. ☎ 415-773-1188, for information only. Internet: www.blueandgoldfleet.com *or* www.telesails.com. *Open: Winter daily 9:15 a.m.–2:30 p.m.; summer daily 9:15 a.m.–4:15 p.m. Ferries run approximately every half hour. Arrive at least 20 minutes before sailing time. To get there: F-Market streetcar; Powell-Mason cable car (the line ends a few blocks away); or 30-Stockton bus, which stops one block south. Admission (includes ferry and audio tour): $13.25 adults, $11.50 seniors 62 and older, $8 children 5–11.*

San Francisco's Top Sights

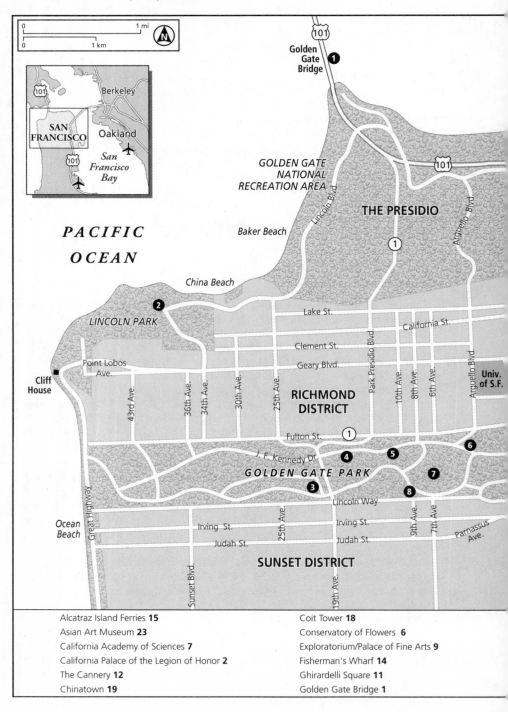

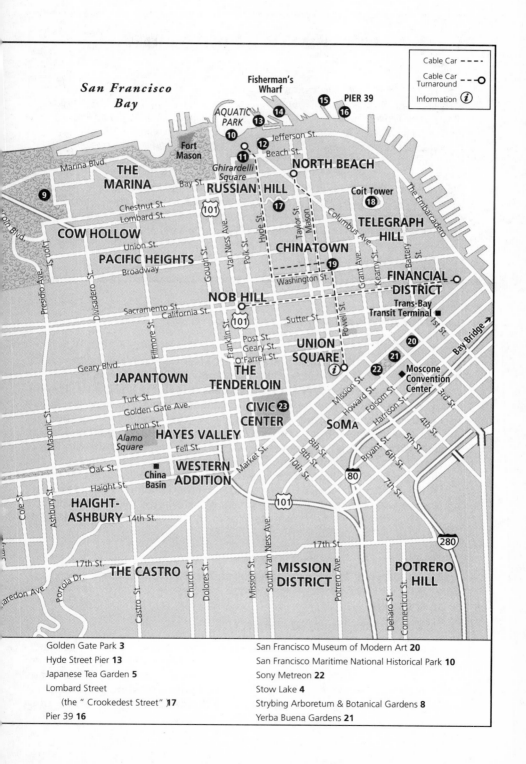

San Francisco Bay

Fisherman's Wharf

PIER 39

Cable Car
Cable Car Turnaround
Information (i)

AQUATIC PARK

Fort Mason

Marina Blvd

THE MARINA

Ghirardelli Square

Jefferson St.

Beach St.

NORTH BEACH

Chestnut St.

Bay St.

RUSSIAN HILL

Coit Tower

Lombard St.

COW HOLLOW

Union St.

PACIFIC HEIGHTS

Broadway

Chinatown

TELEGRAPH HILL

Washington St.

NOB HILL

FINANCIAL DISTRICT

Sacramento St.

California St.

Trans-Bay Transit Terminal

Sutter St.

Post St.

Geary St.

O'Farrell St.

UNION SQUARE

Bay Bridge

JAPANTOWN

THE TENDERLOIN

Turk St.

Golden Gate Ave.

Moscone Convention Center

Fulton St.

CIVIC CENTER

SoMa

Alamo Square

HAYES VALLEY

Fell St.

Oak St.

China Basin

WESTERN ADDITION

Haight St.

Market St.

HAIGHT-ASHBURY

14th St.

17th St.

17th St.

THE CASTRO

MISSION DISTRICT

POTRERO HILL

From maximum prison to maximum attraction

Alcatraz Island was first discovered in 1775. Due to its strategic location in San Francisco Bay, the U.S. Army took notice and began building a military fortress atop "The Rock." From 1850 to 1933, it served as a military post and army prison, housing Civil War, Spanish-American War, and, finally, civilian prisoners. In 1934, it was converted into a maximum-security prison. The prison was home to famous gangsters such as Al Capone; Robert Stroud, the so-called Birdman of Alcatraz (because he was an expert on ornithological diseases — he never kept birds on Alcatraz); and "Machine Gun" Kelly. Twenty-nine prisoners tried to escape from Alcatraz — two made it ashore, only to be captured almost immediately, and five drowned, presumably, although their bodies were never recovered. All 29 attempts are said to have failed. The prison closed in 1963, due to deterioration of the buildings and prohibitive maintenance costs. Alcatraz became part of the Golden Gate National Recreation Area in 1972.

Asian Art Museum of San Francisco
Civic Center

At press time, the brand new Asian Art Museum hadn't actually opened in its new quarters near City Hall, but by the time you get to San Francisco (if you travel after early 2003), the doors should be opened. The museum owns one of the largest collections of Asian art in the Western world, covering 6,000 years and encompassing cultures throughout Asia. Formerly housed in Golden Gate Park, the Asian gathered public and private funds to completely renovate the interior of the old Beaux Arts Main Library and create 37,500 square feet of exhibition space (and if that doesn't invigorate Civic Center, I'm not sure what will). Although the collection itself remains more than enough reason to visit, the renovation will garner plenty of attention. It is designed by Gae Aulenti, the Milanese architect who renovated the former d'Orsay train staion in Paris into the wildly popular Musée d'Orsay.

Larkin at Fulton streets. ☎ **415-379-8800**. *Internet:* www.asianart.org. *To get there: Muni or BART to Civic Center station. Phone for hours and admission.*

Cable Cars
Union Square/Financial District

San Francisco's most notable icon is probably the cable car. These cherished wooden cars creak and squeal up and around hills while passengers lean out into the wind, running the risk of getting their heads removed by passing buses. San Francisco's three existing lines comprise the world's only surviving system of cable cars, and they are a delight to ride. The sheer joy of whizzing down a hill with the bay glistening in the foreground will linger in your memory. But these legendary icons aren't just fun, they're also a useful means of transportation. The **Powell-Mason line** conveniently wends its way from the corner of Powell and Market streets through North Beach and ends near **Fisherman's Wharf.** If you only have time to ride the cars once, this is the one I'd recommend. It will take you most of the way to Fisherman's Wharf, or if you prefer, you can hop off when you get to North Beach. The **Powell-Hyde line,** which starts at the same intersection, ends up near the **Maritime Museum** and **Ghirardelli Square.** The less-thrilling **California line** begins at the foot of Market Street and travels straight up California Street over **Nob Hill** to Van Ness Avenue.

I thought I had a foolproof method of avoiding the crowds at the cable car turnarounds by waiting two blocks from the Powell Street *turnaround* (which is literally where the cars are turned around at the end of the line), but after forcing my visiting brother to watch as one car after another passed us by ("And you do this professionally?" he said, unkindly), my only other suggestion is to get up early to ride. You can also try walking a few more blocks to the next stop. (Stops are indicated by brown signs with a white cable car on them.) Although at first it will appear that there's no room for you among the zillions of passengers already on the car, by magic a foothold may open up. Cars run from 6:30 a.m. to 12:30 a.m. The fare is $2 per person one-way, payable on board; Muni Passports are accepted. See Chapter 11 for more details.

Chinatown

Crowded with pedestrians and crammed with exotic-looking shops and vegetable markets whose wares spill onto the sidewalks, Chinatown is a genuinely fascinating destination. Take your time as you walk through this enclave, housing the largest Chinese population outside of Asia — it's easy to miss something. The **Dragon Gate arch** at Grant Avenue and Bush Street (just a few blocks north of Union Square) marks the entry to Chinatown. To get a more authentic experience, avoid the visiting hordes and explore the side streets and alleys off Grant Avenue. If you stay for lunch or dinner, your adventure will take about a half day. Walking from Union Square is the more sensible way to get here, but you can also reach Chinatown by taking the 30-Stockton bus; parking is nearly impossible, but if you want to try it, your best bet is on Kearny Street at Portsmouth Square. (See Chapter 14 for dining suggestions and Chapter 19 for where to shop.) While you're in Chinatown, don't miss the following highlights.

The Chinese Historical Society of America, 965 Clay St. (☎ **415-391-1188**), is a good place to begin your Chinatown tour. The fascinating history of the Chinese in California is well documented here through photographs and artifacts, and you can browse through a gallery and a gift shop. The museum is open Tuesday 1 to 4 p.m., and Monday and Wednesday through Friday from 10:30 a.m. to 4:00 p.m. Admission is free.

Chinatown

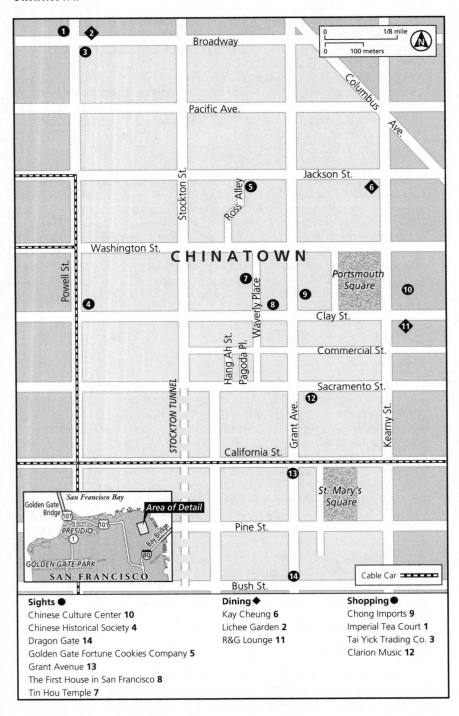

Sights ●
Chinese Culture Center **10**
Chinese Historical Society **4**
Dragon Gate **14**
Golden Gate Fortune Cookies Company **5**
Grant Avenue **13**
The First House in San Francisco **8**
Tin Hou Temple **7**

Dining ◆
Kay Cheung **6**
Lichee Garden **2**
R&G Lounge **11**

Shopping ●
Chong Imports **9**
Imperial Tea Court **1**
Tai Yick Trading Co. **3**
Clarion Music **12**

The steel wheels tour

The famous cable cars you see going up and down the hills of downtown San Francisco were invented in 1869 by Andrew Hallidie. Hallidie saw the need for a new mode of transportation when he witnessed a horse-drawn streetcar slide backward down one of the many steep slopes that make up San Francisco's unique topography. Here's how the cable car system works: A steel cable is housed just under the street in a rail, kind of like an inside-out train rail (it's the cable that makes that clickity-clacking sound). Powered by electricity, this cable constantly runs through the rail. Each cable car has a lever that, when pulled back, closes a pincer-like "grip" on the cable. The person who pulls the lever is called a *gripper*— some would call this person a driver, but he doesn't drive, he "grips" the cable. The cable car is then attached to the cable that runs through the rail under the pavement, and the car begins to move at a constant 9 miles per hour — the speed at which the cable is set to travel.

Tin Hou Temple, 125 Waverly Pl. (an alley off Clay Street between Stockton and Grant), one of the oldest Chinese temples in the United States, is dedicated to the Goddess of Heaven. The temple is open to the public, but please keep in mind this is still an active house of worship. Be prepared to climb a narrow staircase to the top floor, and make an offering or buy some incense on your way out.

Golden Gate Fortune Cookies Company, 956 Ross Alley, between Jackson and Washington streets near Grant Avenue, is a working factory where you can buy bags of fresh, inexpensive almond and fortune cookies. You may find the cramped quarters somewhat claustrophobic, but watching rounds of dough transmogrify into cookies is fun. Open daily from 10 a.m. to 7 p.m.

Portsmouth Square, a park above the Portsmouth Square parking garage on Kearny Street between Washington and Clay streets, marks the spot where San Francisco was originally settled and is the site of the first California public school, which opened in 1848. A compact but complete playground attracts all the neighborhood preschoolers, and in the morning, elderly Chinese practice their tai chi exercises. The landscape includes comfortable benches, attractive lampposts, and young trees. The distinctly San Francisco view includes the **Transamerica Pyramid** looming above the skyline. The garage below is a good place to know about if you're driving. Interestingly, the garage's fourth floor is most likely to have empty spaces, because in Cantonese, the word for *four* sounds like the word for *death.* Superstitious Chinese won't park there.

The pedestrian bridge over Kearny Street leads directly into the third floor of the Chinatown Holiday Inn, where you'll find the **Chinese Culture Center** (☎ 415-986-1822; Internet: www.c-c-c.org). A gift shop leads to the sole gallery, where changing exhibits may feature photographs from pre-earthquake Chinatown, Chinese brush painting, or exquisitely embroidered antique clothing and household items. The center is open from 10 a.m. to 4 p.m. Tuesday through Sunday. Admission is free.

Coit Tower
Telegraph Hill (Near North Beach)

Erected in 1933 with funds bequeathed to the city by Lillie Hitchcock Coit, this 210-foot concrete landmark is visible from much of the city. But everyone needs to take a closer look to see the beauty of the tower. The decor inside features walls with dramatic murals inspired by and commissioned during the Great Depression. Take an elevator to the top for panoramic views of the city and the bay. This diversion will probably take about 30 minutes from start to finish.

Atop Telegraph Hill. ☎ **415-362-0808.** *To get there: Take the 39-Coit bus or walk from Lombard Street where it meets Telegraph Hill Boulevard (two blocks east of Stockton Street). Parking: The drive up and the parking lot are always a mass of cars. Open: Daily 10 a.m.–6 p.m. Admission to top of tower: $3.75 adults, $2.50 seniors, $1.50 kids 6–12.*

Exploratorium/Palace of Fine Arts
Marina District

Scientific American magazine rates the Exploratorium as "the best science museum in the world," and it's certainly an intriguing space that appeals to all ages. The hands-on exhibits explore many different topics, such as technology, human perception, and natural phenomena. Well-written text accompanies the exhibits to further enhance the learning experience. Don't worry about feeling like a science dunce if you're visiting with children; a well-informed volunteer is ready to field any questions you can't answer. Expect to spend about two hours exploring the museum, especially if you're traveling with kids. Allow more time, and make advance reservations, if you want to experience the popular "Tactile Dome," a pitch-black geodesic dome that you have to feel your way through. A walk around the grounds of the **Palace of Fine Arts,** which now houses the Exploratorium but was originally built for the 1915 Panama-Pacific International Exposition, is a great way to unwind after exploring the museum. Better yet, if the weather's balmy, bring a picnic and stay a while.

3601 Lyon St. at Marina Boulevard. ☎ **415-561-0360.** *Internet:* www.explorato rium.edu. *To get there: 30-Stockton bus to Marina stop. Parking: Free and easy. Open: Summer (Memorial Day to Labor Day) daily 10 a.m.–6 p.m., Wed until 9 p.m.; winter Tues–Sun 10 a.m.–5 p.m.; Wed until 9 p.m. Admission: $10 adults, $7.50 students and seniors, $6 kids 5–17, free kids 4 and under. Free first Wed of the month. Tactile dome: $14 all ages.*

Fisherman's Wharf & Vicinity

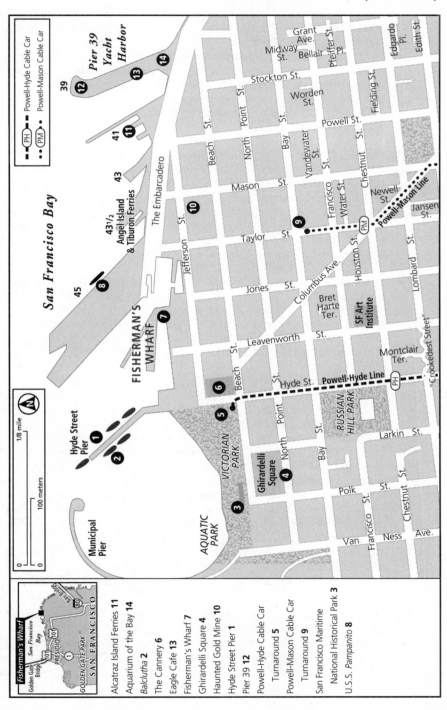

San Francisco Bay

Pier 39
Yacht
Harbor

FISHERMAN'S
WHARF

Hyde Street
Pier

VICTORIAN
PARK

AQUATIC
PARK

Municipal
Pier

Ghirardelli
Square

RUSSIAN
HILL PARK

SF Art
Institute

Bret
Harte
Ter.

Montclair
Ter.

"Crookedest Street"

The Embarcadero

Angel Island
& Tiburon Ferries

Powell-Hyde Line
Powell-Mason Line

PH — Powell-Hyde Cable Car
PM — Powell-Mason Cable Car

1/8 mile
100 meters

Streets: Grant Ave., Midway St., Bellair Pl., Pfeiffer St., Edgardo Pl., Edith St., Stockton St., Worden St., Powell St., Fielding St., Beach St., North Point St., Bay St., Vandewater St., Chestnut St., Mason St., Francisco St., Water St., Newell St., Jansen St., Taylor St., Columbus Ave., Jefferson St., Jones St., Houston St., Lombard St., Leavenworth St., Hyde St., Beach St., North Point St., Bay St., Larkin St., Polk St., Chestnut St., Van Ness Ave., Francisco St.

Fisherman's Wharf

GOLDEN GATE PARK
PRESIDIO
Golden Gate
Bridge
San Francisco
Bay
SAN FRANCISCO
Bay Bridge

Fisherman's Wharf

Don't be confused when you arrive at Fisherman's Wharf and see lots of people wandering around, none of whom appear to fish for a living. This was once a working set of piers, but today it's a seemingly endless outdoor shopping mall masquerading as a bona-fide destination. Some people really enjoy examining the refrigerator magnets and cable car bookends stocked in one olde shoppe after another; others, dazed in the presence of so much kitsch, hastily plan their escape. Still, because most folks make their way to the wharf for one reason or another, here's a rundown of what's there.

Pier 39. No matter the weather, tourists crowd this multilevel, Disneyesque shopper's dream (or nightmare). Video arcade halls, lined with deafening video games, anchor the pier on each end. You can also find T-shirt and sweatshirt shops and plenty of fried food. Join the mob if you want to see the golden views of Alcatraz visible from the end of the pier, or to watch the huge sea lions that loaf around on the west side of the pier (follow the barking). Catch the ferry to Alcatraz or for bay cruises here as well. If you're hungry, stop by the only authentic place to eat, the **Eagle Cafe** (☎ 415-433-3689), open daily from 7:30 a.m. to 3 p.m. on the second floor. This inexpensive breakfast and lunch joint opened in 1920. If you're arriving by car, park on adjacent streets or on the wharf between Taylor and Jones streets. But be advised: The parking garage charges $5.50 per hour! Do your best to avoid these price-gougers and don't bring a car here. Besides, taking the F-Market down the Embarcadero is much more fun (see Chapter 11).

Aquarium of the Bay. Pier 39 at Fisherman's Wharf (☎ **800-SEA-DIVE;** Internet: www.aquariumofthebay.com). This giant fish bowl is dedicated to the creatures that inhabit the San Francisco Bay ecosystem (so don't go looking for tropical species). After a brief introduction to the underwater world, facilitated by the Aquarium's loquacious band of naturalists, visitors decend to a moving walkway that slowly leads through two clear tunnels surrounded by 700,000 gallons of filtered bay water. Many thousands of fish swim by (some seemingly chasing their lunch), and if you've ever wanted to be practically face to face with a *Prionace glauca,* this is your big chance. The last exhibit contains touch pools, always a hit with children. Should a trip to the Monterey Bay Aquarium be in your future, you can easily skip this smaller cousin, but for something with an educational component on the wharf, this is a refreshing stop. The Aquarium is open every day; admission is $12.95 for adults, $6.50 for seniors and kids, $29.95 for a family ticket.

The San Francisco Maritime National Historical Park is a small two-story museum overlooking the bay and Alcatraz. It takes only 15 minutes or so to examine the model schooners, figureheads, and photographs illustrating the city's maritime heritage, although children may lose interest after the first five minutes. Still, it's very sweet and admission is free.

If you have small children along (or anyone interested in history), you won't want to miss touring the **USS *Pampanito*** on Pier 45 (☎ 415-775-1943). This submarine saw active duty during World War II and helped save 73 British and Australian prisoners of war. The $27 family pass (for two adults and up to four children) also gets you into the **Hyde Street Pier** (see following). Otherwise, submarine-only admission, which includes a 20-minute audio tour, is $7 for adults and $4 for seniors, students, and children 6 to 12. Kids under 6 are free. Open daily from 9 a.m. to 6 p.m. in winter, and until 8 p.m. in summer.

At the **Hyde Street Pier,** two blocks east of the Maritime Museum, you can roam around on a number of historic, refurbished ships. Of particular note is the 112-year-old ***Balclutha,*** a square-rigger with an interesting past. During the year, activities that take place on the *Balclutha* include concerts, sea chantey sing-alongs, and children's events. Call ☎ **415-556-3002** for a schedule. Touring the vessels takes at least an hour or so. The pier is open daily 9:30 a.m. to 5 p.m. Summer admission is $4 adults, $2 kids 12 to 17, free for kids 11 and under. Winter admission is half price.

Ghirardelli Square, which is the site of the original Ghirardelli chocolate factory, across the street from the Maritime Park, offers one of the more pleasant shopping mall experiences in the area. Granted landmark status in 1982, the series of brick buildings is home to a roster of special events, including an annual chocolate-tasting benefit in September. Street performers entertain regularly in the West Plaza. Open daily 10 a.m. to 6 p.m. in winter, to 9 p.m. in summer.

Go one block east of Ghirardelli Square and you find what was once a peach canning facility, **The Cannery.** It now features shops, jugglers, musicians, and food. Visitors especially enjoy **Lark in the Morning** (☎ 415-922-HARP), a music haven with an array of early music and modern instruments. Gift shoppers of a practical bent and people with newly formed blisters will also love **Sox, Sox, Sox** (☎ 415-563-7327), which, as the name implies, sells foot coverings, in both silly and conventional patterns. If the kids get wiggly (or if the weather is ugly and you need something to keep them occupied), head to the **Basic Brown Bear Factory** (☎ 415-931-6670), which is located on the second floor of the South Building. Customers stuff and help sew teddy bears to take home. Or you can paint plates, cups, and other useful pottery items at **Handmade Ceramic Studio** (☎ 415-440-2898), which is happy to ship your work home after it has been fired.

At the foot of Polk Street, on the western edge of the Embarcadero. ☎ *415-556-3002. To get there: Take the Powell-Hyde cable car line to the last stop; the F-Market streetcar; or the 19-Polk, 30-Stockton, 42-Downtown Loop, or 47-Van Ness bus. Parking: Pricey lots and garages; street parking is difficult. Open: Daily 10 a.m.–5 p.m. Admission: Free.*

Golden Gate Bridge

This quintessential San Francisco landmark spans 1.7 miles and soars hundreds of feet above the water. Bundle up against the windy conditions, then set out from the **Roundhouse** on the San Francisco side of the bridge lot (see Chapter 17 for information on walking to the bridge). It can get pretty noisy, but the views can't be beat. Remember that the only way to return from the other side is on foot, so know your limits before crossing the whole bridge and finding out you're too tired to make it back. Afterward, take some time to climb below the bridge to see the 5-acre garden there. The bridge is open to pedestrians from 6 a.m. to 6 p.m. daily. The 28-19th Avenue or the 29-Sunset bus deposits you across from the viewing area, right by a parking lot. If you're driving, take 19th Avenue or Lombard Street and pay attention to the sign that indicates when to exit for the parking lot. Otherwise, enjoy your drive across the bridge: There's a $3 toll upon your return to the city.

Golden Gate Park

Once nothing but a sand-covered tract, today's glorious Golden Gate Park features 1,017 acres of greenery and cultural attractions. San Franciscans can be spotted doing just about everything at the park, from playing soccer to sailing model yachts to throwing family reunions. On Sundays, when John F. Kennedy Drive is closed to street traffic, bicyclists ride with impunity and in-line skaters converge for dance parties. From April through the middle of October, also on Sundays, the **Golden Gate Park Band** plays from 1 to 3 p.m. in the **Music Concourse,** between the **de Young Museum** construction and the **California Academy of Sciences.** A massive **Children's Playground** and a beautifully restored carousel sit just past the grand park entrance on Stanyan Street (off Waller Street). This remodeled entrance, for some reason, reduced the rather large number of street people who used to hang out there (the Haight seems to attract youthful transients and burnouts) but didn't completely eliminate the panhandling. In any event, don't let that keep you away. Another entrance at Ninth Avenue on Lincoln Way brings you to the **Strybing Arboretum,** the **Japanese Tea Garden,** and the **Academy of Sciences.**

Joggers and parents pushing baby strollers make regular use of the path around man-made **Stow Lake.** It's the perfect place to take advantage of a sunny day by renting a paddleboat and having a picnic. The **boat house** (☎ **415-752-0347**) also rents bikes and in-line skates by the hour, half day, and full day. If you aren't driving, it's a bit of a walk to the boat house, which is west of the Japanese Tea Garden on Martin Luther King Drive. It's open daily from 9 a.m. to 4 p.m.

To get there: The N-Judah Muni Metro streetcar drops you off on Ninth Avenue and Judah Street; from there it is a three-block walk to the park. Numerous bus lines drive close to or into the park, including the 44-O'Shaughnessy, which you can catch on Ninth Avenue, the 21-Hayes, the 71-Haight-Noriega, and the 5-Fulton. You can also transfer to the 44-O'Shaughnessy from the 38-Geary bus on Sixth Avenue.

Golden Gate Park

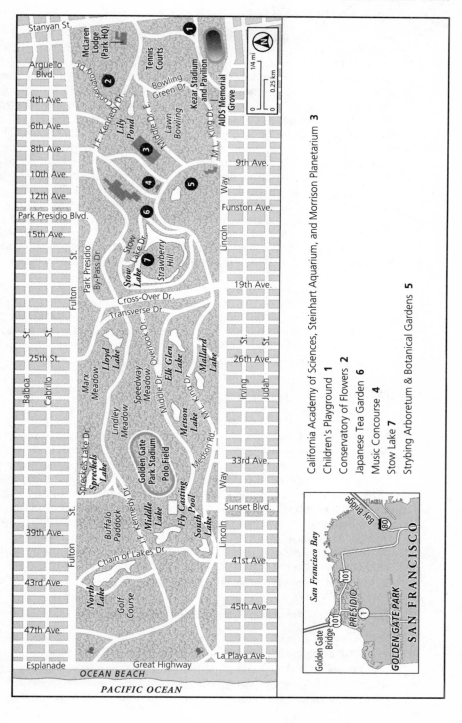

California Academy of Sciences, Steinhart Aquarium, and Morrison Planetarium **3**

Children's Playground **1**

Conservatory of Flowers **2**

Japanese Tea Garden **6**

Music Concourse **4**

Stow Lake **7**

Strybing Arboretum & Botanical Gardens **5**

California Academy of Sciences
Golden Gate Park

The Academy features traveling exhibits on everything from dinosaurs to spiders, which complement the informative permanent natural history exhibits that put to shame the dusty moose dioramas you may remember from grammar school field trips. You'll know you're in California when you visit the **Earth and Space exhibit,** which includes a popular earthquake simulation — it's as close as you want to get to the real thing. Check out the **Morrison Planetarium** and the **Steinhart Aquarium,** too. The highly entertaining and informative Planetarium sky shows, which run about 40 minutes long, are scheduled frequently during summer afternoons, holidays, and weekends, and at 2 p.m. on school days; call ☎ **415-750-7141** for show schedules. At the Steinhart Aquarium, kids love the hands-on tide pool, where they can (gently) handle starfish and sea urchins. They may also enjoy watching the Aquarium's colony of black-footed penguins being fed; mealtimes are at 11:30 a.m. and 4 p.m. You can find rest and relaxation in the cafeteria in the basement and enjoy strategically located gift shops for creative shopping. Plan on spending an hour or two here, longer if you attend a planetarium show.

On the Music Concourse. ☎ **415-750-7145,** *or 415-750-7127 for planetarium show schedules. Internet:* www.calacademy.org. *Open: Memorial Day–Labor Day, daily 9 a.m.–6 p.m.; Labor Day–Memorial Day, daily 10 a.m.–5 p.m. Admission: $8.50 adults, $5.50 seniors and students 12–17, $2 children 4–11; free for all the first Wed of the month. Discount for public transit users (bring your bus transfer). Planetarium show, $2.50 adults, $1.25 seniors and children under 18.*

The Conservatory of Flowers
Golden Gate Park

A fixture in guidebooks and tourist brochures, and nearly as recognizable as the Golden Gate Bridge, the postcard-perfect Victorian Conservatory of Flowers closed in 1995 after sustaining massive damage during a wild storm. Prefabricated in Ireland in 1875 and erected in the park around 1878, the cost to repair the glass and wood greenhouse topped $25 million, all of which was privately donated. At press time construction was yet to be finished, but the Conservatory is scheduled to reopen in Spring of 2003. Its galleries will contain rare orchids, ferns, tropical plants, a 100-year-old philodendron rescued from the wreckage, and other exhibits. Find the Conservatory just off John F. Kennedy Drive, near the Stanyan Street entrance. Expect a small admission fee.

The Strybing Arboretum and Botanical Gardens
Golden Gate Park

This splendid oasis houses over 6,000 species of well-tended plants, flowering trees, and theme gardens. It is exceptionally lovely in late winter when the rhododendrons blossom and wild iris poke up in corners, and there is no more peaceful a place when it's rainy and gray outside. You can catch a free docent tour offered daily at 1:30 p.m.; I recommend it for those, like myself, who are arboreally and botanically challenged when trying to identify any but the most basic of flowers and trees. Plan to spend at least half an hour here just wandering around.

Ninth Avenue at Lincoln Way, left of the tour bus parking lot by the Music Concourse. ☎ *415-661-1316, ext. 314 for docent tour information. Internet:* www.strybing.org. *Open: Mon–Fri 8:00 a.m.–4:30 p.m., Sat–Sun 10 a.m.–5 p.m. Admission: Free.*

Japanese Tea Garden
Golden Gate Park

Enjoying this tranquil spot, with colorful pagodas, koi ponds, bridges, and a giant bronze Buddha, you feel like you're in the Orient. Young children find this part of the park particularly memorable — they can climb over a steeply arched wooden bridge here, just as I did when I was much younger and lots more limber than I am today. The Tea Garden's beauty is slightly marred by its gift shop, full of miniature license plates and other junk. Bus tours overrun this major destination during the day, so try to get here before 10 a.m. or after 4 p.m. during the summer to avoid the onslaught. You can partake of Japanese tea and snacks in the teahouse for $2.95 per person. I think the garden is worth the small admission fee, but you won't be missing anything if you pass on the tea and crackers.

The garden entrance is to the left of the de Young Museum. ☎ *415-752-4227. Open: Oct–Feb, 8:30 a.m.–dusk; Mar–Sept, 8:30 a.m.–6:30 p.m. Admission: $3.50 adults, $1.25 seniors and children 6–12.*

Lombard Street
Russian Hill (Near North Beach)

Lombard Street, or to be exact, the part of Lombard with the moniker "crookedest street in the world," begins at Hyde Street below **Russian Hill.** This whimsical, flower-lined block attracts thousands of visitors each year. If you intend to drive this red-brick street (it's one-way, downhill, so take the curves slowly), go early in the morning before everyone else revs up their Chevys. Better yet, walk down the stairs to fully admire the flowers, the houses with their long-suffering tenants, and the stellar view. This portion of Lombard is between Hyde and Leavenworth streets. Lombard Street is most convenient to the Powell-Hyde cable car line.

San Francisco Museum of Modern Art (MoMA)
SoMa

The handsome Museum of Modern Art houses an impressive collection of 20th-century paintings, sculptures, and photographs. The beautiful interior exudes a warmth that makes viewing the exhibits even more enjoyable. Among the Diebenkorns and Rauschenbergs, you may be surprised to see Jeff Koons's gold and white sculpture of Michael Jackson and his chimp pal Bubbles (an acquisition I think better suited to a Las Vegas hotel lobby, but perhaps the curators know something I don't). The exhibits, the excellent museum cafe, and the artfully stocked museum store keep you there for a good half-day.

151 Third St. (two blocks south of Market near Howard Street). ☎ **415-357-4000.** *Internet:* www.sfmoma.org. *To get there: Take any Muni streetcar to the Montgomery Street Station or the 15-Third, 30-Stockton, or 45-Union/Stockton bus. Open: Thurs 11 a.m.–9 p.m., Fri–Tues, 11 a.m.–6 p.m. Closed Wed and major holidays. Opens at 10 a.m. during the summer. Admission: $10 adults, $7 seniors, and $6 students with ID; half-price Thurs 6–9 p.m.; free for kids under 12. Free to all first Tues of the month.*

Yerba Buena Gardens and Center for the Arts
SoMa

This 22-acre complex is a micro-destination in a setting that once attracted nothing but parking lots and derelicts. It includes a collection of galleries showing a rotating exhibition of contemporary visual and performance art by local artists, lovely gardens, a stage for dance troupes including ODC/San Francisco and Smuin Ballets/SF, and a film/video theater. Interactive amusements include an ice-skating rink, a bowling alley, a children's garden and carousel, and an arts/technology studio for older kids. An entertainment behemoth in a separate building across the street — **Sony's Metreon** — houses restaurants, retail shops, an IMAX theater, and multiplex movie screens. If you take in all that Yerba Buena Center has to offer, you can easily spend the entire day here. Parking is expensive; use public transportation if possible.

East of the carousel you can find the enclosed, but light-filled, **Yerba Buena Ice-Skating Rink** and the tidy 12-lane **Bowling Center** (☎ **415-777-3727**). Public skating session times vary from day to day, so you should phone before trekking over with your figure skates. Admission is adults $6, seniors and children 12 and under $4.50. Skate rental $2. The Bowling Center is open Sunday through Thursday 9 a.m. to 10 p.m., until midnight Friday and Saturday. Admission for adults is $3.50 per game or $18 per hour; seniors and children 12 and under $2 per game or $12 per hour.

Zeum (☎ **415-777-2800**) is a wonderful art/technology center with hands-on labs that give visitors the opportunity to create animated video shorts with clay figures; learn about graphics, sound, and video production in the second floor studio; and interact with the changing gallery exhibits. The center is rare in that it's probably the only city attraction specifically designed for older kids and teens that doesn't rely on video games. Nevertheless, any bored adolescent would find it difficult not to succumb to a Zeum offering. Open: Saturday and Sunday 11 a.m. to 5 p.m. during the school year; Wednesday to Friday 12 to 6 p.m. and Saturday to Sunday 11 a.m. to 5 p.m. in the summer. Admission is adults $7, seniors and students $6, kids 5 to 18 $5.

Yerba Buena Gardens

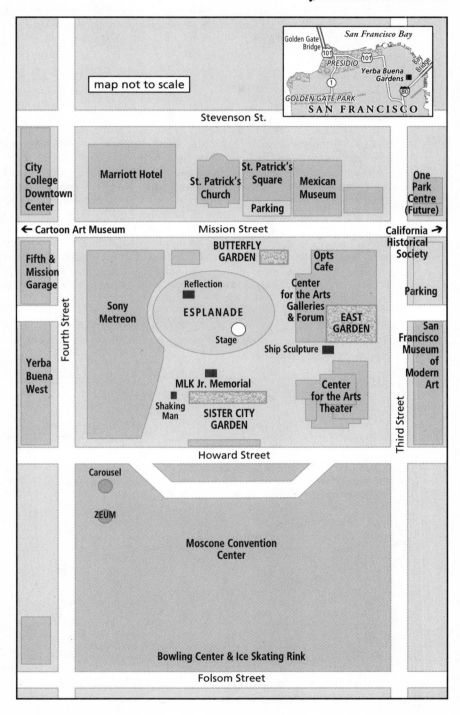

map not to scale

San Francisco Bay
Golden Gate Bridge
101
PRESIDIO
101
Yerba Buena Gardens
1
80
GOLDEN GATE PARK
SAN FRANCISCO
Bay Bridge

Stevenson St.

City College Downtown Center

Marriott Hotel

St. Patrick's Church

St. Patrick's Square

Parking

Mexican Museum

One Park Centre (Future)

← Cartoon Art Museum   Mission Street   California →

Fifth & Mission Garage

Sony Metreon

Fourth Street

BUTTERFLY GARDEN

Reflection

ESPLANADE

Stage

Opts Cafe

Center for the Arts Galleries & Forum

Ship Sculpture

EAST GARDEN

Historical Society

Parking

San Francisco Museum of Modern Art

Yerba Buena West

MLK Jr. Memorial

Shaking Man

SISTER CITY GARDEN

Center for the Arts Theater

Third Street

Howard Street

Carousel

ZEUM

Moscone Convention Center

Bowling Center & Ice Skating Rink

Folsom Street

701 Mission St., between Third and Fourth streets. ☎ **415-978-2700** *or 415-978-ARTS (box office). Internet:* www.YerbaBuenaArts.org. *To get there: Take a streetcar to the Powell or Montgomery Street stations, or take the 14-Mission or 15-Third bus, among others.*

Sony Metreon
SoMa

Noisy and lit like a Vegas casino, the Metreon is best described as awesome. The four stories of glass and brushed metal anchoring one block of Yerba Buena Center are quite the sight. Some are calling it the future of entertainment centers, and, at the moment at least, there isn't anything like it on the planet. Of course, eating and spending are the big themes here — the Metreon has many places to fill your tummy and empty your wallet. Sony has a big presence, naturally — a great showcase in which to ogle what's new in the way of digital cameras and other gadgets. On the third floor are 15 — count 'em 15 — movie screens and the city's very first IMAX theater. And you can also find what Sony refers to as "family-friendly attractions," one of which is cleverly based on the popular children's book *Where the Wild Things Are*. Another is an interactive game arena, likely to swallow up a generation of video-savvy teens and young adults.

Mission at Fourth Street. ☎ **1-800-METREON.** *Internet:* www.metreon.com. *Open: Daily 10 a.m.–10 p.m. Admission: There is no entrance fee; individual attraction prices range from $6–$10.*

Chapter 17

More Cool Things to See and Do

In This Chapter

▶ Keeping the kids content

▶ Indulging fans of history, art, and architecture

▶ Taking to the great outdoors

▶ Finding a spiritual respite

*J*ust because you've visited the top sights doesn't mean you've seen it all. This chapter offers ideas on how to entertain children and teens, how to get a taste of San Francisco history and more than a taste of art, where to take your hiking shoes, where to grab a bike, and much more.

Especially for Kids

The best Web site for finding out what's available for children is www.gocitykids.com. It's kept up to date and includes a great calendar of events.

The **San Francisco Zoo,** Sloat Boulevard and 45th Avenue (☎ **415-753-7080;** Internet: www.sfzoo.org), has just finished a renovation of the main entrance and some of the habitats. You'll find an innovative and noteworthy primate center, a carousel, an expanded children's zoo, and — this is the clincher — a sizable children's playground near the Sloat Boulevard entrance. Stroll the more than 65 acres to see the animals, then park your tired body on a bench within yelling distance and let the under-10 members of the family climb to their heart's content. The L-Taraval Muni streetcar deposits riders in front of the zoo — this is the easiest way to get there from downtown. Open daily from 10 a.m.

to 5 p.m., admission is $10 adults, $7 seniors and kids 12 to 15, $4 kids 3 to 11, and free for babes 2 and under. Take note of the Carousel hot dog parlor across Sloat Boulevard, marked by a fiberglass, chef-hatted dachshund. Formerly one of many Doggie Diners in town, this puppy was the center of heated controversy between those who wanted to grant it landmark status and those who want it moved so the site could be turned into a parking lot. Judging from its new cherry paint job, the doggy won.

Another kid-pleaser, the **Musée Mécanique,** contains a fantastic collection of lovingly restored and maintained mechanical marvels that were the forerunners to pinball machines. Among the treasures, you can try your hand at World Series Baseball, have your fortune told, and giggle wildly with Laughing Sal, all for a quarter a pop. The museum is housed below the Cliff House, 1090 Point Lobos Rd., at the Great Highway, but at press time, the Park Service announced that the Cliff House was to partially close for restoration. The Musée Mécanique may have to relocate, so you'll need to phone them at ☎ **415-386-1170,** or check the Web site (www.museemecanique.com) to find out where. Open daily (somewhere). Admission is free. Bring along a roll of quarters.

China Beach has picnic facilities and awe-inspiring views of the Golden Gate Bridge. It's also one of the few safe swimming beaches in town, but the water is chilly so designing sand castles and picnicking are better activities. The 29-Sunset bus stops at 25th Avenue and El Camino del Mar. From there it's a walk of about six blocks north to the beach.

There's no shortage of parks and playgrounds in nearly every neighborhood, but they do range in quality. In the Nob Hill/Russian Hill area, **Lafayette Park** is appealing for its small, but nicely-equipped and fenced-in playground, walking paths, and views. It's on Clay Street between Washington, Laguna, Gough, and Sacramento streets. Take the 1-California or 12-Folsom-Pacific buses to get there. You have to make a little effort to reach **Mountain Lake Park,** which is close to the Richmond District side of the Presidio on Lake Street (between 8th and 12th avenues), but this is one of the best parks in town for the entire family. The playground is two-tiered; the street-level half is for the under-6 set, while the bottom half is fun even for young-at-heart teens. Hiking trails and a small beach make this spot even more attractive. To get there, take Muni buses 1AX, 1BX, or 28-19th Avenue.

Young Performers Theatre at Fort Mason presents children's plays most weekend afternoons, starring members of the YPT acting classes. The performances are most suitable for kids 10 and under. You can find a schedule of events on the Web (www.ypt.org). Tickets are $5 for kids and $8 for adults. Make reservations in advance by phoning YPT at ☎ **415-346-5550** or e-mail them at reservations@2ypt.com. The theater is located in Room 300, Building C at Fort Mason. To get there, take the 22-Fillmore, 30-Stockton, or 42-Downtown buses.

The Zoo & Lake Merced Area

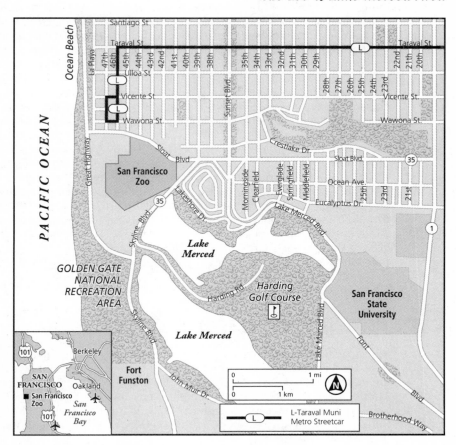

Especially for Teens

The **Cartoon Art Museum,** 655 Mission St., between Second and Third streets in SoMa (☎ **415-495-7000;** Internet: www.cartoonart.org), presents exhibits on all kinds of cartoon art ("The Art of Spiderman" was a recent hit). The museum is open Tuesday through Friday from 11 a.m. to 5 p.m., Saturday from 10 a.m. to 5 p.m., and Sunday from 1 to 5 p.m. Admission is $5 for adults, $3 for seniors, $2 for children 6 to 12. The first Wednesday of each month is free.

San Francisco Centre, on the corner of Market and Fifth streets, is a nine-story mall containing many familiar names beloved by teenaged girls, including a huge **Nordstrom** department store. Your young shopper may be just as happy exploring the stores around Union Square (see Chapter 6), and at least there you'll get a little fresh air on your way in and out of the revolving doors.

Teenagers adore **Metreon** (see Chapter 16) because the technology stores contain all the latest widgets, some of which they can audition. When they tire of gawking at stuff, the video games in the Airtight Garage can occupy as many minutes as you'll allow or that they can pay for. And when you've had enough, you can coax them away from the flashing screens with promises of food at one of the many cafes.

Zeum (see Chapter 16) was designed for 8– to 18-year-olds and is staffed by savvy teens. Even recalcitrant 15-year-olds can find something engaging to do here, whether or not they admit it.

I saved the best for last. Take your teen to Haight Street for some shopping (and shock) therapy. The N-Judah streetcar deposits you a few blocks south of Haight, and it beats parking. One of the best music stores in town, **Amoeba Records,** is here, and both the used and new clothing stores — in particular stop by Villains, 1672 Haight St. (☎ **415-626-5939**) — stock the coolest stuff around. I don't mean to make too much of the street scene, but youthful runaways and poseurs do congregate in this neighborhood and it can feel equally attractive, poignant, and scary to adolescents. At the very least, you'll have something interesting to talk about on the ride back to your hotel.

Especially for History Buffs

To learn about San Francisco's rise during the quest for gold, take the free "Gold Rush City" walking tour offered by City Guides Sundays at 2 p.m. and Wednesdays at noon. Meet by the flower stand at Clay and Montgomery streets. The walk encompasses **Jackson Square** (Jackson and Montgomery streets), a National Historic Register Landmark admired for its many restored Gold Rush–era brick warehouses. Call ☎ **415-557-4266** for details.

The Cable Car Museum explains everything you'd want to know about our 130-year-old road warriors, through photographs, models, actual cable cars, and a close-up look at the mechanisms that make them operate. The museum is inside the cable car barn, 1201 Mason St., at Washington (☎ **415-474-1887;** Internet: www.cablecarmuseum.com). Free admission. Open daily from 10 a.m. to 5 p.m. To get there, take the Powell-Mason or Powell-Hyde cable car lines.

Mission Dolores, at Dolores and 16th streets, is a fine example of Mission architecture and the oldest building in the city. This is one of the 21 missions founded under the auspices of Franciscan Missionary Junipero Serra and built by Native Americans. Services were first held on the site a few days before the Declaration of Independence was signed. It's open daily from 9 a.m. to 4 p.m. A self-guided audio tour takes 40 minutes. Admission is by donation; the audio tour costs $1. The J-Church Muni streetcar stops one block east.

The **Wells Fargo History Museum,** 420 Montgomery St., at California Street (☎ 415-396-2619), displays mining equipment, an antique stage-coach, and gold nuggets in its collection. Be sure to try out the tele-graph machine on the first floor, especially if you have kids in tow. The museum is open weekdays from 9 a.m. to 5 p.m. Admission is free.

Especially for Art Lovers

The inspiring **California Palace of the Legion of Honor,** in Lincoln Park between Clement Street and 34th Avenue in the outer Richmond District (☎ 415-750-3600), exhibits an impressive collection of paint-ings, drawings, decorative arts, and one of the world's finest collec-tions of Rodin sculptures, including an original cast of **The Thinker.** The grounds around the Palace are a draw as well. You can take the 38-Geary bus to 33rd Avenue, then transfer to the 18-46th Avenue bus for a ride to the museum entrance. Open Tuesday through Sunday from 9:30 a.m. to 5:00 p.m. Admission is $8 adults, $6 seniors over 65, $5 chil-dren 12 to 17, and free for children under 12.

Union Square from Grant Avenue to Mason Street and Geary to Post Street is home to a number of fine-arts dealers. Of note are the **Stephen Wirtz Gallery** (☎ 415-433-6879) and **Toomey Tourell** (☎ 415-989-6444), both located in the canvas-rich building at 49 Geary St., at Grant, and the **John Berggruen Gallery** at 228 Grant St., between Sutter and Post (☎ 415-781-4629). The galleries are closed on Mondays.

Combine a walk along the Marina with a tour of the galleries housed at **Fort Mason Center** (☎ 415-441-3400; Internet: www.fortmason.org). They include the **African American Historical & Cultural Society,** the **Craft and Folk Art Museum,** the **Museo ItaloAmericano,** and **SFMoMA's Artists Gallery,** which displays original art for sale and for rent. The galleries are fairly small but often have quirky exhibits. Wandering around Fort Mason is a good way to round out your excursion. A small admission fee is charged by the museums, with the exception of the Artists Gallery, which is free. Days and hours of operation vary, but they're all open Wednesday through Saturday from noon to 5 p.m. and a couple are open on Sunday. To get there, take the 30-Stockton, 47-Van Ness, or 28-19th Avenue buses, which run nearby.

Architectural Highlights

When you visit the **Alamo Square Historic District,** you may feel a touch of déjà vu. That's because this is where the famous picture of the Victorian row houses was photographed. The "Painted Ladies," which front the San Francisco skyline, are still sought by photographers, probably on a daily basis. You'll find this historic block between Steiner, Scott, Hayes, and Grove streets, west of the Civic Center. The 21-Hayes bus takes you right there from Market and Hayes Streets.

Golden Gate National Recreation Area

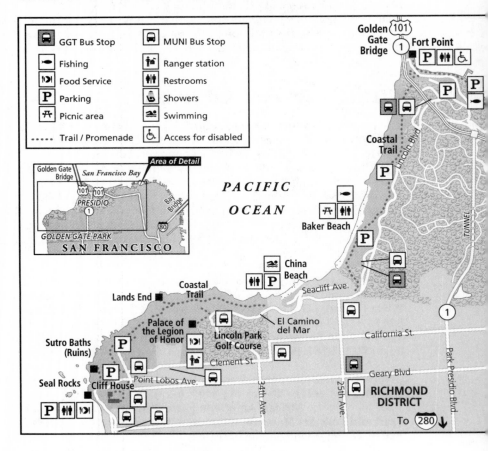

The **Haas-Lilienthal House** (☎ **415-441-3004**), an 1886 Queen Anne
Victorian, is open to the public for one-hour tours on Wednesdays from
noon to 3 p.m. and Sundays from 11 a.m. to 4 p.m. Located at 2007
Franklin, at Jackson Street, this is the only local example of a home
from this period that's open to the public. To get there by bus, take the
12-Folsom, the 27-Bryant, the 42-Downtown Loop, the 47-Van Ness, the
49-Van Ness/Mission, or the 83-Pacific. Admission is $5 for adults, $3 for
seniors 65 and older and for children under 12.

You may also want to check out the **New Main Library,** 100 Larkin St.,
between Grove and Fulton streets. Natural light streams in from a five-
story atrium skylight and windows that encircle the stacks. If you have
kids along, definitely browse the children's section. The library even
has — gasp! — a gift shop. Take any Muni streetcar to the Civic Center
station and walk a block west on Grove Street.

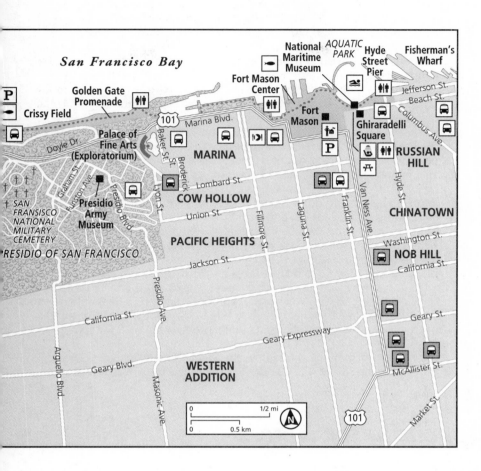

While you're in the Civic Center neighborhood, drop by the refurbished **City Hall** on Van Ness Avenue, between McAllister and Grove streets. The building originally debuted in 1915, but it's never looked better. Not only did the building get a seismic retrofitting (*de riguer* in this earthquake-prone town) and a good cleaning, but also the dome and ornamental balcony railings were regilded, creating an impressive landmark and adding golden highlights to the view.

For more architectural wonders, see Chapter 18 to read about walking tours.

Especially for Bicyclists

If your reflexes are good and you have a reliable helmet, try touring San Francisco from the seat of a bicycle. You can rent bikes and helmets from quite a few locations around town. For a ride in beautiful Golden Gate Park, stop by one of the nearby bike stores such as **Avenue Cyclery,** 756 Stanyan St. (☎ **415-387-3155**). For real convenience, **Holiday Adventures,** 1937 Lombard St. (☎ **415-567-1192**), will pick you up at your hotel and drive you to its store in the Marina, which is convenient for rides over the Golden Gate Bridge or around the Presidio. Both shops charge $5 per hour; per day rates are $25 and $19 respectively for bikes and helmets. **Bike and Roll,** 734 Lombard St., near Columbus Street (☎ **415-771-8735**), offers a special weekend rental rate of $15.99 and the shop is convenient to bayside bike routes (take the Powell-Mason cable car to get there). Finally, the **Bike Hut** at South Beach (on the Embarcadero at Pier 40) is the place to find high-quality bikes to pedal along the waterfront. It's open Friday through Sunday from 10 a.m. to 5 p.m. Rentals are $5 per hour or $20 per day.

Pedaling across the Golden Gate Bridge into Sausalito, where you can have something to eat, do a little sightseeing in this arty, touristy town, then return by ferry, can be good fun. The **Blue & Gold Fleet** (☎ **415-773-1188**) and **Golden Gate Ferry** (☎ **415-923-2000**), depart the Sausalito ferry dock at least half a dozen times a day. Call for a schedule. One-way Blue & Gold Fleet fares are $6.75 adult and $3.25 children 5 to 11; one-way Golden Gate Ferry fares are $5.30 adults, $4 children 3 to 12 (kids ride free on weekends), and $2.65 seniors. The 9-mile ride to Sausalito can be challenging, partly due to the windy conditions and partly due to the other bicyclists you're competing with for space.

For more information on biking in the area, contact the San Francisco Bicycle Coalition (☎ **415-431-BIKE**), or browse their Web site at www.sfbike.org.

Especially for Hikers

Angel Island, a federal and state wildlife refuge that is the largest of San Francisco Bay's three islets, is located 8 miles from San Francisco and is accessible only by ferry (a 20-minute journey) or private boat. Plan to spend the entire day on the island if you decide to go during the week — the ferry departs San Francisco sometime after 10 a.m., and the only return trip departs sometime after 3 p.m. (The schedule changes seasonally.) On the weekends, you have the choice of four return trips. You can bring a picnic with you or get something at the small store and cafe that operate near the dock. Check out the beautiful 12 miles of hiking trails, climb up Mt. Livermore for yet another spectacular view of the Golden Gate Bridge, or take the one-hour tram tour past the historic sites, including the former immigration station. Mountain bike rentals are also available on Angel Island, but for an exorbitant $10 an hour. You'll save money renting a bike in San Francisco and bringing it on the ferry. Call **Blue & Gold Ferry** (☎ **415-773-1188**) for a current ferry schedule. Round-trip fares are $10.50 adult, $5.50 children 6 to 12. For recorded information about the island, call ☎ **415-435-1915**. Ferries leave from Pier 41 in Fisherman's Wharf.

Fort Point (☎ 415-556-1373), which dates from 1857, lies underneath the Golden Gate Bridge at the tip of the peninsula. Along with Civil War–era cannons, you can see surfers who appear to be risking their lives much more than the soldiers once stationed here did. From the Hyde Street Pier, take the easy 3½-mile stroll along the paved Golden Gate Promenade, which hugs the coast as it passes through the Marina Green and Crissy Fields. Or you can get to Fort Point by taking the 28-19th Avenue or the 29-Sunset bus to the Golden Gate Bridge and climbing down from the viewing area to a short trail leading to the premises. You can take a self-guided audio tour of the fort if you like, and afterward backtrack to the Hyde Street cable car turnaround, where you can hop on a cable car to Union Square. Fort Point is open Wednesday through Sunday from 10 a.m. to 5 p.m.

If you're a hiking novice or walking with kids, the **Coastal Trail** to the Cliff House probably isn't the hike for you. It's rigorous and can be dangerous. The trailhead, a bit east of Fort Point, is well marked. Heading south, the trail parallels the Pacific Ocean through the Presidio.

You can see small beaches below the trail on this hike, but if you're tempted to feel sand beneath your toes, please follow the marked paths to get there. Don't climb over any rocky cliffs; the land here isn't stable enough to guarantee your safe return.

When you reach Baker Beach, about 1½ miles from Fort Point, be prepared for the nude sun-worshippers, should there be any sun. As you continue on the trail, you'll pass the Lobos Creek Water Treatment Plant. From there it's a short way to El Camino Del Mar, a street leading through Sea Cliff, a fancy residential neighborhood. At the end of El Camino Del Mar you'll pick up the trail near the Lincoln Golf Course. If you continue along this trail, with the land and the views rewarding your every step, eventually you'll arrive at the Cliff House, which has been serving refreshments to visitors since 1863, but is undergoing renovation at the moment. So keep walking down the Great Highway until you reach the **Beach Chalet** restaurant and brewery (☎ 415-386-8439). After lunch you can return toward the Cliff House and catch the 38-Geary bus at La Playa and Balboa Street, or keep walking to Judah Street and take an N-Judah streetcar downtown.

Named in honor of Sierra Club founder and conservationist John Muir, 553-acre **Muir Woods** is what's left locally of the redwood forests that once dominated the coast of Northern California. Although not as sizable as Redwood National Forest further north, these old-growth redwoods are beautiful, and a range of trails here suits hikers of all levels. From the Golden Gate Bridge, take the Stinson Beach/Highway 1 exit west and follow the signs. Parking is limited, so try setting out early in the day on weekends or go during the week. Muir Woods Park is open from 8 a.m. until sunset. For additional information call ☎ 415-388-2595.

Especially for Sports Fans

The San Francisco Giants Major League Baseball team opened the fabulous, 40,000-seat **Pacific Bell Park** stadium on the bay on opening day in April 2000. The ballpark is sweet — sightlines are clear, you don't freeze to death like you did at Candlestick, the food is pretty good, and home runs splosh into the bay. Season-ticket holders have already bought up all the best seats, but buying bleacher tickets to any but the most sought after games (all Giants versus Dodgers contests, for example) shouldn't be impossible, because they're sold only on game days. However, to purchase regular tickets or tickets from season-ticket holders who are unable to make it to a particular game, log on to the Web site (www.sfgiants.com) before you arrive or call ☎ **888-464-2468** to charge tickets by phone. Transportation to the ballpark is simple — take Muni to the Embarcadero Station and transfer to the King Street extension.

The San Francisco 49ers play at **3Com Park.** Home games have been sold out for the last 12 years or so, but if you want to try your luck, the ticket office number is ☎ **415-656-4900.** Scalpers sell tickets outside the park, but these are often counterfeit. The best method of transport to the park is by Muni bus. The 9X-San Bruno Express bus leaves from Sutter Street near Union Square; the 28X-19th Avenue bus runs along 19th Avenue; and the 47X-Van Ness cruises Van Ness Avenue.

Some Spiritual Pursuits

Arrive a good half-hour early to claim a seat at the 9 a.m. Sunday services (an hour early for the 11 a.m. services) at **Glide Memorial United Methodist Church,** 330 Ellis St. (☎ 415-771-6300). The Reverend Cecil Williams, a genuinely great man, lets the multi-ethnic gospel choir do most of the sermonizing, and they're wildly effective. A cross-section of friendly San Franciscans packs the pews, clapping, singing, and celebrating. It's church, it's theater, and it's amazing.

Grace Cathedral, the magnificent Episcopal Church at the top of Nob Hill, 1100 California St., between Taylor and Jones streets (☎ 415-749-6300), has an outdoor stone terrazzo labyrinth that may promote a meditative moment. It's open to visitors daily, anytime. You can rent a labyrinth audio tour, complete with walking music provided by the Grace Choir, at the gift shop.

Old First Presbyterian Church, 1751 Sacramento St., at Van Ness Avenue (☎ 415-474-1608), sponsors a concert series leaning heavily toward the classical that's low-cost and high-quality. You can call for a list of upcoming events or check the Internet (www.oldfirstcon certs.org). Getting from downtown to the church is a snap on the California Street cable car line.

Completed in 1970, **St. Mary's Cathedral**, 1111 Gough St., between Ellis and Geary (☎415-567-2020), is worth a look for its modern architecture and soaring interior space. Once inside, be sure to lift your eyes toward heaven to admire the cross-shaped skylight.

Garden and Park Respites

San Franciscans cherish the city's open spaces. If you know where to look, you will find little parks and secret gardens in some unlikely places. At the end of Market Street in the Embarcadero, two simple gardens grace the seventh floor of One Market Plaza. Elevators to the gardens are situated in the Spear and Steuart Street lobbies. Upon exiting, walk toward the bay; you'll find two patios surrounded by well-tended expanses of lawn and flowers overlooking a classic bay view.

At **Rincon Center** (corner of Mission and Steuart streets) you'll find a courtyard garden replete with benches sitting among a generous array of ornamental hedges, potted azaleas, and seasonal plantings. You can get a snack inside and enjoy it in the garden. A few blocks away, at 100 First St., you'll find the award-winning second-floor garden in the Delta Tower, which is a lush respite from the madness of the Transbay Terminal and Mission Street. The black granite and green glass fountain sculpture provide a soothing counterpoint to the street traffic. **Yerba Buena Gardens** (see Chapter 16) features willow trees, a sweep of bright green lawn, and a variety of blossoms. Behind the garden's 22-foot waterfall is a memorial to Martin Luther King, Jr., featuring a series of glass panels etched with quotations from Dr. King's speeches and writings.

Levi's Plaza, located between the Embarcadero and Sansome Street, consists of the company's multiple buildings and two plazas separated by Battery Street. The centerpiece of the hard plaza is a fountain you can walk through on paving stones — a big favorite with kids. The soft plaza across the street is really a park with fir trees and grass.

Cross the plaza to Sansome Street and look for the bottom of the Filbert Steps, a steep staircase that rises to Montgomery and Filbert streets. Around the midpoint of the stairway you'll find a sight so profoundly San Francisco that you'll immediately understand what all the fuss is about. This is the **Grace Marchand Garden;** its roses and ferns add a wild elegance to the hillside. The residents don't like the tourists who clog the steps, especially on weekends, but that's the price they have to pay for living next to a minor landmark. In any case, this is a garden to admire from outside the wooden fence only.

Chapter 18

And on Your Left, Golden Gate Park: Seeing San Francisco by Guided Tour

. . . .

In This Chapter

▶ Deciding whether guided tours are right for you

▶ Taking in the sights by bus, on foot, or by boat

▶ Touring on your own

▶ Seeing the city on a special-interest tour

. . . .

1 used to feel self-conscious about taking a guided tour in a new city. Many travelers, myself included, shy away from the idea of being herded on and off large buses like cattle. But lately I've embraced my inner tourist and learned to love them. Actually, guided tours are a sensible way to get your bearings in an unfamiliar place. You may not have much time to explore on your own and just want to catch the major sights in one day. Or perhaps you have difficulty getting around, or you don't want to drive. Maybe you need an overview to find out what interests you in a specific city, or you're traveling alone and want some company.

Fortunately, you can find almost as many varieties of guided tours as there are varieties of people in San Francisco. Not all of them have you peering out a dirty bus window at some unfathomable landmark while straining to hear the muffled voice of your guide over the microphone, or worse, an out-of-date tape. In San Francisco, guided tours happen on foot and ferry boats as well as on buses. And they cover special interests, as well as the major sights. If you think a tour listed in this chapter is for you, call the companies or individual guides for their brochures, or ask your hotel to send you information. Most tours require advance reservations.

Hotels generally have preferred companies that they recommend for bus tours. The hotel often gets a small kickback for every reservation, so they may not have your best interests in mind. If you favor one tour company over another, book it yourself or request that company specifically when you speak to the concierge. Don't leave the decision up to the hotel.

The Bus Stops Here: Touring on Wheels

If you want to be sure you at least catch a glimpse of San Francisco's major attractions, then orientation tours may be just the ticket. Some tour operators spiff up the menu with motorized cable cars or double-decker buses, whereas other companies use lower profile minibuses that appeal to visitors who don't want to stand out in a crowd.

Be advised that not all trips are narrated by the bus driver; some just have recorded commentary. I do not recommend these audio tours. The sound quality is miserable and some of the information is outdated, such as the part about the prices of the houses you pass on the tour. As a matter of fact, I think prices went up another 10% since you've been reading this book. Be sure to ask whether the commentary is recorded or live before you book your tour.

Gray Line Tours (☎ 415-558-9400; Internet: www.graylinesan francisco.com), the big kahuna of the tour industry, schedules a number of orientation tours around the city and beyond in red double-decker buses, motorized cable cars, and smaller vans. The deluxe 4-hour city tour ($37 for adults, $15.50 for children 5 to 11) hits the highlights — Twin Peaks, Mission Dolores, the Cliff House, Golden Gate Park, the Golden Gate Bridge — and there's an option to tack on a trip to Alcatraz.

Tower Tours (☎ 415-434-8687; Internet: www.towertours.city search.com) is popular with many San Franciscans with visiting relatives because the company uses sleek, low-profile minibuses that carry only about two dozen people. Tower's 3-hour city tour stops at the same sites as Gray Line's buses. The cost is $34 for adults and $17 for children 5 to 11.

Saving Money on Muni and DIY

Stopping at every other corner and having a driver that doesn't give much, if any, commentary may not seem like the ideal let's-get-to-know-the-city excursion. But a do-it-yourself tour by Muni bus has its advantages. The outing will only cost you $1 or $2 and no more than three transit hours. They let you come and go at your leisure — if you decide 25 minutes at Golden Gate Park isn't enough, who cares if the bus leaves? You can always catch the next one. These "orientation" tours are not for the impatient traveler or for anyone who requires a great deal of comfort, however — city buses are, after all, creaky and well-worn.

Ask for a free transfer when you board the bus. With the transfer, you can disembark whenever you like and catch another bus or a Muni streetcar at no additional charge (within 90 minutes). Transfers are not valid on cable cars, however.

Muni tour #1: Painted Ladies and Pacific Heights

Here's a tour that introduces you to a section of the city that encompasses the famous Victorians on Alamo Square, Japantown, Fillmore Street shopping in Pacific Heights, the Marina, and Chinatown. Board the 21-Hayes bus at Market and Fourth streets (and remember to ask for a transfer). Exit on Steiner Street, at one side of Alamo Square. When you've gotten your fill of the Painted Ladies, walk one block east to Fillmore Street and look for the 22-Fillmore. That bus runs toward the bay through Japantown and continues up toward Pacific Heights. All kinds of shops line Fillmore Street, and they become swankier as you pass California Street. The bus eventually crosses Union Street and ambles through the Marina District. Exit as close to Chestnut Street as possible, where you can catch the 30-Stockton. See the tour below for a description of your travels on this bus back to Union Square. If you don't stop for breaks (which sort of defeats the purpose), expect to spend two hours on this route.

Muni tour #2: Traveling on the west side

Another do-it-yourself tour takes you around the western perimeter of the city. From any downtown Muni station (Powell Street is closest to Union Square), catch the L-Taraval or N-Judah streetcar, both of which travel through some well-kept residential neighborhoods. Get off at Sunset Boulevard in the outer Sunset District. On Sunset Boulevard, at Taraval Street or Judah Street, depending on which streetcar you rode, pick up a 29-Sunset bus going to the Presidio (*not* to California and 25th Avenue, which enters the former military base). The spectacular views on this part of the ride include the Pacific Ocean and the Golden Gate Bridge. In fact, the bus stops right by a viewing area where you can get off the bus and walk across the bridge and back if that's on your to-do list. The ride also includes a look at a pet cemetery inside the Presidio.

The 29-Sunset terminates at Letterman Hospital in the Presidio, but you can then catch the 43-Masonic bus from the same bus shelter, which takes you down Lombard Street and over to Chestnut Street in the Marina district. From there, the 30-Stockton meanders along Chestnut over to Van Ness Avenue, and then travels down Van Ness to Northpoint Street, close to Aquatic Park and Ghirardelli Square. The route then goes through North Beach, Chinatown, and back to Union Square. Alternatively, you can walk to Pier 39 and catch the F-Market streetcar for a ride down the Embarcadero and up Market Street. Allow three hours without breaks.

Two If by Sea: Touring by Boat

Boat cruises provide a view of the city from an unusual vantage point and are the only way to experience the bay in all its glory. There are quite a few options for riding the waves of the bay, one of which is the commuter ferries. Ferries pick up passengers from Fisherman's Wharf (Pier 41) and the Ferry Building.

The Blue & Gold Fleet (☎ 415-773-1188) operates ferries to and from Marin County. This is also the only company that will take you to Alcatraz Island (see Chapter 16). Blue & Gold's one-hour bay cruise ($17 for adults, $13 for seniors and kids 12 to 18, $9 for kids 5 to 11) sails under the Golden Gate Bridge; past Sausalito, Angel Island, and Alcatraz, and then back to Fisherman's Wharf. This tour will be a satisfying, if brief, encounter with the bay.

You want something a little more exciting than a ferry? Try sailing on **The Ruby (☎ 415-861-2165)**. This 60-foot steel sloop, which holds about 30 passengers, skims the white caps in the bay daily with a lunch cruise from 12:30 to 3:00 p.m. and an early evening sail with hors d'oeuvres from 6:00 to 8:30 p.m. The cost is $35 per person (including food); beer and wine are available at an additional cost. Kids 10 and under are half-price. Reservations are necessary. The Ruby is docked by The Ramp (see Chapter 22), at the foot of Mariposa Street at Third Street. The 22-Fillmore or 15-Kearny bus drops you off a block away.

You could also voyage from Sausalito on the **Hawaiian Chieftain** (☎ 415-331-3214; Internet: www.hawaiianchieftain.com). This is a 103-foot steel-hulled, square-rigged topsail ketch, designed to resemble a late-18th-century European trading vessel. It glides into the sunset April through October only, from 6 to 9 p.m. Wednesday through Friday. The cost is $35 on Wednesday and Thursday, $40 on Friday (hors d'oeuvres and drinks included). The cost for kids under 12 is $15. You can also choose a three-hour Sunday brunch sail with live music for $50 per person ($25 for kids under 12), or a four-hour Saturday adventure sail for $45 per person, including lunch. Phone them for directions on how to get there via public transit.

Hornblower Dining Yachts (☎ 800-ON-THE-BAY or 415-788-8866; Internet: www.hornblower.com) let you sup as you sail, offering dinner and weekend brunch cruises around the bay. Cruises last from one and a half hours for brunch to three hours for the nightly dinner/dance. The food is hotel-like, but this is a festive way to dine — surrounded by superb views. Dinner rates per person are $75 Sunday through Friday, $89 Saturday. Saturday and Sunday brunch cruises cost $59. Kids are half-price. Reservations required.

Taking a Walk on the Wild Side: Walking Tours

Friends of the Library sponsor **City Guides walking tours** (☎ **415-557-4266;** Internet: www.hooked.net/users/jhum). There are 26 different tours to choose from, all for free! All you have to do is pick the tour that interests you and show up at the proper corner on time. You can get an insider's view of Chinatown, admire San Francisco's collection of beautifully restored Victorian homes on the "Landmark Victorians of Alamo Square" tour, or explore the haunts of the original 49ers on the "Gold Rush City" walk. Tours run about two hours on average. Highly recommended!

The Victorian Home Walk (☎ **415-252-9485;** Internet: www.victorian walk.com) combines a trolley-car excursion with a walking tour through a number of celebrated neighborhoods. During the 2½-hour tour, you see an array of houses in areas where tour vans are prohibited from entering. The guide promises the walk isn't strenuous. The cost is $20. Tours leave daily at 11 a.m. from the lobby of the Westin St. Francis, 335 Powell St., between Geary and Post streets in the Union Square neighborhood.

San Francisco Architectural Heritage conducts a Pacific Heights walk (☎ **415-441-3000** for reservations) on Sundays at 12:30 p.m. beginning at the Haas-Lilienthal house (see Chapter 17). The two-hour tour through this swanky neighborhood costs just $5 for adults and $3 for seniors and children under 12.

Eating Your Way through San Francisco

Shirley Fong-Torres, a local writer and personality, has been operating Chinatown food tours for 17 years. The 3½-hour walk manages to demystify the exotic rather irreverently. It includes running commentary about the history of this fascinating neighborhood and stops at an artist's studio, a one-room temple, a market, an herbal shop, and a tea company, where you're treated to a tasting. Shirley's company, **Wok Wiz Chinatown Walking Tours & Cooking Center,** 654 Commercial St., between Kearny and Montgomery streets (☎ **800-281-9255** or 415-981-8989; Internet: www.wokwiz.com), schedules the tours daily. They cost $40 for adults and $35 for kids under 11 (dim sum lunch included). A new evening tour and Chinese banquet runs $60.

The popular North Beach neighborhood reaches new heights of giddiness on Saturdays when food writer GraceAnn Walden leads **Mangia! North Beach,** a 4½-hour, $50 walking, eating, shopping, and history tour. GraceAnn and her followers traipse in and out of a deli, an Irish pub (stout is actually rather bracing in the morning), a truffle factory, a bakery, a pottery store, and two lovely churches, before ending with a multi-course family-style lunch at one of her favorite restaurants. Lots of samples, lots of tidbits about the Italians, and lots of fun. Call ☎ **415-397-8530** to make reservations. Anyone interested in Latin culture should inquire about dates for GraceAnn's new Latino Mission Tour and Mural Walk ($65), which includes lunch at a Nuevo Latino restaurant.

Seeking Out Special-Interest Tours

Get a great introduction to gay and lesbian history from the Gold Rush to the present with the delightful Trevor Hailey, a 30-year Castro resident, on her four-hour **Cruisin' the Castro** walking tour (☎ **415-550-8110**; Internet: www.webcastro.com/castrotour). Lunch is included in the $40 price. Tours depart from the Harvey Milk Plaza, which is atop the Castro Street Muni Station at the corner of Castro and Market streets. Reservations are required.

Caffeine addicts and coffee connoisseurs alike will enjoy **Javawalk** (☎ **415-673-WALK**; Internet: www.javawalk.com), a walking tour devoted entirely to the tasting of java. With your guide, Elaine Sosa, you spend two hours sipping java in the North Beach cafes, learning how to take coffee breaks with finesse. Tours are Saturdays only, beginning at 10 a.m. The cost is $20 for adults and $10 for kids.

The **Precita Eyes Mural Arts Center,** 2981 24th St., near Harrison Street (☎ **415-285-2287**; Internet: www.precitaeyes.org), a not-for-profit arts center, features more than 75 murals on the Mission District walking tours that it sponsors. The six-block walk departs Saturdays and Sundays at 1:30 p.m. from the center itself. The cost is $12 for adults, $5 for seniors, and $2 for children under 18. A slightly different walk leaves from Café Venice, 3325 24th St., near the 24th Street BART station, on Saturdays at 11 a.m.

An easy way to explore the redwood groves of Muir Woods (see Chapter 17) is with Sierra Club guide Tom Martell, of **Tom's Scenic Walking Tours** (☎ **800-909-9255** or 415-381-5106). He'll pick you up (and drop you off) at your hotel, provide a picnic lunch, and drive up to six adventurers to the lovely redwoods just beyond the Golden Gate Bridge for a 2– to 4-mile hike. Cost for the 3½-hour walk with lunch is $50.

Chapter 19

A Shop-'Til-You-Drop Guide to San Francisco

. . . .

In This Chapter

▶ Locating San Francisco's big-name shops and specialty boutiques

▶ Discovering the main shopping neighborhoods

▶ Hunting down bargains

. . . .

Although most people think of Union Square as the hub of San Francisco shopping, the downtown area has plenty of competition. Nearly every San Francisco neighborhood boasts a thriving "Main Street" of locally-owned boutiques, cafes, and bookstores. You can find shops with unique arts and crafts, clothing stores that eschew chain-mentality fashion, even houseware havens that reflect the style of the local clientele. Shopping in San Francisco is never mundane. Depending on where you head, you can try on a different attitude as easily as a different outfit.

Scoping Out the Shopping Scene

If you know where to look, you can do some very interesting shopping around here. Oh, plenty of people complain about the city being Starbucked and Gapped to death, but they aren't looking beyond the obvious retail centers. Not all the entrepreneurs in San Francisco are franchisees or part of some retail conglomerate — some are actually opening boutiques with a personal stamp. In particular, check out Valencia Street for post-modern streetwear and decor, Sacramento Street for contemporary clothing and accessories, upper Grant Street for local clothing designers, and upper Polk Street for home furnishing and decoration design trends.

You'll find that stores are generally open Monday through Saturday from 10 a.m. to 6 p.m. and on Sunday from noon to 5 p.m., even on many holidays. Shops around Fisherman's Wharf tend to stay open later, as do most department stores.

San Francisco Shopping

Belden Place **27**
Bell'occhio **13**
Biordi Art Imports **19**
Books Inc. **1**
Britex Fabrics **32**
Burton's Pharmacy **2**
Carol Doda's Champagne
and Lace **6**
Chong Imports **25**
City Art **16**
City Lights Bookstore **20**
Clarion Music Center **26**
Dandelion **37**
Encantanda Gallery **14**
Esprit Factory Outlet **38**
Fillamento **9**
Forrest Jones **40**
Gallery of Jewels **5**
Gazoontite **4**
Golden Gate Fortune
Cookie Company **24**
Goodbyes **39**
Gump's **31**
Home Remedies **14**
House of Magic **3**

Imperial Tea Court **5**
Kiehl's **10**
Knitz & Leather **17**
La Place du Soleil **23**
La Tulipe Noir **22**
MAC **16**
Macy's **33**
Maiden Lane **32**
Mrs. Dewson's Hats **11**
Mudpie **7**
Neiman Marcus **34**
Nest **8**
Original Levi's Store **29**
Paxton Gate **14**
Polanco **12**
Rolo **36**
Rolo Garage **36**
Saks Fifth Avenue **28**
San Francisco Centre **35**
Show Biz **18**
Wilkes Bashford **30**
Tai Yick Trading
Company **21**
Virginia Breier **41**
XOX Truffles **15**

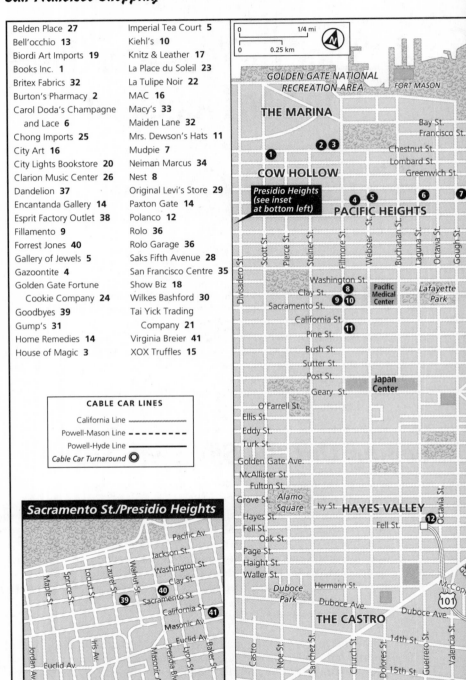

CABLE CAR LINES

California Line ————
Powell-Mason Line — — — — —
Powell-Hyde Line ————
Cable Car Turnaround ◎

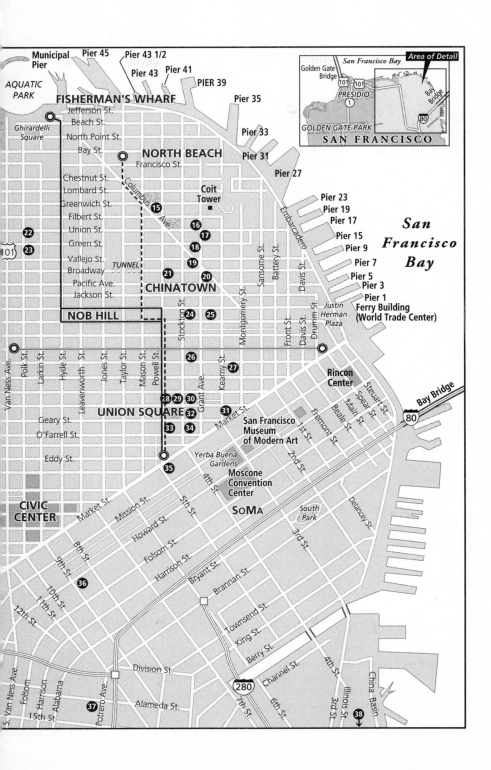

Municipal Pier
Pier 45
Pier 43 1/2
Pier 43
Pier 41
PIER 39
AQUATIC PARK
FISHERMAN'S WHARF
Jefferson St.
Beach St.
Ghirardelli Square
North Point St.
Bay St.
NORTH BEACH
Francisco St.
Pier 35
Pier 33
Pier 31
Pier 27
Chestnut St.
Lombard St.
Greenwich St.
Coit Tower
Filbert St.
Union St.
Green St.
Vallejo St.
TUNNEL
Broadway
Pacific Ave.
Jackson St.
CHINATOWN
Columbus Ave.
Pier 23
Pier 19
Pier 17
Pier 15
Pier 9
Pier 7
Pier 5
Pier 3
Pier 1
Ferry Building (World Trade Center)
San Francisco Bay
NOB HILL
Van Ness Ave.
Polk St.
Larkin St.
Hyde St.
Leavenworth St.
Jones St.
Taylor St.
Mason St.
Powell St.
Stockton St.
Montgomery St.
Sansome St.
Battery St.
Front St.
Davis St.
Drumm St.
Justin Herman Plaza
Grant Ave.
Kearny St.
Rincon Center
UNION SQUARE
Geary St.
O'Farrell St.
Eddy St.
Market St.
San Francisco Museum of Modern Art
Steuart St.
Spear St.
Main St.
Beale St.
Fremont St.
1st St.
2nd St.
Bay Bridge
Yerba Buena Gardens
Moscone Convention Center
CIVIC CENTER
Market St.
Mission St.
Howard St.
Folsom St.
Harrison St.
4th St.
5th St.
SoMa
South Park
3rd St.
Delancey St.
8th St.
9th St.
10th St.
11th St.
12th St.
Bryant St.
Brannan St.
Townsend St.
King St.
Berry St.
Channel St.
Division St.
Alameda St.
7th St.
6th St.
4th St.
3rd St.
Illinois St.
China Basin
S. Van Ness Ave.
Folsom
Harrison
Alabama
Potrero Ave.
15th St.
280
80

Area of Detail
San Francisco Bay
Golden Gate Bridge
101
101
PRESIDIO
1
GOLDEN GATE PARK
SAN FRANCISCO
Bay Bridge
80

Sales tax in San Francisco is 8.5%, and the salesperson will add it at the register for all goods. You don't have to pay the sales tax if the store ships something out of state for you, but shipping can cost as much or more than the tax, unless you're purchasing a very expensive item.

Finding the Stores That Suit Your Style

The worldwide chain-store invasion has not, unfortunately, passed San Francisco by. In fact, we accept the blame for the Gap frenzy — the headquarters are near the Embarcadero — and if you see a Pottery Barn or a Gymboree in your midst, well, those companies originated in the Bay Area, as well. But you can find plenty of truly unique emporiums that will make shopping a joy again. Here's a short list of great places to get started.

The famous names

Gump's, in Union Square at 135 Post St., between Kearny Street and Grant Avenue (☎ 415-982-1616), is famous for its Asian antiques, silver, and china, as well as for longevity — it's been in business since 1861. Anyone who receives a gift from Gump's will shower impressed thanks on the giver because of the name itself. Open Monday through Saturday from 10 a.m. to 6 p.m., until 7p.m. Thursday.

Looking for the perfect place for one-stop-shopping? Then head over to the remodeled **Macy's** on Union Square, at Stockton and O'Farrell streets (☎ 415-397-3333). At 700,000 square feet, this eight-story, glass-fronted fashion legend is bigger than some towns. Open Monday through Saturday 10 a.m. to 8 p.m., Sunday from 11 a.m. to 7 p.m.

The Original Levi's Store, 345 Stockton St., at Post Street (☎ 415-501-0100), is a showcase for more than 501s — you'll see some wild designs stitched onto jackets and jeans. One corner of this three-story monument to denim is dedicated to alterations, in case your shrink-to-fits still need a tuck here and there. Open Monday through Saturday 10 a.m. to 8 p.m., Sunday 11 a.m. to 6 p.m.

Other places you should know about

Bell'occhio (☎ 415-864-4048) has long been a favorite among decorators and wedding planners. But, with its hidden location in an alley off Market Street near Civic Center, it was widely unknown even among locals. When Martha Stewart discovered this bewitching little place, things started to change. Along with cunning decorations and French ribbons, you can buy interesting items the owner has discovered on her travels, such as a bit of chocolate or imported face powder. The shop is at 8 and 10 Brady Alley, off Market Street between 12th and Gough streets. Take the F-Market streetcar to Civic Center. Open Tuesday through Saturday from 11 a.m. to 5 p.m.

Polanco, a bright gallery featuring crafts and artwork from Mexico, is located at 393 Hayes St. (☎ 415-252-5753). This block in Hayes Valley also has a few terrific clothing and home-decor shops, so if you're in the neighborhood, it's worth a side trip. The gallery is open Tuesday through Saturday 11 a.m. to 7 p.m., Sunday 1 to 6 p.m.

Dandelion, 55 Potrero Ave., at Alameda (☎ 415-436-9500), isn't a store you'll find by accident. You have to have heard about this place from a devoted customer, with its out-of-the-way location close to the Design Center south of Market Street. The owners seem to be magnets for beautiful objects. Their prices are very fair, their taste impeccable. The 9-San Bruno bus from Market and Ninth streets can take you right here. Open Monday through Saturday 10 a.m. to 6 p.m., Sunday noon to 5 p.m.

Famed *San Francisco Chronicle* journalist Herb Caen's favorite clothing store, **Wilkes Bashford,** 375 Sutter St., between Stockton Street and Grant Avenue, near Union Square (☎ 415-986-4380), was often mentioned in his columns. And San Francisco's natty mayor, Willie Brown, purchases his Brioni suits here. The store sells sophisticated clothing for women as well. Open Monday through Saturday 10 a.m. to 6 p.m., Thursday to 8 p.m.

For CDs, vinyl (remember that?), and an in-depth selection of previously-owned music, the cognoscenti shop at **Amoeba Records,** 1855 Haight St. (☎ 415-831-1200), in the musically famous neighborhood of the same name. Open Monday through Saturday from 10 a.m. to 10 p.m., Sunday 11 a.m. to 9 p.m.

When those cognoscenti stroll down Haight Street, they often wear really cool clothes from **Rolo,** a locally grown retailer with six stores around town. The flagship store, which carries streetwear for both men and women, is south of Market at 1235 Howard St. (☎ 415-989-7656). Open Monday through Saturday from 10 a.m. to 8 p.m. and Sunday 11 a.m. to 7 p.m.

Finding the Best Shopping Neighborhoods

Looking for that perfect little doodad for Aunt Hermione back home? Or do you just like to browse and see what catches your fancy? Below is a rundown of the city's best shopping areas, with a few highlights in each. Happy hunting!

Union Square

You're never far from a department store in this neighborhood. From one spot in the middle of Union Square you can see **Neiman Marcus** (☎ 415-362-3900) on Stockton and Geary Streets (open Monday, Thursday, and Friday 10 a.m. to 8 p.m., Tuesday and Wednesday 10 a.m. to 6 p.m., Saturday 10 a.m. to 7 p.m., and Sunday noon to 6 p.m.) and **Saks Fifth Avenue** (☎ 415-986-4300) on the corner of Powell and Post streets (open Monday through Saturday 10 a.m. to 7 p.m. and Sunday 11 a.m. to 6 p.m.). Then there's **Levi's** (see the previous section) on Post and Stockton, and **Macy's** (see the previous section) everywhere else. Ah . . . shopping! A half-block north of Neiman's on Stockton Street is Maiden Lane, which is lined with designer shops. You can also find an entrance here to **Britex Fabrics** (☎ 415-392-2910), probably the most well-stocked notions and fabric store in the country (open Monday through Wednesday and Saturday 9:30 a.m. to 6:00 p.m., Thursday and Friday 9:30 a.m. to 7:00 p.m.). Walk another block east and two blocks north and watch for tiny **Belden Place** between Bush and Pine streets (see Chapter 13). A covey of delicious little restaurants lines the alley, and any one of them makes a satisfying place to stop for a meal. At lunchtime on fair days, Belden, which is closed to auto traffic, is filled with cafe tables, giving the street a party-like atmosphere.

Be careful of the multitude of shady salespeople who operate questionable electronics/camera, luggage, and gift shops on certain blocks of Mason, Powell, and Market streets around Union Square. (You'll probably know them when you see them: Most offer too-good-to-be-true deals, and some have someone standing outside the store scoping out potential customers.) Out-of-town customers have been known to discover inflated charges on their credit cards after shopping at these places, so buyer beware.

Chinatown

Chinatown is known for its amusing trinkets and inexpensive clothing. But most of the souvenirs sold in the shops that line Grant Avenue are not the must-haves you come to San Francisco seeking. If you venture off Grant Avenue, however, shop to your heart's content in Chinese herbal shops with strange remedies and unique jewelry stores full of jade of varying quality. The merchants in the less touristy stores don't always speak English, and they may seem less than friendly, but don't let that stop you from looking around.

The "going-out-of-business" signs you see taped to the windows of several Chinatown stores are nearly as old as the grandmothers walking about with babies tied to their backs. These stores have been running their farewell sales for years. Don't expect any bargains.

If you can't tear yourself away from Grant Avenue, the best place to find inexpensive (or expensive) gifts and housewares is **Chong Imports,** 838 Grant Ave., in the Empress of China building between Clay and Washington streets (☎ **415-982-1432**). This basement-level treasure house stocks a little of everything. Open daily from 10 a.m. to 9 p.m.

At the **Clarion Music Center,** 816 Sacramento St., near Grant Avenue (☎ **415-391-1317;** Internet: www.clarionmusic.com), check out the amazing instruments, including traditional Chinese musical instruments like moon-shaped guitars, plus Chinese lion dance masks. Open Monday through Friday from 11 a.m. to 6 p.m., Saturday from 9 a.m. to 5 p.m. Call for a Friday night world concert series schedule.

Tai Yick Trading Company, 1400 Powell St., at Broadway (☎ **415-986-0961**), sells teapots, dishes, lamps, porcelain and pottery vases, and statues at reasonable prices. The owners are helpful and friendly, and native San Franciscans swear that this is the best store of its kind in town. Open daily from 9:30 a.m. to 6:30 p.m.

The Imperial Tea Court, 1411 Powell St., near Broadway (☎ **415-788-6080**), noted as a tranquil place to rejuvenate yourself, sells everything you need to brew a proper cup of Chinese tea. Open daily from 11 a.m. to 6:30 p.m.

Legend has it that fortune cookies were invented at the Japanese Tea Garden in Golden Gate Park. If you want to watch these crispy cookies in the making, head over to the **Golden Gate Fortune Cookie Company** in Chinatown (see Chapter 16). They make wonderful gifts to take back home. The working factory is located at 956 Ross Alley, between Jackson and Washington streets near Grant Avenue. It's open daily from 10 a.m. to 7 p.m.

North Beach

North Beach is more than just a food and drink mecca — you can find all sorts of curiosities and clothing off Columbus Street. The section of Grant Avenue (completely different from the street of the same name in Chinatown) from Green to Greenwich streets has a more Parisian accent, with stylish boutiques for clothes and accessories. Among the finds — and there are many — take a gander at **MAC,** 1534 Grant St. (☎ **415-837-1604**), which stocks local clothing design talent. It's open Monday through Saturday 11 a.m. to 7 p.m. and Sunday noon to 5 p.m. Head to **Knitz & Leather,** 1429 Grant Ave. (☎ **415-391-3480**), for handmade leather jackets. Open Monday through Saturday 11a.m. to 6 p.m., Sunday noon to 5 p.m. Members of your party not interested in clothes may find the music, theater, and movie memorabilia store **Show Biz** more to their liking. It's located at 1318 Grant Ave. (☎ **415-989-6744**) and is open daily noon to 8 p.m., until 10 p.m. Friday and Saturday.

There's no need to comb Italy for ceramics, when you can shop at **Biordi Art Imports,** 412 Columbus Ave., at Vallejo Street (☎ 415-392-8096). You'll find the most beautiful hand-painted Majolica dishes and serving pieces nearly too pretty to eat off. Open Monday through Saturday from 9:30 a.m. to 6 p.m.

City Lights Bookstore, 261 Columbus Ave. (☎ 415-362-8193), is famous for its Beat Generation roots, but it's also a book-fiend's paradise. The first all-paperback bookstore in San Francisco, this city institution dates to 1953, when it was opened by Beat poet Lawrence Ferlinghetti. At the time, most people thought hardcover books were superior to paperbacks in terms of both the quality of the content as well as the quality of the paper. Ferlinghetti challenged this attitude and made great literature available to everyone by stocking his bookstore with less costly paperback editions. The San Francisco Board of Supervisors recently designated the store a cultural and architectural landmark, assuring a long and happy life for the building. Ferlinghetti's brainchild is also on its way to becoming a national historic site. Open daily from 10 a.m. to midnight.

Admirers of chocolate can wedge themselves into **XOX Truffles,** 754 Columbus Ave. (☎ 415-421-4814), a tiny store devoted to nickel-sized truffles in a huge assortment of flavors. These bites of bliss are all handmade by a handsome French chef, who removed himself from the rigors of the restaurant world to bring pleasure to us chocoholics. They're open Monday through Saturday from 9 a.m. to 6 p.m.

Union and Chestnut streets

According to a survey, one out of four visitors to San Francisco plans on visiting Union Street between Fillmore Street and Van Ness Avenue in the Marina district. Folks who love wandering in and out of specialty shops will think they've hit pay dirt. Muni buses 22-Fillmore, 41-Union, 42-Downtown Loop, and 45-Union/Stockton all run on Union Street.

Carol Doda, who shaped a career out of her chest long before implants were considered accessories, runs a lingerie shop, **Carol Doda's Champagne and Lace,** at 1850 Union St. (☎ 415-776-6900). She carries bras in regular and hard-to-find sizes, plus lots of other fun things. Open daily from 12:30 to 7 p.m., to 6 p.m. on Sunday.

Cover yourself with beautiful adornments crafted by local artists at **Gallery of Jewels,** 2101 Union St. (☎ 415-929-0259), open Monday through Friday 10:30 a.m. to 6:30 p.m. and Sunday 11 a.m. to 6 p.m. You'll find unique pieces of jewelry as well as purses and hats on occasion.

If you find yourself sneezing and sniffling on a regular basis, or if you surround yourself with people who do, help now comes in the form of **Gazoontite.** Located at 2157 Union St. (☎ 415-931-2230), useful products for your favorite asthmatic or allergy-prone relative are attractively displayed. Open Monday through Thursday 10 a.m. to 7 p.m., Friday and Saturday 10 a.m. to 8 p.m., and Sunday 11 a.m. to 6 p.m.

Mudpie, 1694 Union St. (☎ 415-771-9262), sells incredibly expensive children's clothes and gifts. Sticker shock is slightly alleviated in the downstairs sale room, where everything is half-price. Open Monday through Saturday 10 a.m. to 6 p.m., Sunday 11 a.m. to 5 p.m.

Another highly attractive, healthy shopping area is **Chestnut Street** in Cow Hollow, patronized by highly attractive and healthy locals with plenty of discretionary cash. Neither Chestnut nor Union Street, a few blocks south, have been able to fight off the invasion by some of the more ambitious chain stores, but local neighborhood and merchant groups are vigilant enough to keep them at a minimum. Muni bus 30-Stockton or 43-Masonic will get you to Chestnut Street.

Among the Banana Republic, Pottery Barn, and Williams-Sonoma stores lining the area is an anomaly, **Burton's Pharmacy,** 2016 Chestnut St. (☎ 415-567-1166), one of the few remaining independent drugstores left. Open weekdays 9 a.m. to 6:30 p.m., Saturday 9:30 a.m. to 6 p.m., and Sunday 11 a.m. to 4 p.m.

On the other end of Chestnut is another independent, **Books, Inc.,** 2251 Chestnut (☎ 415-931-3633), which has a broad inventory of fine reading material for the entire family. Open Sunday through Thursday 9 a.m. to 10 p.m. and Friday and Saturday 9 a.m. to midnight.

Wow your friends and family with some cool magic tricks from the **House of Magic,** 2025 Chestnut St. (☎ 415-346-2218). Plenty of spellbinding tricks and gag gifts are on hand, along with a vast array of masks and wigs. Kids love this place, too. Open Monday through Saturday 10 a.m. to 7 p.m., Sunday 11 a.m. to 4 p.m.

Pacific Heights

The tony neighborhood of Pacific Heights offers shoppers Fillmore Street, which is chock-full of clothing boutiques and other cool places to shop. Between Jackson and Sutter streets, you won't be able to put your credit card away.

Kiehl's manufactures high-end, high-quality cosmetics and hair products for men and women. Their shop at 2360 Fillmore St. (☎ 415-359-9260) is one of only two free-standing retail outlets in the country. Open Monday through Saturday 11 a.m. to 7 p.m., Sunday noon to 6 p.m.

Nest, 2300 Fillmore St., at Clay Street (☎ 415-292-6199), is yet another home store, but one that carries many old French decorative items, including quilts and linens. Open Monday through Saturday 10:30 a.m. to 6:30 p.m., Sunday noon to 6 p.m.

You don't see many hat shops left in the world, so a visit to **Mrs. Dewson's Hats,** 2050 Fillmore St. (☎ **415-346-1600**), is a must if your chapeau is a little tattered. This place is home to the "Willie Brim," a snappy fedora named after Mayor Willie Brown. Open Tuesday through Saturday 10 a.m. to 6 p.m. and Sunday noon to 4 p.m.

Polk Street

The stretch of road from Filbert to Broadway on the Russian Hill end of Polk Street has blossomed into a hot spot for dining and shopping. Along with a second location for **Nest** (see the preceding section), two little shops for the home, **La Place du Soleil,** at 2356 Polk St. (☎ **415-771-4252;** open Tuesday through Saturday 11 a.m. to 6 p.m., Sunday noon to 5 p.m.), and **La Tulipe Noire,** at 2418 Polk St. (☎ **415-922-2000;** open Tuesday through Sunday 11 a.m. to 6 p.m.) will seemingly transport you to a street in the fourth arrondissement of Paris.

Sacramento Street

Some exclusive shops and also some of the best secondhand stores in town can be found in the section of Sacramento Street between Spruce and Divisadero streets in Presidio Heights. The 1-California bus takes you within one block of Sacramento Street.

Virginia Breier, 3091 Sacramento St., near Baker Street (☎ **415-929-7173**), shows the work of local craftspeople and artists. Whatever you find — paintings, jewelry, glass, furniture, or crafts — will be one-of-a-kind, high quality, and expensive. Open Monday through Saturday from 11 a.m. to 6 p.m.

Before housewares were considered a lifestyle choice, **Forrest Jones,** 3274 Sacramento St. (☎ **415-567-2483**), was stocking an array of kitchen tools, linens, lovely porcelain lamp bases and vases, cookbooks, glassware, and other necessities. The variety of goods crowded about makes the store very appealing. Open Monday through Saturday 10 a.m. to 6 p.m., Sunday 11 a.m. to 5 p.m.

If you want to see what the swells have cleaned out of their closets (the locals are going to hate me for this), head to **GoodByes,** 3464 Sacramento St., between Walnut and Laurel streets (☎ **415-346-6388**). This is the place for gently worn men's and women's clothing. Open Monday through Saturday from 10 a.m. to 6 p.m., Thursday until 8 p.m., and Sunday from 11 a.m. to 5 p.m. A second store for women only is across the street (☎ **415-674-0151**).

Valencia Street

In the last three years, Valencia Street in the Mission District has been developing into an up-and-coming shopping district. The blocks from 19th to 23rd streets still hold plenty of storefront churches and used-appliance dens, but the cafes and restaurants that ventured here in the first wave of gentrification have been joined by sellers of youthful fashions, local art, and goods for the home. Of note is **Paxton Gate,** 824 Valencia St. (☎ 415-824-1872; open Sunday through Thursday noon to 7 p.m., Friday and Saturday 11 a.m. to 8 p.m.), part entomological display, part garden store, but neither description does this place justice. Almost next door is **City Art** (☎ 415-970-9900; open Tuesday through Sunday noon to 9 p.m.), a co-op gallery featuring San Francisco artists and photographers. For whimsical linens, festive candles, original art, or perhaps a new sofa, drop into **Home Remedies,** 1026 Valencia (☎ 415-826-2026; open Tuesday through Friday noon to 7 p.m., Saturday 11 a.m. to 6 p.m., Sunday noon to 5 p.m.). And don't pass by **Encantada Gallery of Fine Arts,** 904 Valencia St. (☎ 415-642-3939; open Tuesday through Sunday noon to 6 p.m., until 8 p.m. Friday and Saturday), which has a wonderful collection of Mexican art and pottery, as well as a changing exhibit of paintings and mixed media. From downtown, use BART, exit at the 24th Street Station, and walk one block west. Some of the Valencia Street shops are closed on Mondays.

What a Steal!: Bargain Hunting in SoMa and Beyond

The discount manufacturers based South of Market (SoMa) have made bargain shopping in San Francisco a popular pursuit. Although outlets can be found around SoMa and beyond, the area between Townsend and Bryant streets and Second and Fourth streets is especially great for bargains.

Attention serious factory-outlet and discount-store shoppers: You'll want to get your hands on a copy of Sally Socolich's *Bargain Hunting in the Bay Area.* It's available in local bookstores for the bargain price of $6.95.

Young women flock to the **Esprit Factory Outlet,** 499 Illinois St., at 16th Street (☎ 415-957-2550), for shoes, discounted clothing, and accessories for women and children. Many visitors rank a shopping trip here as important as a visit to Lombard Street. Take Muni bus 15-Third to 16th Street and walk east one block. Open daily from 10 a.m. to 7 p.m., Sunday from 11 a.m. to 5 p.m.

The hip retailer Rolo has an outlet for sale merchandise called **Rolo Garage,** 1301 Howard St., at Ninth Street (☎ 415-861-1999). It's open every day from 11 a.m. to 7 p.m.

Did your son outgrow his sneakers yesterday? Did you? You're gonna go wild in the **Skechers USA** outlet in the Mission at 2600 Mission St. (☎ 415-401-6211). Open Monday through Saturday 10 a.m. to 7 p.m., Sunday 11 a.m. to 6 p.m.

Index of stores by merchandise

Antiques
La Tulipe Noire (Polk Street)

Arts and Crafts
City Art (Valencia Street)
Encantada Gallery of Fine Arts
    (Valencia Street)
Polanco (Hayes Valley)
Virginia Breier (Sacramento Street)

Beauty Products
Kiehl's (Pacific Heights)

Books
Books, Inc. (Union/Chestnut streets)
City Lights (North Beach)

Clothing, Children's
Esprit Outlet (SoMa)
Macy's (Union Square)
Mudpie (Union/Chestnut streets)
Neiman Marcus (Union Square)

Clothing, Menswear
Goodbyes (Sacramento Street)
Macy's (Union Square)
Neiman Marcus (Union Square)
Original Levi's Store (Union Square)
Rolo (SoMa)
Rolo Garage (SoMa)
Saks Fifth Avenue (Union Square)
Wilkes Bashford (Union Square)

Clothing, Womenswear
Esprit Outlet (SoMa)
Goodbyes (Sacramento Street)
Knitz & Leather (North Beach)
MAC (North Beach)
Macy's (Union Square)
Neiman Marcus (Union Square)
Original Levi's Store (Union Square)
Rolo (SoMa)
Rolo Garage (SoMa)
Saks Fifth Avenue (Union Square)
Wilkes Bashford (Union Square)

Edibles
Golden Gate Fortune Cookie Company
    (Chinatown)
Imperial Tea Court (Chinatown)
XOX Truffles (North Beach)

Fabric
Britex (Union Square)

Gifts
Biordi Art Imports (North Beach)
Burton's Pharmacy (Union/Chestnut
    streets)
Chong Imports (Chinatown)
Dandelion (SoMa)
Gazoontite (Union/Chestnut streets)
Gump's (Union Square)
House of Magic (Union/Chestnut
    streets)
Show Biz (North Beach)

Hats

Mrs. Dewson's Hats (Pacific Heights)

Home Decor and Housewares

Bell'occhio (Civic Center)
Forrest Jones (Sacramento Street)
Home Remedies (Valencia Street)
La Place du Soeil (Polk Street)
Nest (Pacific Heights)
Paxton Gate (Valencia Street)
Tai Yick Trading Company
    (Chinatown)

Jewelry

Gallery of Jewels (Union/Chestnut
    streets)

Lingerie

Carol Doda's Champagne and Lace
    (Union/Chestnut streets)

Music

Amoeba Records (Haight-Ashbury)
Clarion Music Center (Chinatown)

Shoes

Macy's (Union Square)
Neiman Marcus (Union Square)
Saks Fifth Avenue (Union Square)
Skechers, USA (SoMa)

Chapter 20

Four Great Itineraries to Make Your Day

In This Chapter

▶ Making the most out of three to five days

▶ Showing the kids a good time

▶ Taking a food-lover's holiday

*T*ourists naturally want to pack as much as possible into a sightseeing trip, fearing that they won't have a chance to return. Having been in that position myself, I've come to the conclusion that travel isn't pleasurable if all you do is run around like a mad person checking off sights as if you're grocery shopping. My idea of a good time is visiting one or two important sights in a day (or sometimes just walking past the front portal and waving) and then finding somewhere to sit and watch the world pass by. (But I must admit that I felt really foolish for missing the Eiffel Tower on my first visit to Paris — and I was in the neighborhood.) You may prefer a compromise between these two approaches, in which case I suggest you decide in advance what you absolutely must see, then fit in whatever else you can based on how much time and energy you have.

On that note, the following suggested itineraries are intended for first-time visitors who want to catch as much as possible without completely exhausting themselves or their companions. I've packed a lot in, but you can pick and choose (or completely ignore) parts of each.

San Francisco in Three Days

Three days is barely enough to "get" San Francisco, so I'm going to keep you within the city limits for the entire time. The following list takes you step-by-step through the city.

✔ **Day 1:** Find Market Street and catch one of the historic F-Market streetcars (see Chapter 11) heading toward Pier 39 and Fisherman's Wharf. If you haven't eaten breakfast, try the **Eagle Café** on the second floor of the pier. If it happens to be a Saturday, stop at Green Street on the Embarcadero and breakfast at the **Ferry Plaza Farmers' Market.** When you reach **Pier 39,** greet the sea lions (follow the barking) and continue to the end of the pier for a dead-on view of Alcatraz Island. Walk to **Aquatic Park** to complete a tour of **Fisherman's Wharf** (see Chapter 16). You'll pass the **Hyde Street Pier** and the **Maritime National Museum** — pop in if you like ships — as well as **Ghirardelli Square.** On Bay Street, catch a 30-Stockton bus to Chestnut Street. If it's not too soon to shop or eat, **Café Marimba** (see Chapter 14) is a great choice for Mexican food. The bus ends up at Beach Street, and your task is to walk from the **Palace of Fine Arts** through the Presidio to the **Golden Gate Bridge.** Follow the joggers along the bay; there's a path. The 29-Sunset bus will also take you there and back. End the afternoon around **Union Square,** window shopping along Stockton and Sutter. Change your clothes, then go to the **Top of the Mark** (see Chapter 14) for an aperitif and a grand view. For dinner, see what's cooking on **Belden Place** (see Chapter 13) and if you still have a bit of steam left, drop by **Biscuits and Blues** (see Chapter 22) for a musical nightcap.

✔ **Day 2:** This day starts with another transportation highlight. Fling yourself on a Powell-Hyde cable car (see Chapter 11) for the brief ride to Lombard Street. Walk down via the staircases on either side and, heading north, find the **San Francisco Art Institute** at 800 Chestnut St. Inside the campus, follow the signs to the cafe for breakfast or a snack. This is a funky place with unobstructed views of the bay and a menu of sandwiches, bagels, and vegetarian entrees priced for starving artists. Follow Filbert Street to **Washington Square Park** in North Beach, a modest pocket of green with plentiful benches on the perimeter and the twin spires of Saints Peter and Paul's Church solidly cutting into the sky to the north. Park yourself on a bench, maybe with a latté in hand from **Mario's Bohemian Cigar** on the corner. Then stroll around North Beach if you like, or walk up Grant Avenue past Union Street and follow the signs to **Coit Tower** (see Chapter 16). From there, return to North Beach for a leisurely lunch at **Moose's** (see Chapter 14), which is on the east side of the park, or pick up a sandwich at one of the delis and have a picnic of sorts in Portsmouth Square (above the parking garage on Kearny Street between Washington and Clay; see Chapter 16), a short walk away. Spend the afternoon exploring **Chinatown** (see Chapter 16). If you're in the mood for Chinese cuisine for dinner, see Chapter 14 for suggestions. Then head back to North Beach for a performance of *Beach Blanket Babylon* (see Chapter 21).

✔ **Day 3:** Enjoy a walk in the park — **Golden Gate Park** (see Chapter 16) — where you can experience an earthquake at the **California Academy of Sciences** and get some fresh air in the **Strybing Arboretum.** Find lunch over on Ninth Avenue and then stroll down Irving Street, a typical neighborhood shopping block. In the afternoon, a trip to the **Museum of Modern Art** (see Chapter 16) finishes the artistic portion of your vacation. Take a rest stop in **Yerba Buena Gardens** (see Chapter 16) across the street. Then dine around **Union Square** if you're ambitious enough to see an 8 p.m. show at ACT or another theater. Otherwise, hail a cab and head to a Mission District restaurant such as **Delfina** (see Chapter 14), and pretend you're a local. Night owls can finish the evening at a salsa dance club such as **El Rio** (see Chapter 22).

San Francisco in Five Days

For a four– or five-day trip, you can add the following days to the itinerary in the preceding section:

✔ **Day 4:** By now, you've already covered a fair portion of the city; it's probably time to hug a tree (you are in Northern California, after all). Rent a car (see Chapter 9) or take a guided tour (see Chapter 18) and cross the Golden Gate Bridge into **Marin.** Hike **Muir Woods** in the morning (take the Stinson Beach exit) and have lunch by Muir Beach at the English Tudor–style **Pelican Inn,** located at the end of Muir Wood Road at Highway 1 (☎ **415-383-6000;** Internet: www.pelicaninn.com). The inn is a short walk from the beach, which lies below a hikable hill. Stop in **Sausalito** on your way back to the city for an ice cream or just a walk along the bayfront — the San Francisco skyline is quite the sight, but Sausalito itself, while postcard pretty, is quite touristy. This evening, eat dinner in Japantown at either **Mifune** in the Japan Center for noodles or **Isuzu** for sushi or tempura (see Chapter 13).

✔ **Day 5:** This may be the morning to get in your trip to **Alcatraz Island** (see Chapter 16) or to trek to the beautiful **Palace of the Legion of Honor** (see Chapter 17) for another dose of culture. For lunch try the **Tadich Grill** (see Chapter 14), the oldest restaurant in California (although it's been in its current location only since 1967). The menu of old favorites, such as lobster thermidor, is accompanied with a side of local history and an active bar. Then spend the afternoon catching up on shopping, or stroll to the **Ferry Building** down on Pier 5 (just to the east of Broadway), where you can hang out on benches and watch skateboarders or just admire the view. In the evening, splurge with an upscale dinner around Nob Hill — **Charles** is romantic (see Chapter 14) — followed by a show at the **Plush Room** (see Chapter 22).

San Francisco with Kids

How to keep the kids engaged and happy (for example, not asking what time it is, what they're doing tomorrow, and when they're eating) depends on their ages and interests, of course. Here's a list to meet any need:

- **For families with little kids:** A day around **Golden Gate Park** is ideal. The **Academy of Sciences** was developed with children in mind, and youngsters with energy to spare will gravitate toward the big, imaginatively designed playground. When lunch beckons, you can feed the family reasonably at **Park Chow** on Ninth Avenue, just a block from the park entrance. The **zoo** (see Chapter 17) is a logical alternative for a morning's activity as well. In the afternoon, consider a **ferry boat ride** to Sausalito and back.

- **For families with slightly older progeny:** Spend a delightful day taking the cable car to **Fisherman's Wharf** (see Chapter 16), where Pier 39 holds sway, with its many shops and video games. You can avoid the scene, if you prefer, with strategically timed tickets to **Alcatraz** (see Chapter 16); think about bringing along sandwiches or snacks because the food around the pier is over-priced and underwhelming. If you can stave off starvation until your return from solitary confinement, hustle everyone over to **North Beach** on the Mason-Powell cable car and eat at **Il Pollaio** (see Chapter 15). **Chinatown** is convenient to North Beach and kids generally love browsing in the shops. For dinner, **Lichee Gardens** (see Chapter 14) is a good family-style Chinese restaurant, or you can eat at one of the North Beach eateries such as **La Felce,** 1570 Stockton St., at Union (☎ **415-392-8321**), where platters of antipasti, pasta, and roast meats satisfy diverse tastes.

- **For families with kids of varied ages:** Yerba Buena Gardens (see Chapter 16) is a godsend. Teens are usually more than happy to hang out in **Metreon's Airtight Garage** and at **Zeum,** while younger siblings can ride the merry-go-round and then run around the Metreon attraction "Where the Wild Things Are." Skating or bowling works for everyone, and there is plenty of food to be had within walking distance. For a step above the center's offerings, **Pazzia** (see Chapter 14) is an excellent choice for dinner. In the evening, play around at **The Great Entertainer,** 975 Bryant St., between Seventh and Eighth streets (☎ **415-861-8833**), a family-friendly billiards hall serving food and drink along with pool, video games, and even table tennis.

San Francisco for Foodies

You could come here and spend a week honing your talents in the kitchen at **Tante Marie's Cooking School** (☎ **415-788-6699;** Internet:

www.tantemarie.com) and that would certainly qualify you as a foodie. Or you could imitate my friend Bev, who flies up from Los Angeles on a regular basis to raid **North Beach** for supplies and then orders huge meals at the restaurant of the moment. Because the cooking classes run until 4 p.m., let's make like Bev for a day instead.

Wake up and smell the cappuccino and a raisin roll at a local favorite, **Caffè Greco,** 423 Columbus Ave., in North Beach (☎ 415-397-6261). While you sip, make a mental note of how much room you have in your suitcase for imported Italian delicacies, then walk a block to **Molinari's** delicatessen on the corner of Columbus and Vallejo Street (☎ 415-421-2337). If you have some way of refrigerating fresh sausages and cheese, you can take better advantage of the selection here — otherwise, consider ordering a sandwich to go for later. Drop by **Liguria** (see Chapter 15) for a sheet of pizza focaccia, which will make you the envy of your fellow airplane passengers on the ride home. If you need a new pizza stone, go to **A. Cavalli & Co.,** 1441 Stockton St., which also sells Italian cards and maps, as well as cooking utensils.

Don't miss immersing yourself in San Francisco's many cultures by eating dim sum and discovering the wealth of ingredients available in its ethnic enclaves. Bev's favorite, **Mayflower** in the Richmond District (see Chapter 14), makes great dumplings and won't be mobbed like the dim sum places in Chinatown (few tourists venture this far out on Geary Boulevard). After lunch, walk or take a bus north down Clement Street, one block west of Geary, and stop by **Green Apple Books,** 506 Clement St., to peruse a sizable selection of used cookbooks. You can find many produce, fish, and meat markets along Clement, as well as houseware stores; **May Wah,** 547 Clement St., is worth a look, as is **Kamei,** 606 Clement. If you're serious about eating you'll probably be ready for a snack by this time. **Pancho Villa** (see Chapter 13) creates a steak and prawn quesadilla that is unparalleled for quality and price. Because you'll find it in the Mission District, you'll also want to visit **La Palma,** 2884 24th St., at Florida (☎ 415-647-1500), for fresh tortillas, dried chilies, and other essentials for cooking Mexican food. Make your way to Civic Center on the F-Market and stop at **Yumm,** 1750 Market St. (☎ 415-626-9866), for more additions to your pantry. You'll find a glorious selection of spices, Blanxart chocolate from Catalonia (the best), plus some unusual sodas and good sandwiches for takeaway. Finally, head south of Market to the **Wine House** at 535 Bryant St., between Third and Fourth streets, where the staff is very knowledgeable. For dinner, consider a leading neighborhood destination such as **Delfina** (see Chapter 14) or a high-end experience such as **Gary Danko** (see Chapter 14). If you have another day, or you're ready for more, see Chapter 23 for additional dining destinations.

Part VI

Living It Up After the Sun Goes Down: San Francisco Nightlife

"For tonight's modern reinterpretation of Carmen, those in the front row are kindly requested to wear raincoats."

In this part . . .

*B*ecause San Francisco appeals to such a diverse populace to begin with, no single form of entertainment has come to be associated with the city in the same way that music is associated with New Orleans or theater with New York, for example. Instead, San Francisco offers an eclectic mix of dance, music, performance art, theater, and opera, with plenty to choose from on any given night. For those who shun anything requiring a trip to a box office, you can choose from plenty of bars and clubs to keep you off the streets until the wee hours.

Even travelers with kids don't have to limit after-hours activities to dinner and a movie. A few clubs offer shows for patrons of all ages, featuring local alternative or blues bands. (Your kid will think you're very cool.) A night at the theater is also a great family alternative; you can usually find something with intergenerational appeal playing.

Chapter 21

San Francisco Really Puts On a Performance

*P*erforming-arts fans can find plenty of interesting offerings in San Francisco. For drama, there's a bit of the tried and true when Broadway road companies drop into town, and our own **American Conservatory Theatre (ACT)** regularly produces works that are visually inspired and well acted. Opera is just as vibrant. Although the great Enrico Caruso never returned to San Francisco after the shock of the 1906 earthquake, plenty of other stars have aria'd their way through town, raising the local opera company to world-class heights. The **SF Symphony** is in a similar league, and while I'm bragging, I'd better mention the ballet. It, too, is as fine a company as you'll see anywhere. But don't let the big brands sway you from trying smaller stages outside the Civic Center, where experimental theater abounds.

Getting Arts Information Before You Go

Three or four weeks before you arrive, order the *San Francisco Chronicle* Sunday paper or a copy of *San Francisco* magazine; or, if you have access to the Internet, look up a local Web site (see Chapter 9).

Whether a particular performance sounds like something you'd enjoy is a trickier matter. On the Web you can search sites such as Citysearch (www.bayarea.citysearch.com) and the *San Francisco Chronicle* Web site (www.sfgate.com/listings) for reviews and synopses; otherwise, take your chances. You may stumble onto something wonderful. If you're looking for something outside the mainstream (and this is a fine place to find that), a month or so before your trip sign up for the hip, new e-mail list sf.flavorpill.net. This free, weekly e-mail highlights the more-elusive cultural events gracing the town, including films, concerts, and theater.

Ticket tips

For tickets to any theater, dance, symphony, or concert performance, you can call the appropriate box office directly and order with a credit card (charges are non-refundable if, for some reason, you don't show up). **City Box Office,** 153 Kearny St., Suite 402 (☎ **415-392-4400**), also sells tickets to most events. If you didn't order tickets before you arrived in town, visit **TIX Bay Area** (☎ **415-433-7827**) for half-price tickets for same-day performances (a $1 to $3 service charge is tacked on). TIX, which is also a **BASS Ticketmaster** outlet, is located on Union Square between Post and Geary streets. It's open Tuesday through Thursday from 11 a.m. to 6 p.m., Friday and Saturday until 7 p.m. If the Union Square renovation project is still underway when you visit, look for TIX in the parking garage.

Don't buy tickets from anyone outside TIX or a box office claiming to have discount or scalper tickets, especially to sporting events. Folks get duped all the time, forking over real cash for counterfeit tickets. Another common scam is to sell tickets to an event that has already taken place.

The concierge at your hotel can be a source for hard-to-get tickets. The larger the hotel, the more likely it is that the concierge will be successful, but in any case, it's worth asking. If he does manage to come through, a $5 to $10 tip is appropriate thanks.

If you're flexible about your plans for the evening, go to the box office of the theater you want to attend and stand in line for last-minute cancellations by season-ticket holders or the release of tickets held for media or VIPs. With luck, you can score seats in the orchestra. Without luck, you'll have wasted an hour or so.

The inside edge

Don't be late to the theater, symphony, or opera. Curtains rise on time, and if you're late, you won't be seated until there's a break in the action.

If you're attending a show at the Geary Theater, avoid the boxes on either side. They're positioned to obscure half the stage, generally the half where the action takes place.

As for what to wear, you'll see a little of everything from tailored evening clothes to jeans. People seem to dress up a bit more Friday and Saturday nights, especially in the orchestra seats, but your Sunday best isn't necessary.

Comings and goings

Cable cars will get you to Union Square theaters if you're coming from North Beach; from the Marina or Union Street, take a 30-Stockton or 45-Union/Stockton bus. If you prefer to take a cab to your lodgings afterward, walk to a big hotel to catch one. You can find a number of parking garages near Union Square with fees beginning at $10 for the evening.

You can reach the **Civic Center,** where the opera, ballet, and symphony are located, by any Muni Metro streetcar or any bus along Van Ness Avenue. I wouldn't walk around this area unescorted after dark to get back to the Muni station, and taxis aren't always immediately available. If you feel stuck, walk to one of the many nearby restaurants and ask the host to call a taxi for you. Relax, and prepare to wait a while at the bar. If you're driving, you can park in the garage on Grove Street between Franklin and Gough streets.

South of Market and Mission neighborhood venues (see "Broadway West: The Theater Scene" later in this chapter for venue listings) have troubles similar to **Civic Center.** You can usually get to the performance by public transportation, but returning late at night by bus is less interesting (or perhaps more interesting, depending on your perspective). Again, if you're attending a show in this area, don't expect to automatically hail a cab afterwards. Instead, walk to a nearby restaurant or bar and call. These numbers for local cab companies can help:

- ✔ **Desoto Cab:** ☎ 415-970-1300
- ✔ **Luxor Cabs:** ☎ 415-282-4141
- ✔ **Pacific:** ☎ 415-986-7220
- ✔ **Veteran's Cab:** ☎ 415-552-1300
- ✔ **Yellow Cab:** ☎ 415-626-2345

Broadway West: The Theater Scene

Yes, I am exaggerating, and no, I would never seriously compare our little theater district to the Great White Way in New York, but there are a fair number of professional stages in town. At least ten in varying sizes are housed around **Union Square,** and experimental theaters are scattered about the **South of Market** and **Mission** districts in converted warehouses and gallery spaces. Productions may include a musical or two, distinguished classics, and world-premiere comedies and dramas.

San Francisco Performing Arts

American Conservatory Theater
(Geary Theater) **11**
Beach Blanket Babylon (Club Fugazi) **2**
Curran Theater **10**
42nd St. Moon (Eureka Theatre) **3**
Golden Gate Theater **14**
Intersection for the Arts **19**
Lorraine Hansberry Theatre **6**
The Magic Theater **1**
New Conservatory Theater **17**
New Langton Arts **18**
Noontime Concerts (St. Patrick's Church) **12**
Old First Presbyterian Church **6**
Orpheum **15**
The Plush Room **5**
San Francisco Ballet **16**
San Francisco Opera **16**
San Francisco Symphony **4**
Smuin Ballets/SF
(Yerba Buena Center for the Arts) **13**
Theater Artaud **20**
Theatre on the Square **7**
Ticket Outlets:
City Box Office **8**
TIX Bay Area **9**

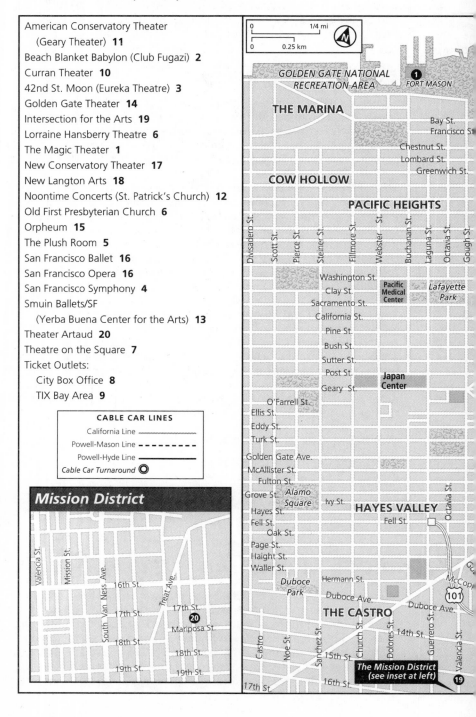

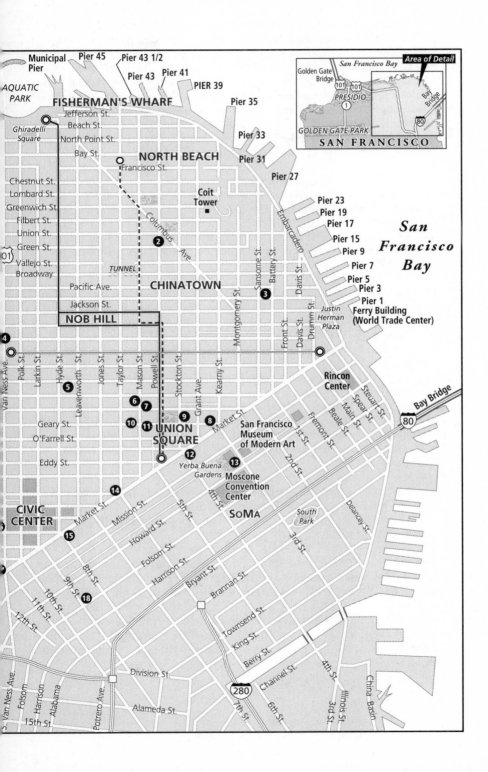

Municipal Pier

Pier 45
Pier 43 1/2
Pier 43
Pier 41
PIER 39
Pier 35
Pier 33
Pier 31
Pier 27

AQUATIC PARK

FISHERMAN'S WHARF
Jefferson St.
Beach St.
North Point St.
Bay St.

Ghirardelli Square

NORTH BEACH
Francisco St.

Chestnut St.
Lombard St.
Greenwich St.
Filbert St.
Union St.
Green St.
Vallejo St.
Broadway

Coit Tower

Columbus Ave.

2

TUNNEL

Pacific Ave.
Jackson St.

CHINATOWN

NOB HILL

Sansome St.
Battery St.

3

Montgomery St.

Front St.
Davis St.
Drumm St.

Embarcadero

Pier 23
Pier 19
Pier 17
Pier 15
Pier 9
Pier 7
Pier 5
Pier 3
Pier 1

San Francisco Bay

Justin Herman Plaza

Ferry Building (World Trade Center)

4

5

Van Ness Ave.
Polk St.
Larkin St.
Hyde St.
Leavenworth
Jones St.
Taylor St.
Mason St.
Powell St.
Stockton St.
Grant Ave.
Kearny St.

Rincon Center

6 7

Geary St.
O'Farrell St.

Eddy St.

10 11 UNION SQUARE

9 8

Market St.

San Francisco Museum of Modern Art

12

13

Yerba Buena Gardens
Moscone Convention Center

Stewart St.
Spear St.
Main St.
Beale St.
Fremont St.
1st St.
2nd St.

Bay Bridge

80

CIVIC CENTER

14

Market St.
Mission St.
5th St.
4th St.

SoMa

South Park

Delancey St.

15

Howard St.
Folsom St.
Harrison St.

3rd St.

8th St.
9th St.

18

Bryant St.
Brannan St.

10th St.
11th St.
12th St.

Townsend St.
King St.
Berry St.

4th St.
China Basin

Division St.

280

Alameda St.

Van Ness Ave.
Folsom
Harrison
Alabama
15th St.

7th St.
6th St.
3rd St.
Illinois St.

Channel St.

Area of Detail

San Francisco Bay

Golden Gate Bridge

101 101

PRESIDIO

1

GOLDEN GATE PARK

SAN FRANCISCO

Bay Bridge

80

The American Conservatory Theater (ACT) is the preeminent company in town and produces a wide variety of plays during its season, which runs October to June. The acting is first-rate, and the costumes and sets are universally brilliant. The choice of material ranges from new works by playwrights such as Tom Stoppard, can't-lose American chestnuts, and Shakespeare, all the way to not-quite-ready-for-prime-time dramas that still receive a careful rendering. The lovely **Geary Theater** is home to ACT productions. You'll find it at 415 Geary St., at Mason Street (☎ 415-749-2228). Ticket prices range from $11 to $55, and the box office is open every day from 10 a.m.

Broadway hits and road shows appear down the block at the **Curran Theater,** 445 Geary St., between Mason and Taylor streets (☎ 415-551-2000); the **Golden Gate Theater,** 1 Golden Gate Ave., at Market Street; and the **Orpheum,** 1192 Market St., at Eighth Street. The phone number listed for the Curran Theater is shared by all three venues, and the recorded message explains what's playing, where to buy tickets, and how to get to the theaters.

You may like your theater a lot less expensive and a little more cutting-edge. If so, check out **The Magic Theater** at Fort Mason Center, Bldg. A (☎ 415-441-8822), where Sam Shepard's Pulitzer Prize–winning play *Buried Child* premiered. Tickets range from $18 to $23. Or try **Intersection for the Arts,** a 72-seat theater in the Mission District at 446 Valencia St., between 15th and 16th streets (☎ 415-626-2787). Ticket prices run between $9 and $15.

The **Lorraine Hansberry Theatre** in the Sheehan Hotel, 620 Sutter St. (☎415-474-8800), features dramas and musicals by black authors such as Langston Hughes and August Wilson, and plays with African-American casts. Recent productions include *Ain't Misbehavin'* and Shakespeare's *Twelfth Night.*

Another Union Square stage tucked inside a hotel is **Theatre on the Square,** 450 Post St., where the Kensington Park Hotel is situated (☎415-433-9500). Lily Tomlin played there recently and the producers have excellent taste.

Close to Civic Center, in an impressive former Masonic Temple built in 1911, is the **New Conservatory Theater (NCT)** complex at 25 Van Ness Ave., a half block off Market Street (☎ 415-861-8972). NCT, which consists of three small theaters, presents a variety of productions throughout the year. From September through July is **"Pride Season,"** during which a series of six plays with gay themes are presented. The summer **Women's Festival** features plays by women writers. NTC also produces children's theater programming all year long.

Admirers of musical theater should keep an eye out for productions by **42nd Street Moon.** This company presents long-forgotten American musicals in concert format and gives audiences an opportunity to hear delightfully clever tunes that somehow "disappeared." Check the Web site (www.capybara.com/42ndStMoon) for shows and dates. Productions take place at the **Eureka Theatre,** 215 Jackson St., at Battery in the Financial District (☎ **415-243-9895**).

Classical Music and Opera

You can find many venues for listening to classical music in San Francisco. Local papers and Web sites are your best source for event listings. You can see major groups such as the **San Francisco Symphony,** which performs in the **Louise M. Davies Symphony Hall,** 201 Van Ness Ave., at Grove Street (☎ **415-864-6000**), in the Civic Center. The season runs from September through July, and tickets cost $15 to $78. Also at Civic Center is the **Herbst Theater,** 410 Van Ness Ave. (☎ **415-621-6600**), home to **San Francisco Performances** (www.sfperformances.org) and other professional groups.

You can also enjoy piano and violin duos, chamber music ensembles, and singers at **Old First Presbyterian Church,** 1751 Sacramento St., at Van Ness Avenue (☎ **415-474-1608**). These less formal concerts are scheduled afternoons and evenings, and tickets are a mere $9 to $12. The California Street cable car takes you to within two blocks of the church. If you're around **Yerba Buena Gardens** at lunchtime on a Wednesday, head to **St. Patrick's Church,** 756 Mission St., which is the site for ½-hour concerts produced by **Noontime Concerts** (☎ **415-777-3211**). These brief shows may be solo or full orchestral performances. Admission is $5. Noontime Concerts also uses the **A.P. Giannini Auditorium** at the Bank of America headquarters, 555 California St., in the Financial District. Concerts are currently held there on the second and fourth Tuesday of the month, but call for an updated schedule.

The San Francisco Opera opens its season with a gala in September and ends quietly in early January. Performances are produced in the **War Memorial Opera House,** 301 Van Ness Ave., at Grove Street (☎ **415-864-3330**), in the Civic Center. Tickets run from $10 to $140. **Pocket Opera** (☎ **415-575-1100**) delivers opera to the masses in stripped-down, English-language versions that are quite entertaining and highly professional. The season begins in February and ends in June; productions are held at different locations, so you'll need to phone for a schedule or check the Web site (www.pocketopera.com).

The Civic Center

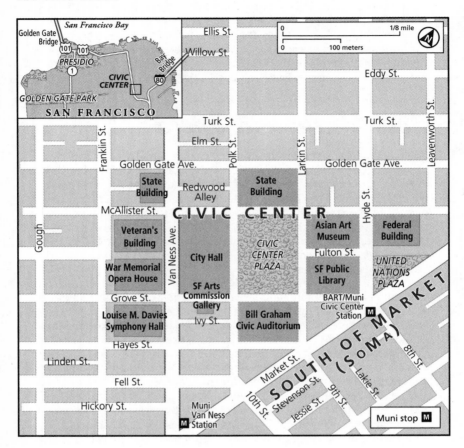

Ballet and Beyond

You can find plenty of classical and modern dance in San Francisco, the **San Francisco Ballet** being the best-known dance company. Their season runs from February to June and they perform in the War Memorial Opera House, 301 Van Ness Ave., at Grove Street. Call ☎ **415-865-2000** for tickets. Prices run from $7 for standing room to $100 for orchestra seats.

You can find an adventurous season of modern dance, performance art, and theater at the **Theater Artaud,** 450 Florida St., at 17th Street (☎ **415-621-7797**), in the Mission District. Ticket prices are $20 or less, depending on the day and type of show.

Some of the most interesting dance companies, including **Smuin Ballets/ SF,** appear on stage at the **Yerba Buena Center for the Arts,** 700 Howard St. (☎ 415-978-2787). It's easy to reach, and there are many fine restaurants in the neighborhood for pre– or post-theater supper.

New Langton Arts, a nonprofit, artist-run performance space in SoMa, may have an art show, a theater performance, video pieces, or all three at the same time — it's experimental and won't be mistaken for *Beach Blanket Babylon* in any case. Check it out at 1246 Folsom St., between Eighth and Ninth streets (☎415-626-5416). Gallery and box office hours are Wednesday through Saturday, noon to 5 p.m.

A San Francisco Institution: Beach Blanket Babylon!

You may not want to miss *Beach Blanket Babylon,* by now a San Francisco ritual. The musical revue is known for wildly imaginative hats that seem to live lives of their own. The spectacle is so popular that even after celebrating 27 years of poking fun at stars, politicians, and San Francisco itself, seats for the constantly updated shows are always sold out. Purchase tickets ($25 to $62) through TIX or by mail at least three weeks in advance (especially if you want to attend a weekend performance). You must be 21 to attend evening performances; minors are only admitted for Sunday matinees, when no liquor is sold. You can enjoy this spectacle in North Beach at Club Fugazi, 678 Green St., between Powell Street and Columbus Avenue (☎ 415-421-4222). You've got to see it to believe it.

Pre– and Post-Theater Dining

You have plenty of dining choices before attending any 8 p.m. performance. After the show, however, your dining choices are somewhat more limited. On Union Square, a branch of **The Cheesecake Factory** has arrived on the eighth floor of Macy's. It's open until 11 p.m. **The Grand Cafe** (reviewed in Chapter 14) also serves until 11 p.m. from a bar menu. If you're attending an event around Civic Center and want to eat before the show, be sure to make reservations. **The Hayes Street Grill** (reviewed in Chapter 14) originally opened to accommodate the culture crowd, and this restaurant has been joined by a great many more on and around Hayes Street. Down around Yerba Buena Center, **Bacar,** 448 Brannan, between Third and Fourth streets (☎ 415-904-4100), has the most extensive wine list around and serves tempting dishes like wok-cooked Maine lobster. **XYZ** at the W Hotel, 181 Third St., at Howard (☎ 415-817-7836), has a cafe as well as a restaurant so you can go casual or upscale, depending on how quickly you need to eat.

Chapter 22

Seeking Out the Nightlife

. . . .

In This Chapter

▶ Checking out the hippest clubs and bars for live music

▶ Shaking your thang at the hoppin'est dance clubs

▶ Aiming for atmosphere

▶ Getting a good laugh

▶ Broadening your horizons at some unique establishments

. . . .

*O*ne thing I love about this city: There's no end to the good times. You can have a night at the theater, followed by a night shimmying through a few bars and clubs, followed by a night listening to some great jazz. There are so many places for drinking and dancing and socializing, you'll have no excuse (except maybe exhaustion) for hanging around your hotel room.

Livin' It Up with Live Music

Bars, all of which by law must remain closed from 2 to 6 a.m., are self-explanatory. Clubs are a different story altogether. South of Market, dance clubs that have different styles and names may share the same space. For example, a particular club may feature 1970s-revisited disco catering to the Velvet Elvis crowd on Friday, and then play Gothic industrial "music" for body-piercing aficionados on Monday. Take a careful look at the listings in the *SF Weekly* or *Bay Guardian* so you'll know what you're getting into. Because most clubs don't get going until after 10 p.m., plan to take cabs anywhere not within walking distance of your hotel.

San Francisco Clubs & Bars

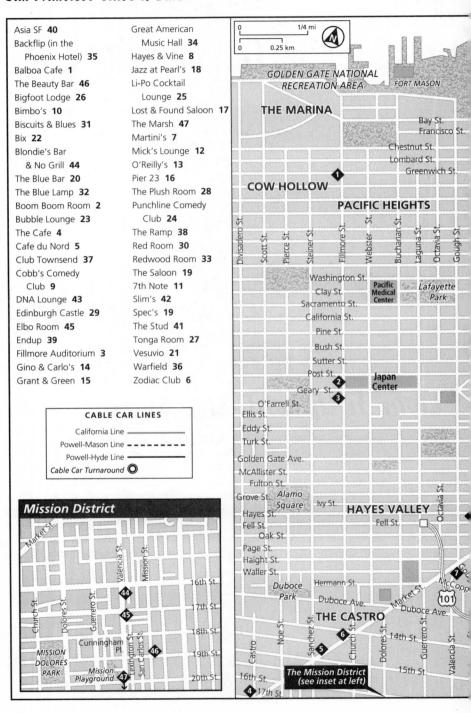

Asia SF **40**

Backflip (in the Phoenix Hotel) **35**

Balboa Cafe **1**

The Beauty Bar **46**

Bigfoot Lodge **26**

Bimbo's **10**

Biscuits & Blues **31**

Bix **22**

Blondie's Bar & No Grill **44**

The Blue Bar **20**

The Blue Lamp **32**

Boom Boom Room **2**

Bubble Lounge **23**

The Cafe **4**

Cafe du Nord **5**

Club Townsend **37**

Cobb's Comedy Club **9**

DNA Lounge **43**

Edinburgh Castle **29**

Elbo Room **45**

Endup **39**

Fillmore Auditorium **3**

Gino & Carlo's **14**

Grant & Green **15**

Great American Music Hall **34**

Hayes & Vine **8**

Jazz at Pearl's **18**

Li-Po Cocktail Lounge **25**

Lost & Found Saloon **17**

The Marsh **47**

Martini's **7**

Mick's Lounge **12**

O'Reilly's **13**

Pier 23 **16**

The Plush Room **28**

Punchline Comedy Club **24**

The Ramp **38**

Red Room **30**

Redwood Room **33**

The Saloon **19**

7th Note **11**

Slim's **42**

Spec's **19**

The Stud **41**

Tonga Room **27**

Vesuvio **21**

Warfield **36**

Zodiac Club **6**

CABLE CAR LINES

California Line ————

Powell-Mason Line – – – – – – –

Powell-Hyde Line ━━━━

Cable Car Turnaround ◎

Municipal Pier
Pier 45
Pier 43 1/2
Pier 43
Pier 41
PIER 39
Pier 35

AQUATIC PARK

FISHERMAN'S WHARF
Jefferson St.
Beach St.

Ghirardelli Square
North Point St.
Bay St.
NORTH BEACH
Francisco St.
Pier 33
Pier 31
Pier 27

Chestnut St.
Lombard St.
Greenwich St.
Filbert St.
Union St.
Green St.
Vallejo St.
Broadway

Coit Tower

Columbus Ave.

TUNNEL

Pacific Ave.
Jackson St.
CHINATOWN

NOB HILL

Sansome St.
Battery St.
Embarcadero

Pier 23
Pier 19
Pier 17
Pier 15
Pier 9
Pier 7
Pier 5
Pier 3
Pier 1
Ferry Building
(World Trade Center)

San Francisco Bay

Davis St.
Front St.
Drumm St.
Davis St.

Justin Herman Plaza

Van Ness Ave.
Polk St.
Larkin St.
Hyde St.
Jones St.
Taylor St.
Mason St.
Powell St.
Stockton St.
Grant Ave.
Kearny St.
Montgomery St.

Rincon Center

Bay Bridge
80

Geary St.
O'Farrell St.
Eddy St.
UNION SQUARE
Leavenworth St.

Market St.

San Francisco Museum of Modern Art

Steuart St.
Spear St.
Main St.
Beale St.
Fremont St.
1st St.
2nd St.

CIVIC CENTER

Yerba Buena Gardens
Moscone Convention Center
SoMa
South Park

Delancey St.

Market St.
Mission St.
Howard St.
Folsom St.
Harrison St.
8th St.
9th St.
10th St.
11th St.
12th St.
5th St.
4th St.
Bryant St.
Brannan St.
3rd St.

Townsend St.
King St.
Berry St.
Channel St.

Division St.
Alameda St.
280
7th St.
6th St.
4th St.
3rd St.
Illinois St.
China Basin

S. Van Ness Ave.
Folsom
Harrison
Alabama
15th St.
Potrero Ave.
Division St.

Area of Detail

San Francisco Bay
Golden Gate Bridge
101
101
PRESIDIO
1
GOLDEN GATE PARK
Bay Bridge
80
SAN FRANCISCO

Finding some cool jazz

Jazz at Pearl's, 256 Columbus Ave., at Broadway (☎ 415-291-8255), showcases a Monday Big Band Night and local jazz musicians Tuesday through Saturday. Pearl's also serves a menu of burgers, ribs, pizza, and other popular items. There's no cover charge, but there is a two-drink minimum. The ever-cool **Elbo Room,** 647 Valencia St., near 17th Street (☎ 415-552-7788), blasts acid jazz for a well-dressed younger crowd, or, depending on the night, you can move to Latin and funk bands. Cover starts at $3 upstairs; downstairs the bar has a fine menu of microbrews. The comfortably dark and hip **Blue Bar,** downstairs from the Black Cat restaurant at the corner of Kearny and Broadway (☎ 415-981-2233), serves from the upstairs menu, so you can sup while you listen to the band. There's no room for dancing, though. Cover is $5 to $10 depending on the band. Around Union Square, the **Blue Lamp,** 561 Geary St. (☎ 415-430-2160), has live jazz on Sundays and an acoustic open-mike event on Monday nights starting at 9:30 p.m. There's a cover charge of $2 to $4 Thursday through Saturday night.

Feelin' blue: Blues bars

The **Boom Boom Room,** 1601 Fillmore St., at Geary Street (☎ 415-673-8000), is open every night for dancing, cocktails, and jiving. Lines often form on the weekends, so it doesn't hurt to arrive on the early side and sip your drink slowly. Cover charges vary depending on the night and the act. Check the Web site (www.boomboomblues.com) for more information.

Follow the crowds to **The Saloon,** 1232 Grant Ave., at Fresno Street near Vallejo Street (☎ 415-989-7666), as your first stop on a walking tour of North Beach blues bars. If you can get close enough to get inside, the cover is usually around $4 to $5. Also in North Beach, check out the **Lost and Found Saloon,** 1353 Grant Ave., between Vallejo and Green streets, (☎ 415-675-5996). It's close to The Saloon and just as crowded weekend nights; there's no cover. **Grant & Green,** 1371 Grant Ave. (☎ 415-693-9565), is the third in the North Beach blues triumvirate. No cover here, either.

Jammin' with the locals

During the day, **Pier 23,** The Embarcadero, at Front Street (☎ 415-362-5125), serves lunch to fashionable business executives on the patio. At night, hot local blues and funk musicians play for fans ages 21 to 70. There's a $5 cover on weekends. A bit outside the tourist neighborhoods is **Storyville,** 1751 Fulton St., at Masonic Avenue (close to the upper Haight — take a cab), ☎ 415-441-1751. This bistro/dance club started out as a jazz venue but expanded to showcase hip-hop, soul, funk, and DJs. An inexpensive New Orleans–inspired dinner menu, served Thursday through Saturday night, is sincere if not exceptional. Cover ranges from none to $10. It's closed Sunday and Monday. Chief among our Irish bars is **Edinburgh Castle,** 950 Geary St., near Polk Street (☎ 415-885-4074), which hosts a mix of entertainment ranging from live music to readings. A pool table and active bar add to its stellar reputation. There's no cover charge.

Catching the big-name acts

You'll want to contact the box office directly or purchase tickets from **BASS** at ☎ 415-776-1999 for major acts. Ticket prices vary at the following clubs, depending on the performers.

The **Great American Music Hall,** 859 O'Farrell St., near Polk Street (☎ 415-885-0750), books everything from rhythm and blues to Cajun bands to Grammy Award–winning artists such as Bonnie Raitt. Although you'll notice the club isn't in a squeaky-clean neighborhood, safety isn't a problem because so many people are going in and out of the place. If you're driving, use the valet in front (if available) or park in the AMC 1000 garage across the street. Take a cab home after the show if you aren't driving. You can find the club schedule on the Web at www.musichallsf.com (you can also order tickets online).

It won't be the Grateful Dead, but you can find out who's playing **The Fillmore,** 1805 Geary St., at Fillmore Street, by checking out its Web site (www.thefillmore.com) or by calling the box office at ☎ 415-346-6000. **The Warfield,** 982 Market St. (☎ 415-775-7722), is a huge theater that hosts big-time musicians, mostly rock 'n' roll. **Slim's,** 333 11th St., between Folsom and Harrison streets (☎ 415-522-0333), is a smaller, fairly comfortable club owned by singer Boz Scaggs, who plays here every now and then. A much bigger room that some grownups I know find extra-palatable is **Bimbo's 365 Club,** in North Beach at 1025 Columbus Ave., at Chestnut Street (☎ 415-474-0365). It's a roomy, '30s-style ballroom with an ornate bar and an attendant in the ladies' restroom. Music varies from rock to alternative, and you can check the schedule at www.bimbos365club.com. **Bottom of the Hill,** 1233 17th St., at Texas Street (☎ 415-621-4455; Internet www.bottomofthehill.com), is a small venue that caters to nationally known indie rock acts. This Potrero Hill–based club also serves bar and grill food and hosts an all-you-can-eat barbecue/music hoedown Sunday afternoons. You can get there on the 22-Fillmore or 19-Polk buses.

Moving Your Feet

The Ramp, 855 China Basin, off Third Street at Mariposa Street (☎ 415-621-2378), is an indoor/outdoor bar/restaurant. It isn't open year-round, but between May and October you can dance to live jazz on Fridays from 5:30 to 8:00 p.m. Saturdays feature salsa bands, and Sundays bring world music (both days from 4:30 to 7:30 p.m.). There's no cover charge. The ultra-hip but friendly **Cafe du Nord,** 2170 Market St., at Sanchez Street (☎ **415-861-5016;** Internet: www.cafedunord.com), is a basement-level club and restaurant that features swing to experimental dance bands or DJs every evening. Cover runs from $3 to $7. The restaurant serves Wednesday through Sunday. Under-21 bohemians are allowed in if accompanied by adults. **DNA Lounge,** 375 11th St., at Harrison Street (☎ **415-626-1409;** Internet: www.dnalounge.com), holds popular 1970s dance parties on Saturday nights, other styles on other nights. Cover is around $12 on weekends.

Swing and ballroom dancers, and those who've never completely let go of their Ginger Rogers fantasies, will adore the **Metronome Ballroom,** 1830 17th St. (☎ **415-252-9000;** Internet: www.metronomeballroom. com). You can swoop by at 7:30 p.m. to take a class, and then stay for a dance party on Friday, Saturday, and Sunday night, or simply arrive at 9 p.m. to trip the light fantastic. This is strictly a social dancing venue; only snacks and nonalcoholic beverages are available. There's a cover charge of $7 to $9.

There's much more to local nightlife than South of Market dance halls. For a little fiesta in the Mission District, reserve a seat on **El Volado,** the Mexican Bus (www.mexicanbus.com), as it cruises the dance clubs. The $35 ticket price includes cover charges at three clubs. Call ☎ **415-546-3747** for reservations two or three weeks ahead. **El Volado** rides Friday and Saturday night. Thursday is Salsa Picante Night. The $35 charge includes a salsa lesson as well as club cover charges.

Sunday afternoons in the Mission call out for a *cervaza* on the patio at **El Rio,** 3158 Mission St. (☎ **415-282-3325**), where they pack 'em in for salsa parties. Thursday nights, drop by to listen and dance to Middle Eastern music. Usually there's no cover; for special events they sometimes charge $4 or $5.

Drinking in the Atmosphere

San Francisco undeniably offers a special ambience. From coffee shops and dance clubs to art galleries and restaurants, there's something to appeal to every persuasion. If atmosphere is what you're after, check out these favorites:

Hitting the singles scene

The **Balboa Cafe,** 3199 Fillmore St., between Greenwich and Filbert (☎ **415-921-3944**), has withstood the test of time. The bar/restaurant gets lots of repeat customers — they come here after every divorce. In and around the Tenderloin, they line up to enter the **Red Room,**

827 Sutter St., between Jones and Leavenworth streets, next door to the Commodore Hotel (☎ **415-346-7666**). Look sharp. **Backflip,** at the Phoenix Hotel, 601 Eddy St., at Larkin Street (☎ **415-771-3547**), is to blue what the Red Room is to . . . well, you can guess. Good cocktail fare, house music nightly, and the staff wears vinyl. **Blondie's Bar and No Grill,** 540 Valencia St., between 16th and 17th streets (☎ **415-864-2419**), is on the sizzling Valencia Street corridor in the Mission District. The young and the restless make good use of the free jazz jukebox. The **Make-Out Room,** also in the Mission at 3225 22nd St. (☎ **415-647-2888**), attracts a very attractive, young crowd and features alternative bands (cover ranges from free to about $6).

Check out a four-hour, four-club tour, **Three Babes and a Bus** (www.threebabes.com), for a great time on a Saturday night. It's hassle-free — no parking to deal with and no lines. Local gals in cele-bratory moods usually fill the luxury tour bus, and the fun is infectious. The $35-per-person fee includes club cover charges, VIP entry, and transportation to and from Union Square. Call ☎ **800-414-0158** for reservations at least a week in advance.

Mixing with the sophisticates

A cool Art Deco supper club, **Bix,** 56 Gold St., off Montgomery Street between Pacific and Jackson streets in the Financial District (☎ **415-433-6300**), will make you want to wear a bias-cut gown and appear very glamorous. The **Redwood Room,** at the Clift Hotel, 495 Geary St., at Jones Street (☎ **415-775-4700**), isn't the same as in my mother's day (and yes, I am perturbed), but the clientele appears like it dropped in from a *Vanity Fair* photo shoot. The **Tonga Room** at the Fairmont Hotel, 950 Mason St., at California Street (☎ **415-772-5278**), features a happy hour buffet weekdays from 5 to 7 p.m. For the price of a drink (about $7) you can enjoy hors d'oeuvres and entertainment — a tropical rain-storm hits every half hour. Okay, okay, maybe that isn't so sophisti-cated, but at least it's cheap.

The Plush Room, inside the York Hotel, 940 Sutter St., between Hyde and Leavenworth streets (☎ **415-885-2800**), features torch and stan-dards singers of some repute. (More than one songbird has started a career in this intimate room and ended up playing clubs in New York City.) At other times, you may find a musical revue or duo. Cover is around $15, with a two-drink minimum. This is one of my favorite clubs, but then I also like Mel Tormé.

Finding places to entertain the kids

Biscuits and Blues, 410 Mason St., at Geary Street (☎ **415-292-2583**), is near the theater district on Union Square in a basement room. The all-ages venue has inexpensive food ($9.95 entrees), and the music — blues musicians of varied repute — is really good. If you aren't dining here, cover starts at $4. The **Great American Music Hall,** 859 O'Farrell St., near Polk Street in the Tenderloin (☎ **415-885-0750**), allows children over 6 into some shows; call for an events calendar to see who's playing an early show. Because it offers food service, **Jazz at Pearl's,** 256 Columbus Ave., at Broadway (☎ **415-291-8255**), can also accommodate minors. The same is true of **Slim's.** (See "Catching the big-name acts," earlier in this chapter.)

Laughing it up: Comedy clubs

I probably don't have to remind you that San Francisco is where Robin Williams got his start. Although the city is no longer the hotbed of chuckles that it was in the 1970s, the comedy clubs are still packin' 'em in. Bring along your monologue — you never know when an open mike may beckon you.

Cobb's Comedy Club, 2801 Leavenworth at The Cannery (☎ **415-928-4320;** Internet:www.cobbscomedyclub.com), has shows Tuesday through Sunday and a three-hour marathon of comics on Monday nights. A Cajun/Creole restaurant is now part of the mix; inquire about getting into the show free if you eat dinner there. No one under 16 admitted; tickets range from $7 to $20. Next door to Embarcadero 1 is the **Punchline Comedy Club,** 444 Battery St., between Washington and Clay streets (☎ **415-397-7573**). Local and nationally known comics play here Tuesday through Sunday at 9 and 11 p.m. These shows are only open to folks 18 and over; tickets range from $5 to $15. The Valencia Street corridor in the Mission District is one hot property, but before it was the place to be, it was the longtime 'hood of **The Marsh,** 1062 Valencia St. (☎ **415-641-0235;** Internet: www.themarsh.org), a complex of theaters devoted to developing performances. On Friday and Saturday nights in one of these theaters, you'll find the **Mock Café,** with scheduled performers at 8 and 10 p.m. and open mike at 9 p.m., for a cover charge of $7. You won't normally find the polished acts that show up at the other clubs (although Robin Williams himself makes the occasional appearance), but you'll certainly be closer to the cutting edge of comedy. Monday nights showcase works-in-progress.

Defying Categorization: Unique Bars

A manicure *and* a martini can be yours at **The Beauty Bar,** 2299 Mission St., at 19th Street (☎ **415-285-0323**), where the decor is straight out of a 1959 beauty parlor. (In case you were wondering where all those enormous hair dryers with the hoods ended up, look no further.) Wednesday through Friday happy hour from 6 to 10 p.m. includes a manicurist making the rounds. There's a drag show every other Thursday night. Our local suburbanites join the fun on the weekends, and during the week around midnight, hipsters drape themselves over the chrome barstools to exude cool.

If you have stars in your eyes, you may enjoy a gin-and-tonic at the **Zodiac Club,** 718 14th St., around Church and Sanchez streets (☎ 415-626-STAR). This is a locals' hangout with Mediterranean-style eats (served until midnight), high-quality booze, and a DJ on Sunday and occasional Thursday nights. **Li-Po Cocktail Lounge,** 916 Grant Ave., at Washington Street (☎ 415-982-0072), is an authentic, dark, Chinatown dive, complete with dusty Asian furnishings, a huge rice-paper lantern, and a shrine to Buddha behind the bar. If you want to drink with professionals, head to North Beach and grab a bar stool at **Gino and Carlo's,** 548 Green St., between Columbus and Grant avenues (☎ 415-421-0896), which opens early so the regulars can get in a fortifying scotch before lunch. **Spec's,** 12 Saroyan Alley, off Columbus Avenue and Broadway (☎ 415-421-4112), is another North Beach institution — dark and dingy, but historic.

Fancy yourself an undiscovered singing sensation? Make your way to the back room at **Martuni's,** 4 Valencia St., at Market (☎415-241-0205), where customers croon and the piano player is kind.

Missing Guinness? Head to **O'Reilly's,** 622 Green St. (☎ 415-989-6222), an Irish pub (no kidding), with the two-toned stout, weekend brunch, and an authentic crowd of employed locals. Literary types always make a pilgrimage to **Vesuvio,** also in North Beach, where Jack Kerouac passed the time. It's at 255 Columbus (☎ 415-362-3370), next to Kerouac Alley, where the author used to pass out.

Wine aesthetes can hover at the bar comparing flights or simply quaffing by the glass at **Hayes and Vine,** a lovely wine bar with a world-beat list and knowledgeable staff. It's near Civic Center at 377 Hayes St. (☎ 415-626-5301). Champagne lovers unite in the Financial District at the **Bubble Lounge,** 714 Montgomery St. (☎415-434-4204). The bar has over 300 sparkling wines, plush sofas, and an array of financial-center types reminiscing over their expense accounts.

If you're around Polk Street for dinner, stop in afterward at the new **Bigfoot Lodge,** a retro, log-cabin-like bar with good taped music, a cool crowd of singles, and a wooden likeness of Bigfoot, as we imagine him to be. Find all this and more at 1750 Polk St., near Washington Street (☎ 415-440-2355).

Tracking Down Gay and Lesbian Bars and Clubs

In this section, I give you a short list of the many clubs and bars that cater to the gay and lesbian community in the city. Find specific listings in the weekly entertainment guides, *SF Weekly* and *Bay Guardian,* and look for the free *Bay Area Reporter* in bookstores, cafes, and bars around town.

The Cafe, 2367 Market St., near Castro (☎ **415-861-3846**), is currently *the* place for both sexes to go dancing. It's also *the* place to stand in line on busy weekend nights. **The Stud,** 399 Ninth St., at Harrison Street (☎ **415-863-6623**), is a long-time institution in the city. Different nights feature different music, but Tuesdays are infamous for "Trannyshack" hosted by Heklina. (And if you're scratching your head in wonder, perhaps you don't want to know.) Cover $2 to $6 on weekends. **Endup** is another gay icon, a hangout as well as a dance club. Located south of Market at 401 Sixth St. (☎ **415-357-0827**), it's a San Francisco institution like the cable cars or Coit Tower. Cover is $5.

Part VII

Exploring beyond San Francisco: Great Day and Overnight Trips

The 5th Wave   By Rich Tennant

"The problem with wine tastings is you're not supposed to swallow, and Clifford refuses to spit. Fortunately, he studied trumpet with Dizzy Gillespie."

In this part . . .

You'd think it would be enough for me to help you plan your trip to San Francisco, a marvel among big cities, but no . . . I toss in a few extra treats for your dining and sightseeing pleasure. Chief among them are the gorgeous Napa and Sonoma valleys, where the sights and scents of grapes and olives act like a restorative. Closer still is Berkeley, a microcosm of Northern California life that revolves around the university and a vibrant dining scene. Finally, nature boys and girls will have a veritable field day hiking or relaxing on the coast in verdant Point Reyes and Inverness.

Chapter 23

Checking Out Berkeley

· ·

In This Chapter

▶ Amusing yourself around town

▶ Taking advantage of shopping opportunities

▶ Satisfying your hunger

· ·

A s you approach Berkeley, a mere 20 minutes over the Bay Bridge, you'll know you aren't in San Francisco anymore. The weather is an immediate giveaway — while the temperature isn't dramatically different, San Francisco's ever-present summer fog disappears. Berkeley is also smaller, and much of its cultural life revolves around the University of California at Berkeley (UCB) campus. One thing both cities have in common is a devotion to fine dining. In fact, one excellent reason to visit Berkeley is to eat a great meal.

Getting There

You can use BART to reach Berkeley, but taking a car is better. Most people drive over the Bay Bridge and follow the signs to Highway 80. The exits include Ashby Avenue, University, and Gilman. If you intend to begin your day on Fourth Street (see "Shopping delights" later in this chapter), take the University Avenue exit. If you intend to make the University your first stop, an alternate route is Highway 24, exiting on scenic Claremont Avenue. Claremont intersects College Avenue, which leads directly to the campus while avoiding the less handsome flatlands of Berkeley. If you visit on a Thursday, you get free admission to UCB museums and the botanical garden.

Doing Berkeley

To my mind, an ideal day in Berkeley revolves around lunch or dinner at **Chez Panisse** (see "Dining Pleasures"). The food is as close to perfect as food gets. The question, then, is how do you keep busy before your reservation? If it's for dinner, you can easily fritter away your time shopping on **Fourth Street** (see "Shopping delights"), walking around

Tilden Park, and seeing what's up at the **University campus.** If you've made lunch reservations, break up the day by touring UCB in the morning and hiking in Tilden Park or checking out the merchandise on **Telegraph Avenue** or Fourth Street in the afternoon.

Seeing the sights

The attractive, active campus of **University of California at Berkeley** is the biggest sight in Berkeley, so to speak. The **Visitor Information Center** is at 101 University Hall, 220 University Ave., at Oxford Street (☎ 510-642-5215). You can join a free 10 a.m. campus tour there Monday through Friday.

Other notable UCB stops include the **Hearst Museum of Anthropology** (☎ 510-642-3682; open Wednesday through Sunday; admission $2 adults, $1 seniors, 50¢ children, free on Thursdays), the **University Art Museum** at 2625 Durant Ave. (☎ 510-642-0808; open Wednesday through Sunday; admission $6 adults, $4 seniors and children), and the 307-foot-tall **Sather Tower** (also known as the Campanile) in the center of campus, where you can take an elevator to the top for excellent views of Berkeley and the bay (open daily; admission: $2 adults, $1.50 kids 12–17, $1 kids 3–11).

Above the campus in the lush hills is the **UC Berkeley Botanical Garden** (☎ 510-642-3343). It features 13,000 plants, including cactus and rose gardens. A good place for an easy hike. Farther up the road, the kid-friendly **Lawrence Hall of Science** (☎ 510-642-5132; open daily; admission: $8 adults, $6 seniors and students, $4 kids 3 to 4) brings science up close and personal.

The campus is bounded by shops, cafes, and well-stocked bookstores. To get a sense of Berkeley street life, walk along **Telegraph Avenue** from Bancroft to Ashby, and get your fill of cappuccino, street vendors, psychic readers, and the occasional weirdo. And consider taking a breather in **O₂ Bar House**, a funky two-level club where patrons relax while breathing flavored air through their own personal nose cord. (It makes a nice souvenir.) The bar is located at 2525A Telegraph Ave., and it's open weekdays from 3 to 11 p.m., weekends from 1 to 11 p.m.

Shopping delights

Close to the University exit off I-80 is **Fourth Street,** a little Mecca for shoppers from all over the Bay Area. It started out small, with a few outlet stores and a popular diner, but over the years it developed into a full-fledged destination for fashion, food, and home decor. Begin by oohing over the gorgeous accessories for home and garden at **The Gardener,** 1836 Fourth St. (☎ 510-548-4545; open daily), and keep going on down the block.

Berkeley

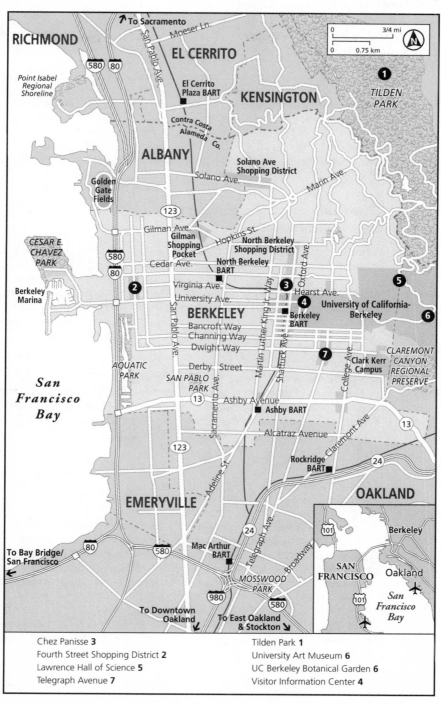

RICHMOND

To Sacramento

Moeser Ln.

San Pablo Ave.

580 80

EL CERRITO

KENSINGTON

Point Isabel
Regional
Shoreline

El Cerrito
Plaza BART

TILDEN
PARK

1

Contra Costa
Alameda Co.

ALBANY

Solano Ave
Shopping District

Golden
Gate
Fields

Solano Ave.

Marin Ave.

123

Gilman Ave.

CESAR E.
CHAVEZ
PARK

Gilman
Shopping
Pocket

Hopkins St.

North Berkeley
Shopping District

Oxford Ave.

Cedar Ave.

North Berkeley
BART

5

Berkeley
Marina

2

Virginia Ave.

University Ave.

3

Hearst Ave.

4

6

Martin Luther King Jr. Way

BERKELEY

Bancroft Way

Berkeley
BART

University of California-
Berkeley

Shattuck Ave.

Channing Way

Dwight Way

AQUATIC
PARK

Derby Street

SAN PABLO
PARK

7

College Ave.

Clark Kerr
Campus

CLAREMONT
CANYON
REGIONAL
PRESERVE

*San
Francisco
Bay*

13

Ashby Avenue

Sacramento Ave.

Ashby BART

Alcatraz Avenue

123

Claremont Ave.

13

Rockridge
BART

24

Adeline St.

EMERYVILLE

OAKLAND

24

Telegraph Ave.

101

Berkeley

To Bay Bridge/
San Francisco

80

580

Mac Arthur
BART

Broadway

SAN
FRANCISCO

Oakland

MOSSWOOD
PARK

101

*San
Francisco
Bay*

980

580

To Downtown
Oakland

To East Oakland
& Stockton

Chez Panisse **3**	Tilden Park **1**
Fourth Street Shopping District **2**	University Art Museum **6**
Lawrence Hall of Science **5**	UC Berkeley Botanical Garden **6**
Telegraph Avenue **7**	Visitor Information Center **4**

0   3/4 mi
0   0.75 km
N

Dining Pleasures

Bette's Oceanview Diner
$ AMERICAN

You can sit down here for a homey breakfast or lunch featuring tender baked goods, tasty salads, and Bette's famous pancakes. Expect huge crowds and a long wait on the weekends. Next door, Bette's sells take-out sandwiches, salads, and desserts, to take care of impatient hungry people.

1807 Fourth St., Berkeley. ☎ *510-644-3230. No reservations. Main courses: $5.95–8.95. MC, V. Open: Mon–Thur 6:30 a.m.–2:30 p.m.; Fri–Sun 6:30 a.m.–4:00 p.m.*

Chez Panisse and Chez Panisse Café
$$$$ CALIFORNIA

Alice Waters, the owner of Chez Panisse, is an icon in the food world, respected for adhering to her vision of food as a gift we give daily to our loved ones (including you) and for serving beautifully constructed dishes. Eating here in the cafe or restaurant is one of the nicer things you'll do for yourself. Dinner downstairs is $45 to $75 prix fixe, depending on the night. The cafe is moderately priced, comparatively speaking, but expect to spend a lot more than you think prudent for lunch. It's worth it.

1517 Shattuck Ave., Berkeley. ☎ *510-548-5525; Internet:* www.chezpanisse. com. *Advance reservations a must for dinner in the restaurant; recommended for dinner in the cafe. AE, DC, MC, V. Main courses: $45–$75 prix fixe downstairs; $16–$19 in the cafe. Open: Restaurant Mon–Sat 6:00–9:30 p.m.; cafe Mon–Thur 11:30 a.m.–3:00 p.m. and 5:00–10:30 p.m., Fri–Sat 11:30 a.m.–3:30 p.m. and 5:00–11:30 p.m.*

Cafe Rouge
$$$ MEDITERRANEAN

Those living in the Fourth Street neighborhood don't have many reasons to stray. Everything you need is nearby, including a lovely meal in this French-style bistro opened by a kitchen alumnus of Chez Panisse. Meat eaters will be greatly charmed by the menu (go admire the butcher counter in the back), while mollusk fans can turn happily to the oysters. Desserts shine as well.

1782 Fourth St., Berkeley. ☎ *510-525-1440; Internet:* www.caferouge.net. *Reservations advised. Main courses: $15–$30. AE, MC, V. Open: Mon 11:30 a.m.– 2:00 p.m.; Tues–Sun 11:30 a.m.–10:00 p.m.*

Chapter 24

Coastal Scenes: Point Reyes and Inverness

. . . .

In This Chapter

▶ Avoiding the crowds

▶ Going where the wild things are

▶ Eating and lodging in the woods

. . . .

A one-hour drive through the small towns of Marin County and Samuel P. Taylor State Park leads you to **Point Reyes National Seashore,** a mix of wild coastline and forest of unequivocal appeal to hikers, nature lovers, and wildlife-watchers. The rocky shore along this part of the coast is a direct result of earthquake activity — you can even get a close-up look at the San Andreas fault. **Point Reyes Station,** the minuscule town nearby, is a bit of a tourist magnet on the weekends, so you can find a selection of excellent restaurants and interesting shops within its four-block radius. **Inverness,** a tiny community on Tomales Bay, a few miles farther north, has a handful of picturesque inns and B&Bs.

Deciding When to Visit

When planning your trip, keep in mind that the **Point Reyes Lighthouse** is closed Tuesdays and Wednesdays. If you can manage to come later in the week (avoiding the crowded weekends), you'll be treated to relatively empty roads, even during the summer. The best times to view seasonal flora and fauna in **Point Reyes National Seashore** area are as follows:

✔ **Wildflowers:** February through July

✔ **Elephant seals:** November through March

✔ **Harbor seals:** Mid-March through mid-June

✔ **Gray whales:** January through March

Point Reyes National Seashore

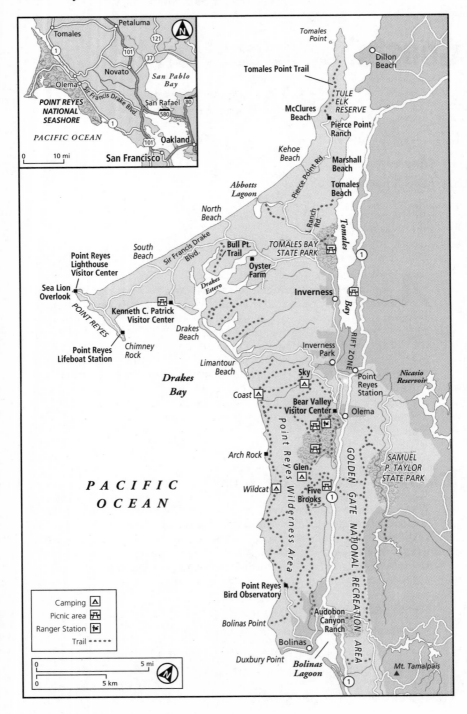

Petaluma

Tomales

121

101

Novato

37

San Pablo
Bay

Olema

Sir Francis Drake Blvd

San Rafael

80

POINT REYES
NATIONAL
SEASHORE

580

1

PACIFIC OCEAN

101

Oakland

0   10 mi

San Francisco

Tomales
Point

Dillon
Beach

Tomales Point Trail

TULE
ELK
RESERVE

McClures
Beach

Pierce Point
Ranch

Kehoe
Beach

Marshall
Beach

Pierce Point Rd.

Abbotts
Lagoon

Tomales
Beach

North
Beach

L Ranch Rd.

Tomales

South
Beach

Sir Francis Drake Blvd.

Bull Pt.
Trail

TOMALES BAY
STATE PARK

1

Point Reyes
Lighthouse
Visitor Center

Oyster
Farm

Drakes
Estero

Inverness

Bay

Sea Lion
Overlook

Kenneth C. Patrick
Visitor Center

POINT REYES

Drakes
Beach

RIFT ZONE

Point Reyes
Lifeboat Station

Chimney
Rock

Inverness
Park

Nicasio
Reservoir

Limantour
Beach

Sky

Point
Reyes
Station

Drakes
Bay

Coast

Bear Valley
Visitor Center

Olema

Point Reyes Wilderness Area

GOLDEN GATE NATIONAL RECREATION AREA

Arch Rock

Glen

SAMUEL
P. TAYLOR
STATE PARK

PACIFIC
OCEAN

Wildcat

Five
Brooks

1

Point Reyes
Bird Observatory

Camping

Picnic area

Ranger Station

Trail

Bolinas Point

Audobon
Canyon
Ranch

Bolinas

Duxbury Point

Bolinas
Lagoon

Mt. Tamalpais

1

0   5 mi

0   5 km

And another word of advice: Bring warm clothes. The weather in Point Reyes is often cold and sometimes foggy in the summer.

Getting to the Point

To reach Point Reyes, cross the Golden Gate Bridge and exit on San Anselmo/Sir Francis Drake Boulevard. Then turn left, heading west on Sir Francis Drake, and stay on this road as it passes through the high-priced burgs of San Anselmo, Ross, Woodacre, and Lagunitas. It takes about an hour (with light traffic) to reach seashore headquarters.

We're Here — Now What?

At the junction of Highway 1 and Sir Francis Drake Boulevard in Olema, follow the signs to the **Bear Valley Visitor Center** (☎ 415-663-1092), about one minute away. The Center has maps, informative park rangers, a book/gift section, and some interesting exhibits on the ecology of the area. Many trails begin here, including an under-1-mile earthquake trail along the San Andreas Fault. Another park attraction is **Kule Loklo,** a Coast Miwok Native Indian village replica.

Hiking is the prime activity in the park, but a drive to **Limantour Beach** is another option. You get to the beach by turning left on Bear Valley Road and left again on Limantour Road. Swimming is not recommended (and it's usually too cold), but you can bird-watch and picnic here.

Point Reyes Lighthouse is a big attraction in these parts all year long, but especially from January through March when migrating gray whales pass by. From the Bear Valley Visitor Center, the lighthouse is a 20.5-mile drive along Sir Francis Drake Boulevard through dairy farms and pastures. At the end of the road is a parking lot. The lighthouse is a half-mile walk away, and down 300 steps. The cliffs all around this area are not stable enough to climb on, and you'll see lots of warnings to that effect. **Sea Lion Overlook** near the lighthouse is the place to watch those creatures as well as harbor seals.

From this stop, it's a short drive to **Drake's Beach** (just follow the signs as you drive to or from the lighthouse). Another fine visitor center with friendly park rangers is on the beach parking lot, next to a cafe specializing in fried foods. As is the case at all the area beaches, there is no lifeguard on duty and the undertow can be dangerous, so swimming is not encouraged. At the end of Drake's Beach, past the Point Reyes Lifeboat Station, is **Chimney Rock.** The **Elephant Seal Overlook** nearby is a good vantage point for observing elephant seals in the winter months.

At the northernmost tip of the seashore at **Tomales Point** is the **Tule Elk Reserve,** where over 500 of these once-nearly-extinct creatures live on 2,600 protected acres. The reserve is a 30-minute drive from

Inverness. Stay on Sir Francis Drake Boulevard until you reach Pierce Point Road, which takes you directly into the reserve.

If you happen to be making this trip in August in warmer weather, with or without kids, there are some wonderful swimming beaches along Tomales Bay in Inverness. Look for signs along Sir Francis Drake Boulevard leading to **Chicken Ranch Beach** or **Shell Beach.**

We've Got Tonight . . .

For more inn or B&B choices, contact Point Reyes Lodging (☎ **800-539-1872;** Internet:www.ptreyes.com).

Manka's Inverness Lodge
$$$ **Inverness**

Inverness consists of a few stores and restaurants, private homes, and some inns. At the high end is Manka's, a handsomely rustic, 80-year-old former hunting and fishing lodge that looks as if Ralph Lauren would feel at home there. Rooms contain fireplaces, comfy beds, privacy, and that woodsy feeling Red Riding Hood's grandmother must have known and loved. Manka's is also known for its $48 to $68 gourmet prix-fixe dinners served Thursday through Monday — it's by far the best place in town to eat.

Argyle Road, Inverness. ☎ 415-669-1034; Internet: www.mankas.com. *Rack rates: $185–$465 double; two-night minimum on weekends. Call months ahead for reservations. MC, V. Look for the sign pointing to Argyle Road, off Sir Francis Drake Boulevard.*

Eating at the Point

If you're hungry or want to gather a picnic, continue on Sir Francis Drake Boulevard until it meets Point Reyes–Petaluma Road. Drive across the little bridge and you'll be in Point Reyes Station. The **Pine Cone Diner,** 60 Fourth St. (☎ **415-663-1536**), is open for breakfast, lunch, and dinner. **The Station House,** 111180 State Route 1 (☎ **415-663-1515**), is also immensely popular and moderately priced (and there's live music on Friday, Saturday, and Sunday nights). For takeout, **Tomales Bay Foods,** 80 Fourth St. (☎ **415-663-9335**), has a small but fantastic menu of seasonal salads and sandwiches ready to go. It shares a building with a small creamery and a shop featuring lovely handwoven clothing.

Chapter 25

California Wine Country

● ●

In This Chapter

▶ Finding your way to Wine Country

▶ Exploring great wineries

▶ Tasting wine like a pro

▶ Enjoying other valley pastimes

▶ Lodging and dining in the best places

● ●

*A*bout an hour's drive north of San Francisco is the gorgeous Napa Valley, America's most celebrated wine-growing region. Less than 30 miles from end to end, this fertile area brims with world-class wine-tasting rooms, excellent restaurants, and marvelous resorts and inns.

Just to the west of Napa Valley along Highway 12 is the peaceful Sonoma Valley. Sonoma Valley is quieter and less tourist-oriented — but equal to its neighbor as a wine-growing region. Although both counties are vacation destinations, many visitors arrive for a day of wine tasting and then turn around and head back to San Francisco. That's not the ideal way to get the most out of this bucolic piece of earth. If at all possible, stay a few days to relax and renew before heading back to tackle the big city.

The Taste of a Lifetime: Planning a Visit to Wine Country

This chapter tells you everything you need to know to tour the wineries and outlines the etiquette of wine tasting. To get a jump on the intricacies of wine making and tasting, call **Beaulieu Vineyard** (☎ 707-963-2411) and request a copy of *From the Grapes to the Glass* by Helene Le Blanc. For $7.95 plus postage, the winery will mail you this beginner's guide to wine. Another great book is *Wine For Dummies,* 2nd Edition, by Ed McCarthy and Mary Ewing-Mulligan.

The Wine Country

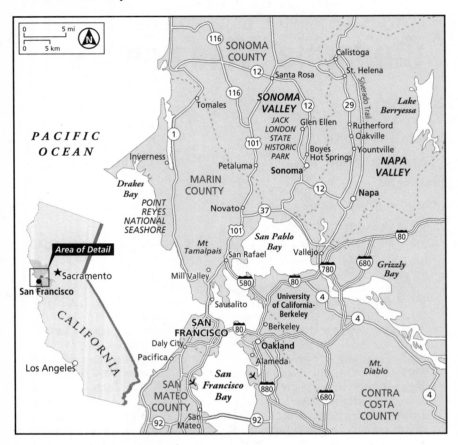

Journeying to Wine Country

Earlier in this book, I warn you against renting a car during your stay in San Francisco. In this chapter, I change my mind — for your Wine Country tour, anyway, because the best way to tour Napa or Sonoma Valley is by car (see Chapter 9 for car rental information). If you really don't want to drive, you can join an organized tour. But if you're interested in spending a night or two in Sonoma or in one of the charming towns near Napa, or if you want to visit smaller, less commercial wineries than those the tour companies choose, you will need to drive yourself.

You can take one of two roads to get there. The faster, less scenic route is across the San Francisco–Oakland Bay Bridge (I-80). The more scenic route crosses the Golden Gate Bridge and meanders up through Marin County on U.S. 101. For the return trip, from Napa, I highly recommend taking I-80 rather than U.S. 101 over the Golden Gate Bridge, especially if you're traveling on a weekend. But to get back from Sonoma, use the Golden Gate Bridge.

If you decide to go the Bay Bridge route to Napa, drive east over the bridge (I-80) and then north to the Napa/Highway 29 exit near Vallejo. Highway 29 is the main road through the Napa Valley. The trip takes approximately 70 minutes.

If you decide to go over the Golden Gate Bridge, continue on U.S. 101 north to Novato, where you need to pick up Highway 37 east. Then, if you're interested in a pleasant drive and aren't in a big hurry, take Highway 121 (the Sonoma Highway) north toward Sonoma and then east to Napa, if that's your destination, where you'll end up on Highway 29. If Sonoma is your destination, take Highway 12. Make sure to have a map handy. This drive takes about 90 minutes.

Contact the **Napa Valley Conference & Visitors Bureau,** 1310 Napa Town Center, Napa, CA 94559 (☎ **707-226-7459;** Internet: www.napa valley.com) for maps to help get you on your way.

Picking the best time to visit

The most popular seasons for touring Napa and Sonoma valleys are summer and fall. The summers are hot in Wine Country, which is one reason why it's so popular with fog-bound San Franciscans. September and October are extremely busy due to the *crush,* or grape harvest, when the sweet aroma of *must* (crushed grapes) fills the air.

Wine Country is delightful any time of year. In the winter, restaurants aren't jammed and traffic is light. Spring is beautiful and still relatively uncrowded. However, if the forecast calls for rain, I recommend you save this trip for another time. If you do plan to visit Wine Country during summer or autumn, make lodging reservations early.

You'll meet with a lot more traffic and tourists on the weekends than on the weekdays. Also, Golden Gate Bridge traffic heading north on Friday afternoons and south on Sunday afternoons is amazing, and I don't mean that in a positive way. Let the guys with their weekend plans sit and stew on 101. Go while everyone else is at work.

Looking out for your safety

Although you may taste wines all along the 35-mile route through Napa and on the scenic roads through Sonoma, the rules of drinking and driving (and good common sense) are still intact. All those little sips add up more quickly than you think. Every winery tasting room has containers for spitting out the wine so you can taste without actually letting it go to your head.

Highway 29 is dangerous, even if you're not drinking. This two-lane thoroughfare through the Napa Valley has been the scene of many accidents, especially at night.

Taking an organized Wine Country tour

A good option for people who don't feel comfortable driving, or for those on a very tight schedule, are local companies that offer one-day Wine Country tours to the Napa and Sonoma valleys. On these six– to nine-hour tours you can usually visit two to three wineries and have lunch in one of the picturesque villages along the way. The downside of a tour like this is that you won't see some of the great wineries that aren't part of the tour package, you won't have time to relax in places that catch your eye, and you may not be able to choose where you want to eat.

But if you're interested in the package tours, here are a few of the good ones to look into:

- ✔ **Great Pacific Tour Company (☎ 415-626-4499)** picks you up at your San Francisco hotel and delivers you back after tastings at two Sonoma wineries, a picnic lunch, and a tour of Domaine Chandon, a sparkling wine producer in Napa. The cost, including lunch, is $72 for adults, $70 for seniors, and $62 for children 5 to 11.

- ✔ **Grayline (☎ 800-826-0202;** Internet: www.grayline.com) offers several Wine Country outings, as well as a few overnight packages. Its nine-hour tour includes two wineries and a stop in Calistoga for lunch and shopping. The price is $55 for adults and $27.50 for children.

- ✔ **Tower Tours (☎ 415-434-8687)** takes you to Napa and Sonoma valleys for the day, with stops at three wineries and lunch in Yountville or the town of Sonoma. The charge is $48 for adults and $31 for children.

- ✔ **Wine Country Jeep Tours (☎ 800-539-5337;** Internet: www.jeep tours.com) will plan a custom three– to four-hour winery tour that can include some off-road trailblazing and a picnic lunch. The cost is $19 per hour per person.

- ✔ You can also ride the **Napa Valley Wine Train (☎ 800-427-4124** or 707-253-9264). The train is basically a gourmet restaurant on wheels that choo-choos 36 miles through the valley, from the town of Napa to the village of St. Helena. You can get a lunch, brunch, or dinner tour ranging in price from $35 to $110. These primarily involve dining and watching the gorgeous scenery go by. The only train that makes a stop is the Grgich Hills Private Winery Tour and Tasting, a luncheon ride that costs $79 per person and stops at one winery. On board the train there is a wine-tasting car with an attractive bar and knowledgeable host. The three-hour tours depart from the train station in downtown Napa, at 1275 McKinstry St. You must make reservations for a spot on the train. If you don't want to drive to Napa, **Grayline** (☎ **800-826-0202**) arranges, for $99 per person, passage via a Blue and Gold Ferry from Pier 39 to Vallejo, where a bus takes everyone to the wine train station in Napa for the three-hour lunch excursion.

Mapping Out Your Winery Journey

A single day in Wine Country can't do the area justice and will leave you wanting more. But if that's all the time you have, plan to visit no more than three to four wineries, one before lunch and two or three after, followed by a late-afternoon snack or an early dinner.

If you spend two days and a night, you'll have the chance to do some other enjoyable activities such as checking out Copia (see "Napa excursions" later in this chapter), biking down a sleepy road, or taking a spa treatment. You could also cut down on your winery visits the first day, and instead take advantage of whatever your inn has to offer, such as a swimming pool, a garden walk, or just some peace and quiet. On your second day, have a substantial breakfast and consider one of the 11 a.m. reservation-only winery tours, such as Niebaum Coppola or Benziger. To occupy any extra time you may have left in your schedule, there's always outlet shopping in Napa and along Highway 29 past St. Helena.

Creating a wine-tasting itinerary isn't easy, because there are so many vineyards to choose from. The wineries suggested in this chapter are great for first-time tasters because they make a special effort to accommodate visitors. These vineyards offer tours, exhibits, and/or an extra-friendly staff. But there are plenty more vineyards to choose from, so get a map of the area and, time permitting, explore those back roads.

Touring the Wineries

The Napa Valley is home to more than 220 wineries (Sonoma has just four dozen or so), some owned by corporations, and others the domain of individuals so seduced by the grape that they abandoned successful careers to devote themselves to *viticulture* (the cultivation of grapes). Although no correlation exists between the size of a winery and the quality of the product — which has more to do with the talents of the vintners and variables such as weather and soil conditions — the bigger wineries offer more to visitors in terms of education and entertainment.

You can greatly enhance your knowledge of wine by tasting correctly — and what better classroom than a French-style chateau smack in the middle of a vineyard? Remember that wine appreciation begins by analyzing color, followed by aroma, then taste. You do this with your eyes

Becoming a wine connoisseur: The basics

Cabernet Sauvignon, Pinot Noir, and Zinfandel grapes (grown for red wines), and Chardonnay and Sauvignon or Fume Blanc grapes (grown for white wines) are the most prominent grape varieties produced in the area. Telling the difference between them takes a great deal of knowledge. Each one of these varieties contains identifiable flavors and aromas you can only begin to recognize through careful sipping.

Reading the label on the bottle is really the best way to tell the difference between Cabernet and Pinot. The label identifies the type of grape used if the wine contains at least 75% of that particular variety, among other bits of information. The appellation of origin indicates where the grapes were grown. The label may state that the grapes were grown in either a viticulture area, such as the Carneros region of the Napa Valley, in a certain county, or just in the state itself. Check the vintage date as well, which explains when at least 95% of the grapes were crushed. You also should make a note of the vintage date because many wines taste better aged, and some years produce better grapes than others.

first, then your nose, then your mouth. Don't be shy about asking questions of the person pouring — he will happily talk, because the more you learn about his product, the more likely you are to become a steady customer. And that makes everybody happy!

For wine-tasting newbies, the first winery you visit should be one that offers an in-depth tour, so you can familiarize yourself with the winemaking process. If you're traveling from north to south, Sterling Vineyards in Calistoga is a good bet, or Robert Mondavi in Oakville. In Sonoma, the tram operators at Benziger are both knowledgeable and accessible. If you're already somewhat of a connoisseur, ask your local wine merchant for suggestions on smaller wineries that you may enjoy.

You won't be able to get a deal on wine that you purchase directly from the producers at the wineries. They sell their wines at the full retail price so as not to undercut their primary market, the wine merchants. If you can't get a particular vintage at home, most wineries will mail order it for you.

Wineries in Napa Valley

Start in Calistoga and work your way down the valley along Highway 29 to make your return to San Francisco a bit shorter. But don't take this drive on a summer weekend. The bumper-to-bumper traffic on Highway 29 will ruin your day.

Napa Valley

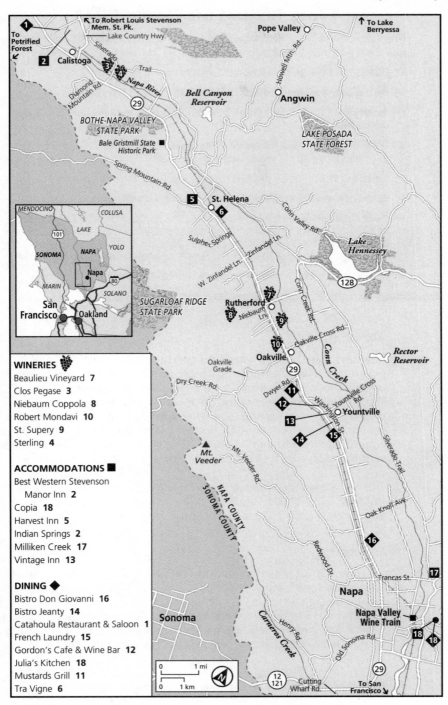

To Robert Louis Stevenson Mem. St. Pk.
Lake Country Hwy.
Pope Valley
To Lake Berryessa
1
To Petrified Forest
2 Calistoga
3
4
Silverado
Trail
Napa River
Diamond Mountain Rd.
29
Howell Mtn. Rd.
Angwin
Bell Canyon Reservoir
BOTHE-NAPA VALLEY STATE PARK
Bale Gristmill State Historic Park
LAKE POSADA STATE FOREST
Spring Mountain Rd.
5 St. Helena
6
Conn Valley Rd.
Lake Hennessey
Sulphur Springs
W. Zinfandel Ln.
Zinfandel Ln.
128
Conn Creek Rd.
SUGARLOAF RIDGE STATE PARK
Rutherford
7
8 Niebaum Ln.
9
Conn Creek
Rector Reservoir
Oakville Grade
10 Oakville
Oakville Cross Rd.
Dry Creek Rd.
29
Dwyer Rd.
11
12
13
14
15
Washington St.
Yountville
Yountville Cross Rd.
Mt. Veeder
Mt. Veeder Rd.
Silverado Trail
SONOMA COUNTY
NAPA COUNTY
Oak Knoll Ave.
16
Redwood Dr.
Trancas St.
17
Napa
Napa Valley Wine Train
18
18

Inset map

MENDOCINO
COLUSA
LAKE
101
SONOMA
NAPA
YOLO
Napa
80
MARIN
SOLANO
San Francisco
Oakland

WINERIES
Beaulieu Vineyard 7
Clos Pegase 3
Niebaum Coppola 8
Robert Mondavi 10
St. Supery 9
Sterling 4

ACCOMMODATIONS ■
Best Western Stevenson
   Manor Inn 2
Copia 18
Harvest Inn 5
Indian Springs 2
Milliken Creek 17
Vintage Inn 13

DINING ◆
Bistro Don Giovanni 16
Bistro Jeanty 14
Catahoula Restaurant & Saloon 1
French Laundry 15
Gordon's Cafe & Wine Bar 12
Julia's Kitchen 18
Mustards Grill 11
Tra Vigne 6

Sonoma
Henry Rd.
Carneros Creek
Old Sonoma Rd.
0 1 mi
0 1 km
N
12 121
Cutting Wharf Rd.
29
To San Francisco

Wine tasting do's and don'ts

When you taste wines, keep in mind the following suggestions and you'll fit right in — even if it's your first time:

✔ **Before the pour, sniff your glass.** It should have a clean aroma.

✔ **Do not pour the wine yourself.** Winery staff will pour it for you.

✔ **Taste wines in the appropriate order: whites first, reds second, and dessert wines last.**

✔ **Swirl the wine to coat the inside of the glass.** Swirling introduces more oxygen and helps open up the wine flavors and aromas.

✔ **Smell the wine.** Notice the different aromas — spice, fruit, flowers.

✔ **Take a sip and cover the back of your tongue with the wine.**

✔ **Taste, then spit.** Wine tasting is one of the few sports where spitting is not only allowed, it's encouraged. (Just make sure you hit your target, a bucket, or some other container available for this purpose.) Tasting, then spitting, is also a nifty way to sample many wines without becoming cloudy-headed.

✔ **Do not bring a bottle of wine from one winery into another.**

Robert Mondavi

Mondavi was the first winery to conduct public tastings, and it continues to take pride in educating people about wine. The free one-hour tour offered daily is well worth your time. And for fees ranging from $30 to $95, you can benefit from the once– or twice-weekly seminars on grape-growing, essence tasting, and wine and food pairing. Reservations are required for the seminars. During July, you can catch a Saturday evening concert sponsored by the winery. The shows sell out quickly, so call or visit Mondavi's Web site for a schedule and tickets.

7801 St. Helena Hwy. (Highway 29), P.O. Box 106, Oakville, CA 94562. ☎ 800-MON-DAVI or 707-226-1395. Internet: www.robertmondavi.com. *Open: Daily May–Oct 9:30 a.m.– 5:30 p.m.; until 4:30 p.m. Nov–Apr.*

St. Supery

Learn about aromas common to certain varietals with this self-guided interactive tour featuring "SmellaVision." You'll also hear about growing techniques at the winery's demonstration vineyard. You'll need at least 1 hour and 15 minutes for the tour and wine tasting alone. Have $3 on hand for the tasting fee. You can get a half glass of the really good stuff in the "Divine Wine" room (the reserve tasting room) for $8.

8440 St. Helena Hwy. (Highway 29), Rutherford, CA 94573. ☎ 800-942-0809. Open: Daily May–Oct 9:30 a.m.– 6 p.m.; until 5 p.m. Nov–Apr.

Niebaum Coppola

Yes, Coppola, as in the movie director, Francis Ford. His wines are fairly sophisticated, but that's fitting for this impressive estate. The property is home to a museum tracing the history of the winery and the two families connected by its ownership. You'll see movie memorabilia on the second floor of the museum, including the desk used by Al Pacino in *The Godfather,* Oscar statuettes, and costumes. Make reservations two weeks in advance in summer for an 11 a.m. or 2 p.m. in-depth historical tour, which costs $20 a person. Enjoy a formal sit-down tasting in one of the wine cellars after the 1½-hour tour. You'll pay $7.50 for regular tastings — you can even keep the glass. There are no picnic facilities at the winery so leave your sandwiches in the car.

1991 St. Helena Hwy. (Highway 29), Rutherford, CA 94573. ☎ *707-968-1100. Open: Daily 10 a.m.–5 p.m.*

Beaulieu Vineyard

At this well-regarded establishment, the vintners pass out glasses of Chardonnay as you walk in to set you in the right mood. After you've enjoyed a glass or two, you can take a free half-hour tour of the production facility, open daily from 11 a.m. to 4 p.m. Each tasting thereafter is $5, or $18 for five delicious reserve vintages.

1960 St. Helena Hwy. (Highway 29), Rutherford, CA 94573. ☎ *707-967-5230. Open: Daily 10 a.m.–5 p.m.*

Sterling

Arrive at this hilltop winery by aerial tram and swoon over the spectacular vista. Wine tasting is included in the ticket price of $6. After you reach the winery, take the self-guided tour that leads you through the entire operation and into the tasting room, where the friendly staff serve you wine at tables rather than at a bar. Plan on spending at least one hour here.

1111 Dunaweal Lane (½ mile east of Highway 29), P.O. Box 365, Calistoga, CA 94515. ☎ *707-942-3344. Open: Daily 10:30 a.m.–4:30 p.m.*

Clos Pegase

The official tour takes only about 30 minutes and is offered at 11 a.m. and 2 p.m. You can spend the rest of your time at this winery joyfully studying the art collection, walking around the sculpture garden, or picnicking on the vast lawn. You need to reserve a picnic table, but reservations aren't required for the complimentary tour. Wine tasting is $2.50 for current releases and $2 each for reserve wines.

1060 Dunaweal Lane (between Highway 29 and the Silverado Trail), Calistoga, CA 94515. ☎ *707-942-4981. Open: Daily 11 a.m.–5 p.m.*

Wineries in Sonoma Valley

The Sonoma Valley includes the towns of Sonoma, Glen Ellen, and Kenwood and is frequented a bit less than the Napa Valley because of its smaller size. Day-trippers may enjoy the smaller, more intimate atmosphere of Sonoma Valley. You can drive here in just over an hour, tour a few wineries, shop, have a great meal, and be back in the city — traffic willing — in time for dinner. You may choose to spend the night, in which case you can find many B&Bs and hotels, plus a few resorts sprinkled around the country roads.

Enter the Sonoma Valley by way of Highway 121, and then turn north on Highway 12. This path takes you directly into the charming town of Sonoma. (If you want to go directly to Glen Ellen, take Highway 116 instead.)

This tour includes stops at some smaller wineries that are simply too delicious to miss; all provide a little wine education and tastings. You'll see country roads bedecked by acres of grapes, old oaks, and flowers. And although the destinations are worthy, the drive itself is divine.

Benzinger

Tractor-pulled trams take visitors up the flower-lined path of this beautiful 85-acre ranch for a 45-minute tram tour. The winery, owned by the Benzinger family since 1981, is situated near Jack London State Park. The tram operators enthusiastically explain how vines work, how insects are controlled, and how the sun and soil together affect the taste of the final product. You can choose from two tasting opportunities, one of which is complimentary; the other costs $5 for the reserve wines.

1883 London Ranch Rd., Glen Ellen, CA 95442 (take Highway 12 to Arnold Drive and left on London Ranch Road). ☎ *707-935-4046. Open: Daily 10 a.m.–5 p.m.*

Matanzas Creek Winery

Your attention may stray from the grape when you notice the fragrant and expansive gardens cascading down the hill from the tasting room at this scenic winery. Matanzas produces a line of gift items featuring the lavender they grow and dry on the property, as well as producing high-quality, award-winning wine. A flight of wines for tasting costs $3, refundable with a wine purchase. A 30-minute tour shows you the basics of barrel-making, viticulture, and corks. (Tour times are 10:30 a.m., 1 p.m., and 3 p.m.)

6097 Bennett Valley Rd. (take Highway 12 to Arnold Drive to Warm Springs Road), Santa Rosa, CA 95404. ☎ *707-528-6464. Open: Mon–Sat 10 a.m.–5 p.m., Sun 11 a.m.–5 p.m.*

Sonoma Valley

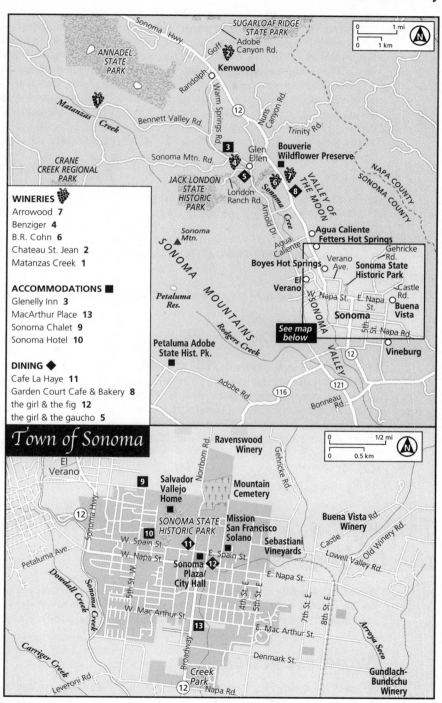

WINERIES
Arrowood 7
Benziger 4
B.R. Cohn 6
Chateau St. Jean 2
Matanzas Creek 1

ACCOMMODATIONS
Glenelly Inn 3
MacArthur Place 13
Sonoma Chalet 9
Sonoma Hotel 10

DINING
Cafe La Haye 11
Garden Court Cafe & Bakery 8
the girl & the fig 12
the girl & the gaucho 5

Town of Sonoma

Chateau St. Jean

Driving back on Warm Springs Drive toward Kenwood, turn left on Highway 12 to find a Mediterranean-style mansion on a 250-acre estate. This winery is a great place for a picnic on the expansive front lawn or in shady groves. (You can pick up picnic food at Cafe Citti, 9049 Sonoma Hwy.) The magnificent magnolia tree here was planted by Luther Burbank. You can wander the property (self-guided tours only) and climb the observation tower for a view of the valley. Downstairs, wine tasting is complimentary; $5 is charged for three tastes of reserve wines.

8555 Sonoma Hwy., Kenwood, CA. ☎ 707-833-4134. Open: Daily 10 a.m.–4:30 p.m.

Arrowood

Arrowood is an intimate, high-end, and somewhat exclusive winery with a small production but national distribution. You need to make an appointment for the one-hour tour. Call a day or two in advance. If you don't go on the tour, you can still sit on the verandah overlooking grapevines and mountains and try some great wines. There is a $3 tasting fee.

14347 Sonoma Hwy., Glen Ellen, CA 95442. ☎ 707-938-5170. Open: Daily 10 a.m.–4:30 p.m.

B.R. Cohn

This tiny tasting room flanked by olive trees is just down the road from Arrowood. The wines are worth trying, although the winery is not as fancy as some of its neighbors. Besides the wines, some of which are only available at the winery, the olive oil produced here is of the highest quality and makes a great gift. Friendly staff who are happy to talk wine and olives preside over the tasting room. Tastings are free.

15140 Sonoma Hwy., Glen Ellen, CA 95442. ☎ 707-938-4064. Open: Daily 10 a.m.–5 p.m.

Taking Advantage of Other Fun Stuff the Valleys Have to Offer

Wine Country offers many other activities besides wine tasting. If you're staying overnight, be sure to check out the following sites, sports, and downright sumptuous pleasures in Napa and Sonoma.

Napa excursions

Copia: The American Center for Wine, Food, and the Arts, 500 First St., Napa (☎ 707-259-1600; Internet: www.copia.org), opened in the fall of 2001 in the city of Napa and has quickly become one of the must-see attractions in the valley. There are obvious reasons for its immediate popularity: Copia celebrates the finer things in life in a modern museum-like setting, but it's neither solemn nor overly reverential. One permanent exhibit, an interactive presentation on the role of food and wine in American society, is both accessible and amusing. In addition, there's a state-of-the-art theater for concerts, lectures, and films; a full roster of wine and food courses are offered year-round; and a 500-seat concert terrace overlooking the Napa River, surrounded by Copia's orchard and organic gardens, provides warm-weather amusement. A great restaurant (see "Dining Delights," later in this chapter), a wine bar, and, of course, a gift shop round out the experience. Check the Web site for programming during your trip, and try to take in an exhibit, a class, a concert, or a meal — all four if time allows. Admission is $12.50 adults, $10 seniors and students, $7.50 children 6 to 12. Open fall and winter Thursday to Monday 10 a.m. to 5 p.m.; spring and summer Monday, Tuesday, and Thursday 10 a.m. to 5 p.m., Friday to Sunday 10 a.m. to 9 p.m.

Art turns up in the most unexpected places, but none more so than the **di Rosa Preserve** (☎ **707-226-5991**). This is a 53-acre indoor/outdoor gallery located 6½ miles west of Napa on Highway 121 that displays over 1,700 works amid meadows, hanging from trees, and throughout the former winery. Rene di Rosa, a former journalist and viticulturist, owns the property. Guides conduct two-hour tours Tuesday through Saturday. You must make a reservation for the tour; admission is $10.

Ride horseback through the beautiful countryside here with the help of the **Sonoma Cattle Company and Napa Valley Trail Rides** (☎ **707-996-8566**). The stable offers 1½– or 2-hour rides through Bothe-Napa Valley State Park (between St. Helena and Calistoga off Highway 29), available for adults and kids 8 years old and up. Rides start at $46.

Soaring over the vineyards under a colorful balloon, with just a few other souls sharing your basket, is a breathtaking experience. **Bonaventura Balloon Company** (☎ **800-FLY-NAPA** or 707-944-2822; Internet: www.bonaventuraballoons.com) is one of Napa's most trusted hot-air balloon operators, with a range of packages available. Or call **Napa Valley Aloft/Adventures Aloft** (☎ **800-944-4408** or 707-944-4408; Internet: www.nvaloft.com), whose early-morning lift-off includes a preflight snack and a postflight brunch with bubbly. However, at $195 to $250 per person (depending on the number of persons and the extras you choose), you may want to keep those feet on the ground.

If you want to join the many bicyclists you see pedaling down Napa's scenic roads, **St. Helena Cyclery,** 1156 Main St., St. Helena (☎ **707-963-7736**), will set you on the Silverado Trail for $7 per hour or $25 per day.

Getaway Adventures BHK (Biking, Hiking, and Kayaking), 1117 Lincoln Ave., Calistoga (☎ **800-499-BIKE** or 707-942-0332), runs full-day bike trips with lunch and winery tours.

Wind down after a busy day of vacationing with a mud bath. People have been immersing themselves in Calistoga mud for more than 150 years, but if you're prone to claustrophobia, get a massage only. You can reserve a tub and a follow-up massage at **Dr. Wilkinson's Hot Springs,** 1507 Lincoln Ave. (☎ **707-942-4102**); **Indian Springs Resort and Spa,** 1712 Lincoln Ave. (☎ **707-942-4913**); or **Calistoga Spa Hot Springs,** 1006 Washington St. (☎ **707-942-6269**). A mud bath and one-hour massage is $92 at Calistoga Spa Hot Springs, which is a very good buy.

Sonoma activities

Olives are also an important crop in Wine Country, and olive-oil tastings have become a popular activity. You can debate the merits of various extra-virgin olive oils in Glen Ellen at **The Olive Press,** 14301 Arnold Dr. (☎ **707-939-8900**). The press works 24 hours a day between October and March. Watch the process from the tasting room, while sampling the olive oil and checking out the olive-themed merchandise.

Jack London State Historic Park, 2400 London Ranch Rd. (☎ **707-938-5216**), is where the prolific author of *The Call of the Wild* lived before his death in 1916 at age 40. You can walk on trails to the ruins of Wolf House, London Lake, and Bath House. You can also visit the museum/library, which displays first editions of London's works and some of his personal memorabilia. Open daily from 9:30 a.m. to dusk. Take a two-hour group trail ride through the park with **Sonoma Cattle Company and Napa Valley Trail Rides** (☎ **707-996-8566**), which has stables on the property. The two-hour ride costs around $45. You can also rent horses for private rides at $45 per hour.

The Good Time Bicycle Shop, 18503 Hwy. 12, Boyes Hot Springs (☎ **707-938-0453**), delivers bikes to your lodgings and also offers 4½-hour picnic/winery rides for $55, which includes lunch. Rental is a reasonable $5 per hour or $25 per day.

If you have an intense interest in food, sign up for a 3– to 4-hour class at **Ramekins,** 450 West Spain St., Sonoma (☎ **707-933-0450**), a small B&B and culinary school next to the General's Daughter restaurant. During the day, take in the demonstration classes; then in the evening, glean culinary tips from some major Bay Area chefs. Students have lots of opportunity to sample the goods with a few glasses of wine. Call for a catalog. You can register over the phone, in person, or on the Web at www.ramekins.com.

Finding Fabulous Places to Stay in Wine Country

Although country inns and bed-and-breakfasts interspersed with spas and motels are sprinkled throughout both valleys, supply and demand keep the room rates and the occupancy on the high side. Even if you're taking your chances on finding a hotel in San Francisco at the last minute, you need to make reservations in the Wine Country as far in advance as possible, especially for stays between May and October. Most lodgings have a two-night minimum on the weekends during the high season. The good news: Parking is free at all the accommodations I've listed in this section.

Here is a breakdown of what the dollar signs represent in the following hotel listings:

- ✔ $: Under $100
- ✔ $$: $100 to $150
- ✔ $$$: $150 to $200
- ✔ $$$$: Over $200

Finding a substantial and well-prepared meal won't be quite as hard as finding a room, although you still need to make reservations. Some great chefs have settled their lives and businesses around the valleys, perhaps realizing that well-to-do tourists and urbanites with second homes love to eat out. Eating out is also one of the few evening activities in Wine Country — there's not much else to do here after 10 p.m.

Contact **The Napa Valley Conference & Visitors Bureau,** 1310 Napa Town Center, Napa, CA 94559 (☎ **707-226-7459;** Internet: www.napa valley.com), for information on accommodations.

The **Sonoma Valley Visitors Bureau** is located on the Sonoma Plaza at 453 First St. E. (☎ **707-996-1090;** Internet: www.sonomavalley.com). They keep an availability sheet of hotel/B&B/motel rooms in case you didn't make reservations.

Lovely lodgings in Napa

Best Western Stevenson Manor Inn
$–$$$$ Calistoga

Situated just east of town, this new motel offers great value in an expensive neighborhood. The motel-basic rooms are boosted up a notch by fireplaces or whirlpool tubs, cable TV, fridges, coffeemakers, and hair dryers, as well as on-property extras including a pool, a hot tub, a sauna, and steam rooms. Guestrooms with two queen beds won't crowd the family, and kids under 12 stay free.

1830 Lincoln Ave. (west of Silverado Trail), Calistoga. ☎ *707-942-1112. Fax: 707-942-0381. Internet:* www.callodging.com. *Rack rates: $99–$244 double. Rates include continental breakfast. AE, CB, DC, DISC, MC, V. Check the Web site for Internet-only discounts. Guests get 10% off spa services at a nearby spa.*

Harvest Inn
$$$$ St. Helena

This Tudor-inspired complex was renovated in 1999, making all the rooms light, attractive, comfortable, and roomy enough for a family. Two pools and two Jacuzzis are set in lovely gardens against a dramatic backdrop of mountains and vineyards. Lots of little luxuries help justify the price, including feather beds, CD players, and VCRs. The mid-valley location is central to everything.

1 Main St., St. Helena. ☎ *800-950-8466 or 707-963-9463. Fax: 707-963-4402. Internet:* www.harvestinn.com. *Rack rates: $240–$319 double, $399–$675 suite. Rates include continental breakfast. AE, DC, DISC, MC, V.*

Indian Springs
$$$–$$$$ Calistoga

Each of these comfortable, old-fashioned bungalows has a kitchen with a refrigerator and microwave, and there are picnic tables and barbecue grills nearby. The resortlike atmosphere is complete with *surreys* (bikes with bench seats and awnings) and Ping-Pong tables for guests to use. Lounge chairs surround a warm, Olympic-size mineral pool. The spa, which is located in a bath house from 1913, offers a full range of services. Booking a bungalow in the summer isn't easy, but try edging out the families that come here year after year by calling 48 hours ahead to find out whether you can get in on a cancellation.

1712 Lincoln Ave., Calistoga, CA 94515. ☎ *707-942-4913. Fax 707-942-4919. Rack rates: $185–$245 double studio or 1-bedroom; $265–$295 2-bedroom; $450–$500 3-bedroom. MC, V.*

Milliken Creek
$$$$ Napa

Cushy, chic, and romantic, the airy, large rooms in this intimate new inn resemble photos out of *Metropolitian Home*. No luxury has been overlooked, from Frette bed linens and L'Occitane bath products to candlelight turndown service. The 3-acre creekside gardens are equally stunning and private; you'll find it difficult to tear yourself away, although many excellent small wineries await along the Silverado Trail.

1815 Silverado Trail, Napa. ☎ *888-622-5775 or 707-255-1197. Fax: 707-942-2653. Internet:* www.millikencreekinn.com. *Rack rates: $225–$450 double. Rates include breakfast and afternoon wine and cheese. DC, MC, V.*

Vintage Inn
$$$$ Yountville

This big, attractive French-country inn is conveniently situated near some of the finest restaurants in the valley. Recently refurbished in a French renaissance decor, rooms are clustered throughout the lovely flowering grounds, and are equipped with fireplaces, fridges, Jacuzzi tubs, and coffeemakers. Tennis courts and a heated pool make this a comfortable mini-resort, good for couples exploring the area.

6541 Washington St., Yountville. ☎ *800-351-1133 or 707-944-1112. Fax: 707-944-1617. Internet:* www.vintageinn.com. *Rack rates: $210–$420 double. Rates include continental champagne breakfast and afternoon tea. AE, CB, DC, DISC, MC, V.*

Retreats down Sonoma way

Glenelly Inn
$$ Glen Ellen

A secluded and peaceful family-run B&B, the modest rooms here are small but quaintly decorated. They each have a private entry and down comforters, and most have clawfoot tubs with shower heads. A spa in the garden adds to the quiet magic, and you can sit and gaze at the mountains on the verandahs on both levels in comfortable chairs.

5131 Warm Springs Rd., Glen Ellen, CA 95442. ☎ *707-996-6720. Fax: 707-996-5227. Internet:* www.glenelly.com. *Rack rates: $150–$175 double; includes breakfast and afternoon snacks. MC, V. From Highway 12 take Madrone Road to Arnold Drive.*

MacArthur Place
$$$$ Sonoma

This divine inn is a renovated Victorian masterfully connected to newer buildings. The rooms are spacious and comfy, with wonderful four-poster beds that'll make you think twice about getting up. Contented guests relax at the small, well-staffed spa where the practiced hands of a masseuse work out pre-vacation tension. Manicured gardens surround a swimming pool, and a steakhouse restaurant, located in the 100-year-old barn, supplies room service.

29 E. MacArthur St., Sonoma. ☎ *800-722-1866 or 707-938-2929. Fax: 707-933-9833. Internet:* www.macarthurplace.com. *Rack rates: $199–$625 double. Rates include continental breakfast. AE, MC, V.*

Sonoma Chalet
$$–$$$ **Sonoma**

Although all you see from this Swiss-inspired farmhouse inn are mountains and the ranch next door, it is located less than a mile from the Sonoma town square. Antiques and collectibles decorate the three delightful, spacious cottages. Inside the farmhouse, the upstairs rooms have private facilities while the two downstairs rooms share a bathroom. The simple and delicious breakfast includes fresh pastries.

18935 Fifth St. W., Sonoma, CA 95476. ☎ *800-938-3129 or 707-938-3129. Internet:* www.sonomachalet.com. *Rack rates: $110–$210 double with continental breakfast. AE, MC, V.*

Sonoma Hotel
$–$$$ **Sonoma**

The location of this historic building, on Sonoma's town square, makes shopping and dining convenient. A new restaurant and remodeled rooms add to its appeal. Bright bathrooms and stylish furniture make the lodgings attractive and cozy. The small suites work well for families, and the kids will have a great time in the park across the street. An excellent restaurant, the girl & the fig (see "Dining Delights"), is on-site.

110 West Spain St., Sonoma, CA 95476. ☎ *800-468-6016 or 707-996-2996. Fax: 707-996-7014. Internet:* www.sonomahotel.com. *Rack rates: $95–$245 double with continental breakfast. MC, V.*

Dining Delights

Wine tasting certainly isn't the only reason to make the trek from San Francisco to Wine Country: The food here is sublime. Take a look at these recommendations and savor the possibilities.

In Napa

Bistro Don Giovanni
$$–$$$ **Napa** **ITALIAN**

Share a pizza, some antipasti, and a bottle of Chardonnay for a delightful, light Italian meal, or go all out with the aged Porterhouse for two. This inviting place attracts a crowd that gathers at tables on the porch overlooking vineyards. It's just heavenly.

4110 St. Helena Hwy. (Highway 29), Napa. ☎ *707-224-3300. Reservations recommended. Main courses: $12.95–$23.50. AE, DISC, MC, V. Open: Sun–Thur 11:30 a.m.–10:00 p.m.; Fri–Sat 11:30 a.m.–11:00 p.m.*

Bistro Jeanty

$$$ Yountville FRENCH

Much applauded around the Bay Area for its great menu, authenticity, and vivacious dining room, this French bistro satisfies both the appetite and the spirit. Rustic dishes like lamb tongue and potato salad or rabbit and sweetbread ragout make up the seasonal menu. Timid and adventuresome eaters will be equally pleased with typical bistro items such as steak frites and coq au vin.

6510 Washington St., Yountville. ☎ *707-944-0103. Reservations recommended. Main courses: $14.50–$24.50. MC, V. Open: Daily 11:30 a.m.–10:30 p.m.*

Catahoula Restaurant and Saloon

$$$ Calistoga AMERICAN/SOUTHERN

You will detect a strong hint of New Orleans in the food and atmosphere of this fun restaurant, both a critical and local favorite. If you didn't make reservations, dine at the bar in front of the wood-fired ovens, where you can watch in awe as busy chefs crank out plate after plate of seasonal Southern-accented dishes, such as an oven-roasted tomato pizza topped with andouille sausage and onion confit; spicy seafood paella with house-made chorizo; and cornmeal-fried catfish with lemon-jalapeño meuniére and Mardi Gras slaw.

In the Mount View Hotel, 1457 Lincoln Ave., Calistoga. ☎ *707-942-2275. Internet:* www.catahoularest.com. *Reservations recommended. Main courses: $12–$24. MC, V. Open: Mon–Thur 5:30 p.m.–10:00 p.m.; Fri 5:30 p.m.–10:30 p.m. (call for Fri daytime hours in summer); Sat 10:00 a.m.–3:30 p.m. and 5:30–10:30 p.m.; Sun 10:00 a.m.–3:30 p.m. and 5:30–10:00 p.m.*

French Laundry

$$$$$ Yountville FRENCH

Regarded as one of the finest chefs in the United States, Thomas Keller prepares superb multicourse meals for a lucky crowd in his intimate, elegant, universally celebrated restaurant. If you're serious about food, book a table well in advance (it's easier to reserve for lunch), and arrive hungry — you won't want to overlook a crumb. The French Laundry experience is sublime on every front.

6640 Washington St. (at Creek Street), Yountville. ☎ *707-944-2380. Internet:* www.sterba.com/yountville/frenchlaundry. *Reservations required. Prix-fixe meals: $80–$105; chef's tasting menu $120. AE, MC, V. Open: Mon–Thur 5:30–9:30 p.m.; Fri–Sun 11 a.m.–1 p.m. and 5:30–9:30p.m.*

Gordon's Cafe and Wine Bar

$–$$ Yountville AMERICAN

Chef-owner Sally Gordon's delicious food is served in a congenial atmosphere reminiscent of a general store. Besides comfort-food favorites at breakfast and creative sandwiches at lunch, Gordon's serves a three-course prix-fixe dinner on Friday nights, making the cafe a prime destination for food lovers. The shop is well-known for its meticulous selection of fine wines and gourmet condiments, including more kinds of olive oil than you ever imagined existed.

6770 Washington St., Yountville. ☎ *707-944-8246. Reservations essential at dinner. Main courses: $3.50–$8 at breakfast and lunch; $32 prix-fixe dinner. AE, MC, V. Open: Sat–Thur 7:30 a.m.–6:00 p.m.; Fri 7:30 a.m.–5:00p.m. and 6:00–8:30 p.m.*

Julia's Kitchen

$$$ Napa CALIFORNIA/FRENCH

Food preferences are entirely personal, but because you asked, I think this bustling restaurant inside Copia (see "Taking Advantage of Other Fun Stuff the Valleys Have to Offer") served the most delicious meal I ate on my last trip to the valley. Named in honor of Julia Child, the kitchen uses organic produce raised on the grounds so even a simple green salad shines with bright flavor, and life only gets better from there. The menu changes often, but I loved the seared day boat scallops and the roasted winter squash skewer. Portions are moderate, which is kind because desserts must be given their due. You can eat here without paying an entrance fee to Copia.

500 First St. (at Copia), Napa. ☎ *707-265-5700. Internet:* www.copia.org/pages/juliaskitchen.html. *Reservations advised. Main courses: $16.50–$26. AE, MC, V. Open: Oct 1–May 15, Mon 11:30 a.m.–3:00 p.m., Thur–Sun 11:30 a.m.–3:00 p.m. and 5:30–9:30 p.m.; May 16–Sept 30, Mon and Wed 11:30 a.m.–3:00 p.m., Thur–Sun 11:30 a.m.–3:00 p.m. and 5:30–9:30 p.m.*

Mustards Grill

$$$ Yountville AMERICAN

Bustling, fun, and relaxed, the lengthy menu and specials board at this valley institution are filled with scrumptious American dishes that will even cause picky eaters to salivate. The restaurant, the bar, and even the menu are always overflowing, as is the parking lot. If you don't have room for dessert, loosen your belt and give it a go anyway.

7399 St. Helena Hwy. (Highway 29), Yountville. ☎ *707-944-2424. Reservations recommended. Main courses: $12–$19. CB, DC, DISC, MC, V. Open: Mon–Fri 11:30 a.m.–9:00 p.m.; Sat–Sun 11:30 a.m.–10:00 p.m.*

Tra Vigne
$$$ St. Helena ITALIAN

This elegant (but not stuffy) restaurant is what people dream of when they dream of eating in the Italian countryside. You have two choices where to take your meal — either the more formal dining room inside, or outside on the lovely courtyard patio (probably the better spot if the kids are with you). The Cantinetta delicatessen is the place to pick up reasonably priced pizza, wine, and prepared foods to eat down the road at a winery.

1050 Charter Oak Ave., St. Helena. ☎ *707-963-4444. Reservations recommended. Main courses: $12.50–$19. CB, DC, DISC, MC, V. Open: Sun–Thur 11:30 a.m.– 10:00 p.m.; Fri–Sat 11:30 a.m.–10:30 p.m.*

In Sonoma

Cafe La Haye
$$ Sonoma CALIFORNIA

This casual little cafe serves some of the best food around, and. unlike many other Wine Country restaurants there's no attempt to pretend you're in Italy or France. Plain tables and chairs are carefully set about, as if to not disturb the art that fills the walls, making La Haye's single room resemble a gallery. The menu selection, spare but complete, features whatever's seasonal and offers organic produce.

140 East Napa St., Sonoma. ☎ *707-935-5994. Reservations accepted. Main courses: $11.95–$17.95. MC, V. Open: Tues–Sat 5:30–9:00 p.m.; Sun 9:30 a.m.–2:00 p.m.*

Garden Court Cafe and Bakery
$ Glen Ellen AMERICAN

Get a modest breakfast and lunch-to-go, or a tasty, filling breakfast that keeps you going most of the day. Wine glasses and a tablecloth can be included in picnic lunches for added panache. If you're in town on the second Wednesday of the month, the four-course prix-fixe at $28.95 is the bargain of the valley.

13875 Sonoma Hwy. 12, Glen Ellen. ☎ *707-935-1565. No reservations. Main courses: $4.95–$10.95. MC, V. Open: 7:30 a.m.–2:00 p.m. Dinner served second Wed of the month.*

the girl & the fig
$$ Sonoma COUNTRY FRENCH

This upscale little country French bistro moved to the Sonoma Hotel from its Glen Ellen location in 2001, adding outdoor dining to the delight of its many admirers. The seasonal menu meets the needs of seafoodies, vegetarians, or carnivores with one or two dishes in each category. The grilled fig salad with arugula and local goat's cheese is a must-order when fresh figs are available. The three-course plat du jour for $25 (served Sunday through Thursday) is the only reason you need to visit during the week.

110 West Spain St., Sonoma, CA. ☎ *707-938-3634. Reservations accepted. Main courses: $10.95–$19.75. MC, V. Open: Daily 11:30 a.m.–2:30 p.m. and 5:30–9:30 p.m.*

the girl & the gaucho
$$$ Glen Ellen   CALIFORNIA

Yes, there are other restauranteers in Sonoma Valley besides the owners of these last two places, but why argue with success? Anyway, none serve a menu of mouth-watering Latin-inspired dishes like they do at this A-framed room, filled with art and kitschy doo-dads. You can make an evening of it, listening to jazz, sampling the international wine list, and ordering small plates of Spanish cheeses, cured meats, ceviche, roasted corn cakes . . . the list goes on.

13690 Arnold Dr., Glen Ellen. ☎ *707-938-3634. Reservations advised. Small and large plates: $5–$22. AE, MC, V. Open: Daily 5:30–9:30 p.m.*

Part VIII
The Part of Tens

"Fisherman's Wharf? Naw–this is TV Repairman's Wharf.
Fisherman's Wharf is about a quarter-mile down on
your right."

In this part . . .

Whipping up this top-ten list was a challenge. I'm just glad I didn't have to come up with my ten favorite restaurants (too challenging) or my ten favorite parking places (the first ten available spots, wherever they are). But here I give you my humble opinions on the greatest views, the best pastimes in foul weather, and the best ways to look less obviously like a tourist — not that I have anything against tourists, mind you.

Chapter 26

The Top Ten Views

*P*eople like views. That much is clear from the wrangling that goes on to get a table with a view in restaurants, or the extra tariff imposed on a room with a view, not to mention a home with a view. San Francisco is one major view, owing to all those hills. I admit to a permanent sentimental attachment to the views of San Francisco. Following are some of my favorites.

From Twin Peaks

The mother of all views — if the weather cooperates — is surely from **Twin Peaks,** which sits in the center of San Francisco in a residential neighborhood at the top of Market Street. The sightline encompasses the entrance to the bay and reaches all the way 'round to Candlestick Point. If you're driving, head southwest on Market Street, which becomes Portola Drive past 17th Street. The first light past Corbett Street is a right turn only; this is Twin Peaks Boulevard, the road that takes you up the hill.

The 37-Corbett bus, which you can easily catch on Market and Church streets, takes passengers near, but not all the way to, Twin Peaks. And the rest of the trip is quite a hike uphill. If you'd prefer something slightly less strenuous and want to see one of San Francisco's beautiful "hidden" staircases, here's a tip: Exit the bus at Corbett and Clayton streets, and look for an old concrete wall on the west side of Clayton marked by a street sign that says "Pemberton." This leads to the Pemberton Stairs. You won't get to the top of Twin Peaks by climbing them, but you'll be treated to bay views in quiet, green surroundings.

From Bernal Heights Park

Look southeast from downtown and you'll spot a prominent hill with a few trees decorating the top. That's **Bernal Heights Park,** the favored dog-walking and fireworks-viewing area for the Bernal Heights neighborhood. The weather in this part of town is far superior to the weather around Twin Peaks, which can get really foggy, much to the dismay of the camera-toting folk on the tour buses. The views here are equally wonderful to my mind, partly because Bernal Hill is closer to downtown and the bay. The 67-Folsom bus drives to the end of Folsom at Esmeralda. Exit and walk up the hill on any of a number of paths.

From Lincoln Park

Lincoln Park is one of the prettiest golf courses in creation, situated as it is around the Palace of the Legion of Honor and above the entrance to the San Francisco Bay at Land's End. Standing in front of the museum, you can see in the distance a snippet of downtown framed within the green branches of fir trees. From here, walk west down the street. You'll be stunned by a postcard-perfect view of the Golden Gate Bridge from a unique perspective — facing north as if you're entering the bay. Take a seat on one of the benches thoughtfully placed along the street so you can survey the vista in comfort. The 18-46th Avenue bus stops in the museum parking lot.

From the Beach Chalet Restaurant

The waves along **Ocean Beach,** at the end of Golden Gate Park on the Great Highway, are at times soothing, and at times violent enough to discourage beachcombing. In either case, you'll be as comfy as a babe in his crib if you get a table upstairs in the **Beach Chalet** restaurant (☎ **415-386-8439**) overlooking the Pacific (ideally, as the sun sets). The building was designed by Willis Polk, and the first-floor visitor center is adorned by murals painted in the 1930s by the same artist who painted the frescoes at Coit Tower. The restaurant is particularly popular for its menu of house-brewed beers, and it serves throughout the day and evening starting at breakfast. If you don't want to wait for a table in the dining room, you can take a seat in the bar and turn toward the view, dramatic in any season. The 5-Fulton, which you can pick up on Market and Powell streets, takes you to Ocean Beach, a block or so from the Beach Chalet.

Above Dolores Park

From any Muni Metro station (the Powell Street Station being the closest to Union Square) take the J-Church toward Daly City. Exit on 18th and Church streets, above Dolores Park. The city and bay views over this stretch of green on a clear day have been responsible for more than one decision to relocate to the Bay Area. After soaking in the scenery and taking a stroll through the park, walk two blocks north on Dolores Street until you reach **Mission Dolores** at 16th and Dolores streets, the oldest building in San Francisco.

From Top of the Mark

If you feel like having a cocktail as you drink in a view, head to the **Top of the Mark** in the Mark Hopkins Intercontinental Hotel, 1 Nob Hill, at California and Mason streets (☎ 415-392-3434). Sometimes it's so busy you have to wait in line at the elevator, but the city views are mesmerizing when you get a table.

From the Cheesecake Factory

Union Square is a compact, urban hub, immensely appealing, especially when it's crowded and bustling. Up until recently, there wasn't a handy place to be among, but not in, the madding crowd, but now **Macy's** (see Chapter 19) has alleviated that problem by installing a branch of the **Cheesecake Factory** (☎ 415-397-3333) on the eighth floor of the department store. Management shrewdly included a heated patio for diners who favor a city view in all its skyscrapered glory. The restaurant is open from 7 a.m. until 11 p.m.

From Fisherman's Wharf

If for some unfathomable reason you've skipped to this section without reading what's come before, you won't know that I, like all upstanding San Franciscans, generally avoid **Fisherman's Wharf** (see Chapter 16) like I avoid the Oakland A's baseball team. However, I recently discovered a way to escape the folks crowding the sidewalks, yet still take advantage of the views and freshly cracked crab.

The crab stands are plopped in front of their namesake restaurants along one block off Jefferson Street. Just to the left of Fisherman's

Grotto #9 are glass doors marked "Passageway to the Boats," the boats being what remains of the fishing fleet. Take your cracked crab, your beer, and plenty of napkins and push through. You'll be on a pier that leads to the tiny **Fisherman's and Seaman's Memorial Chapel** on your right, and views of the bay and Telegraph Hill in front and to your left. The pier is parallel to Jefferson Street but may be gloriously close to empty even on a weekend. You can eat your crab in peace sitting on the dock of the bay, watching . . . well you know. Close by, sea lions jump, swim, and beg in the waters below.

From Fort Point

The remains of **Fort Point,** an 1861 brick artillery fortress, occupy the land at the edge of the bay nearest the Golden Gate Bridge. I remember the first time I visited this area because heavy fog obscured everything around me except the uppermost portion of the bridge. It was a dramatic vision. On a clear day, you'll be treated to the bridge, of course, but also to bright views of the downtown skyline and Alcatraz. The 29 bus stops as close as the parking lot next to the bridge visitor center, a downhill walk to a particularly pretty viewpoint in the midst of eucalyptus trees. If you're up for a hike, follow the joggers past the Marina Green and through the Presidio (see Chapter 17).

From UC Berkeley Botanical Gardens

Drive to the **UC Berkeley Botanical Gardens,** high in the hills behind the campus. Find the rose garden. Beyond the plants you can see the bay and San Francisco, small and glowing in the distance. See Chapter 23 for other ideas on what to do in Berkeley after you finish admiring the view.

Chapter 27

Ten Things to Do If It's Raining (Or Just Too Foggy)

. . . .

In This Chapter

▶ Making the most of a soggy day

▶ Pampering yourself at the hot springs or spa

▶ Finding entertaining indoor activities

. . . .

San Francisco isn't Seattle by any means, but our rainy days can get
in the way of enjoying our city. Actually, a foggy morning is what
bothers people most, I think — fog is always cold and damp and gray.
But you don't have time to grouse about the weather. You have things
to do, places to see, people to meet . . . oh, you don't like getting wet?
Okay. Here are a few rainy/foggy-day options.

Taking High Tea

High Tea at one of the many hotels that offers it is probably the only
civilized way to keep dry. Try the dowdy (in an English way) **King
George Hotel,** 334 Mason St. (☎ 415-781-5050); the **Westin St. Francis,**
335 Powell St. (☎ 415-397-7000); the **Sheraton Palace,** Market and
New Montgomery streets (☎ 415-546-5010); or the **Ritz-Carlton,** 600
Stockton St. (☎ 415-296-7465). **Neiman Marcus** also has a lovely, reasonably priced tea service in the **Rotunda** restaurant, 150 Stockton St.
(☎ 415-362-4777), from 2:30 to 5 p.m. daily.

Checking Out Japantown

Head to Japantown and take cover inside the **Kinokuniya Building** at
1581 Webster St., between Post Street and Geary Boulevard. Although
this and the other buildings in the area aren't much to look at from the
outside, inside you can get a delicious bowl of comforting noodles at
Mifune (see Chapter 13), the most authentic noodle house in town, and
then entertain yourself in any of a number of interesting stores, such as

Mashiko Folkcraft (open from 11 a.m. to 6 p.m., Wednesday through Monday) and the **Kinokuniya Bookstore** (open daily from 10:30 a.m. to 7 p.m.). If the sky still hasn't cleared up, take in a movie at the **Kabuki Theater** next door. This multiplex gets all the latest films. There's an underground parking lot off Webster Street. Muni buses 2-Clement, 3-Jackson, 4-Sutter, 22-Fillmore, and 38-Geary will all drop you in Japantown.

Luxuriating at Kabuki Hot Springs

Staying indoors can turn into a modest luxury at **Kabuki Hot Springs,** 1750 Geary Blvd., at Webster Street (☎ 415-922-6000), a most respectable communal bathhouse. You can soak your feet, have a massage, and take a steam bath. Women may use the facilities on Sundays, Wednesdays, and Fridays; Tuesdays are coed; and men get the rest of the week. Shy people may not feel comfortable at first walking around the premises *au natural,* but no one will bother you. Massages are by appointment. To get here, take the 38-Geary bus. Open daily from 10 a.m. to 10 p.m.

Rock Climbing (Or Working Out) at the Mission Cliffs Rock Climbing Center

Rather than let the kids climb the walls in your hotel room, take everyone rock climbing (indoors of course) at Mission Cliffs Rock Climbing Center, located in the Mission District at 2295 Harrison St., at 19th Street (☎ 415-550-0515), and open every day. This world-class facility caters to beginners and experts of all ages and even folks who never dreamed of making like flies. *Belay* (rope handling) classes are taught regularly, so you can act as assistant to your *compadres* and vice versa. You don't even need any special equipment — you can rent whatever is necessary (including shoes) — and there goes your final excuse. There's also a gym on site with locker rooms and a sauna, perfect for those who prefer to keep their feet on the ground.

Watching the Weather from the Cliff House

Admire the storm from the confines of the Cliff House, 1090 Point Lobos Ave., on the Great Highway (☎ 415-386-3330), open every day. Although this historic property is undergoing renovation through spring of 2004, sections are still open for dining, drinking, and admiring the vistas. I can't recommend the food, but the view of Seal Rocks and the vast Pacific Ocean is impressive, especially if waves are crashing about. The closest museum to this spot is the **Palace of the Legion of Honor** (see Chapter 17), another wonderful place to wait out the weather (there's a good cafe). The 18 bus will bring you to both locations.

Finding Activities for Everyone at the Metreon and Yerba Buena Gardens

The Metreon and Yerba Buena Gardens (see Chapter 16) make up a one-stop rainy-day haven, particularly if you're traveling with your family. Depending on everyone's ages, you don't have to stick together for the entire day. Teens can flex their independence at **Zeum** or in the **Airtight Garage,** while kids needing direct supervision will enjoy the **Metreon play areas.** The elders, if they aren't needed, can shop, play pool at **Jillian's** (the large restaurant on the first floor), or even dash across the street to the **Museum of Modern Art.** Bowling and ice-skating work for everyone, and when it's time to regroup, you can see what's playing at the movies.

Defying the Weather at the California Academy of Sciences

Head for Golden Gate Park and the **California Academy of Sciences** (see Chapter 16). You can find enough to see here to keep you busy until the sun comes back out, but even then, stick around to watch one of the planetarium shows. If the rain turns to drizzle, put on your base-ball cap and take a walk in the **Strybing Arboretum,** across the street. Outside of a few gardeners and squirrels, you'll likely be undisturbed on the paths through this very beautiful garden.

Sightseeing and Staying Dry on the F-Market Streetcar

The **F-Market streetcar** (see Chapter 11) is my current public transport ride of choice. Grab an umbrella, then grab a seat for a ride to **The Cannery** (see Chapter 16). Yes, it's really just an enclosed shopping mall, if you want to be blunt and unromantic; but still, it's an attractive enclosed shopping mall with some fun things to do with the kids (see Chapter 17). Then take the streetcar all the way toward **upper Market Street** and reward yourself with a late lunch at **Zuni** (see Chapter 14).

Babying Yourself at Nordstrom

See if you can get an appointment for a manicure, pedicure, and/or a facial at Nordstrom in the **San Francisco Centre shopping mall** at Fifth and Market streets (☎ 415-977-5102). If you have co-visitors to deal with, send them to the fourth floor grill for lunch or a snack. You can find lots of shopping opportunities here as well, although most of the stores are your typical mall flavors.

Doing Business on a Rainy Day

A great thing to do is sit around your hotel lobby and complain like the locals. Grab a copy of the *Chronicle* and maybe the *Wall Street Journal* for good measure. Whisper into a cell phone while gripping a cup of coffee in your free hand. Then hail a cab and dash to the nearest Internet cafe to check your e-mail: **Club-I,** 850 Folsom St. (☎ 415-777-1448), and **Cafe.com,** 970 Market St., between Fifth and Sixth streets (☎ 415-922-5322), are closest to Union Square. And if you think the rain is bad, be thankful you haven't been inundated with foggy mornings for 40 days straight. Now you know why anyone who can afford a summer home in Napa puts up with the traffic on Friday afternoons.

Chapter 28

Ten Ways to Avoid Looking Like a Tourist

● ●

In This Chapter
▶ Eating, shopping, and dressing like the locals
▶ Avoiding tourist traps

● ●

I don't understand why being a tourist is considered so beneath some people. Even my own dear husband scoffs at tourists — or people he presumes are tourists — and when we travel he does his well-meaning best to look like a local. This generally leads to amusing misunderstandings on behalf of actual citizens, who either ask him something in a language he doesn't understand, or presume he knows where he's going when he hasn't a clue. So, why live a lie, I say. If you're visiting for pleasure and have a keen interest in looking around, you're a tourist. Be proud. Wear that camera around your neck (but maybe leave the bum bag at home). Rattle a map in frustration. Ask a stranger for directions.

Otherwise, memorize the following tips.

Dress for the Weather

This is not the 90210 zip code; you cannot tan here. In summer, it's foggy and cold in the morning, turning to sunshine in the afternoon, with temperatures in the upper 60s or low 70s. I know this, because the weathermen repeat the same forecast every morning in July and August. Dress in long pants, not shorts. Wear a sweater over your T-shirt and a jacket over that. You can always tie extraneous clothing around your waist when you enter one of our famous microclimates. In San Francisco, the temperature changes from neighborhood to neighborhood, so if you're shivering in Golden Gate Park, head to the Mission to warm up.

September and October are the warmest months here. If you look good in shorts, wear them then.

Don't Trust Your Map

Those darn hills have a way of interrupting the streets in ways that may not be apparent to the untrained eye. Telegraph Hill is the worst offender. If you can't go through, you'll have to go around.

Don't Gawk at Tall Buildings

An article in the *San Francisco Chronicle* noted that San Franciscans do not gawk at tall buildings, although I don't know if that includes sky-scrapers in other towns. Probably. But the author also noted that San Franciscans are breaking their own rule and gawking like mad at the new downtown ballpark. So, if you don't want to look like a tourist, don't stare at the Transamerica Pyramid — a quick glance should do — but feel free to drool while admiring Pac Bell Park. You'll then resemble a local who didn't buy season tickets.

Don't Eat or Shop like a Tourist

Be picky about where you spend your time and money. Places most residents wouldn't be caught dead in include the Hard Rock Cafe, any restaurant on Fisherman's Wharf, Ripley's Believe It or Not, and the camera/luggage stores on Powell Street.

Wait 'til You Get Back to the Airport to Buy That Delicious San Francisco Sourdough

Don't walk around with loaves of bread wrapped in plastic for the trip home. Around here we buy our baguettes for same-day consumption. Anyway, you can buy that particular brand of bread at the airport, where no one will see you.

Cross the Bridge Before or After — but Not During — Rush Hour

Don't cross the Bay Bridge between 3 and 7 p.m. unless you want to be mistaken for a suburban commuter. Anyway, no one, not even the com-muters, are actually crossing the Bay Bridge at this time; rather, they're sitting and fuming and occasionally inching their way forward. This is important to remember if you have friends on the East Bay who invite you to come over for dinner.

Don't Stare at the Locals

Don't point/gasp/shriek at the man/woman/other with the attention-getting tattoo/leather chaps/chartreuse wig no matter how unusual he/she/it appears. That would be unseemly.

Don't Shout at People You Suspect Don't Speak English

Don't raise your voice or speak extra slowly to your waiter if you suspect he doesn't speak English. In fact, he does speak English. He's merely trying to turn your table as quickly as possible.

Do the Farmer's Market Thing

Hang around the Ferry Plaza Farmer's Market on a Saturday morning. Have breakfast, circle the stalls, eat all the samples, buy something nonperishable to take home.

Remove Any Incriminating Evidence

Remember the plastic name tag you attached to your lapel upon entering the Moscone Convention Center? It's okay to remove it now.

Appendix

Quick Concierge

*W*here do you go if you need a doctor? How do you find a public restroom? The Quick Concierge contains answers to a variety of "Where do I?" and "How do I?" questions like these. Some of this information is found elsewhere in this guide but repeated here for your convenience; some of it is new.

Fast Facts

American Automobile Association (AAA)

The office at 150 Van Ness Ave. in the Civic Center provides maps and other information for members traveling by car. Call ☎ 800-222-4357 for emergency service or ☎ 415-565-2012 for general information.

American Express

The sole location is now at 455 Market St., at First Street (☎ 415-536-2600), open Monday through Friday from 8:30 a.m. to 5:30 p.m., Saturday from 9 a.m. to 2 p.m.

ATMs

ATMs are easy to find, especially downtown but also on any main business corridor. (See Chapter 12.)

Baby-sitters

Your hotel concierge can probably arrange for a baby-sitter. Otherwise, try American Child Care Service (☎ 415-285-2300; Internet: www.americanchildcare.com). Their rates are $13.50 per hour with a four-hour minimum plus $5 transportation fee.

Camera Repair

It's getting harder to find any places to fix cameras, but try Mission Camera Shop, 1089 Valencia St. (☎ 415-641-8396).

Convention Center

The Moscone Convention Center, 747 Howard St., between Third and Fourth streets (☎ 415-974-4000), is within easy walking distance of the Montgomery Street Muni and BART stations.

Dentists

Call the San Francisco Dental Society for 24-hour referrals (☎ 415-421-1435).

Doctors

Saint Francis Memorial Hospital, 900 Hyde St., between Bush and Pine streets (☎ 415-353-6000), offers 24-hour emergency-care service. The hospital's physician-referral service number is ☎ 415-353-6566. Your hotel can also contact on-call doctors. Before receiving any treatment, check with your health insurance company to find out how emergency treatment is handled when you're out of your provider area.

Earthquakes

California will always have earthquakes, most of which you'll never notice. However, in case of a significant shaker, you should know a few basic precautionary measures. When you're inside a building, seek cover; do not run outside. Stand under a doorway or against a wall and stay away from windows. If you exit a building after a substantial quake, use stairwells, not elevators. If you're in a car, pull over to the side of the road and stop — but not until you are away from bridges, overpasses, telephone poles, and power lines. Stay in your car. If you're out walking, stay outside and away from trees, power lines, and the sides of buildings. If you're in an area with tall buildings, find a doorway in which to stand.

Emergencies

Dial ☎ 911 from any phone for police, an ambulance, and the fire department.

Hospitals

San Francisco General Hospital, 1001 Potrero Ave. (☎ 415-206-8111), accepts uninsured emergency patients, but the wait can be brutally long and uncomfortable. The patient referral and assistance number is ☎ 415-206-5166.

Hotlines

Poison Control Center (☎ 800-523-2222); Rape Crisis Center (☎ 415-492-5970); Family Service Agency (☎ 415-474-7310).

Information

The San Francisco Convention and Visitors Bureau is in the lower level of Hallidie Plaza, 900 Market St., at Powell Street (☎ 800-220-5747 or 415-391-2000).

Internet Cafes

You can check your e-mail while on the road at Cafe.com, 970 Market St., near Fifth Street, open Monday through Saturday.

Liquor Laws

You can't drink or purchase alcohol legally if you're under 21. All the clubs, bars, supermarkets, and liquor stores ID anyone who looks younger than 30 (try not to be offended if you don't get carded). Bars do not serve liquor from 2 to 6 a.m.

Maps

The visitors bureau (see "Information" in this Appendix) has maps of the city, or stop by the California State Automobile Association (see "AAA" in this Appendix) if you are a member of AAA.

Newspapers/Magazines

The major papers are the morning *San Francisco Chronicle* and the afternoon *San Francisco Examiner.* They are distributed from sidewalk kiosks and boxes. The free weekly *San Francisco Bay Guardian* includes excellent events listings. Find it in cafes and in sidewalk boxes around the city. *San Francisco* magazine is the monthly city magazine. You can find it at newsstands everywhere.

Pharmacies

Walgreens, the Starbucks of drugstores, has taken over the city, and you should be able to find one almost anywhere. Call ☎ 800-WALGREEN for the address and phone number of the nearest store. Around Union Square, Walgreen's is at 135 Powell St. (☎ 415-391-4433), open Monday through Saturday from 8 a.m. to midnight and on Sunday from 9 a.m. to 9 p.m., but the pharmacy has more limited hours. A branch on Divisadero Street at Lombard has a 24-hour pharmacy.

Police

Call ☎ 911 from any phone. No coins are needed. The non-emergency number is ☎ 415-553-0123.

Radio Stations

Find KQED, our National Public Radio affiliate, at 88.5 FM. News and sports may be found at KCBS 710 AM.

Reservation Service

For hotel reservations, call SF Reservations (☎ 800-667-1500 or 415-227-1500).

Restrooms

Dark green public bathrooms are located on the waterfront at Pier 39, on Market Street near the cable car turnaround on Powell Street, and by the Civic Center. The restrooms cost 25¢ and are clean and safe. Also try hotels, museums, and service stations. Restaurants usually let only patrons use their bathrooms.

Safety

Walking around alone late at night is never a good idea. San Francisco is relatively safe, but it still has its share of muggings and more heinous crimes. Areas to be particularly careful in include the Tenderloin (see Chapter 6); the lower Haight; the Mission District anywhere between 16th and 24th streets east of Mission Street; lower Fillmore Street; and South of Market, particularly on Sixth and Seventh streets. Keep your wallet in an inside coat pocket and don't carry around wads of cash. Try to avoid using ATMs at night.

Smoking

Since January 1998, smoking has been prohibited in bars. It is also illegal to smoke in restaurants and public buildings, which is why you see so many well-dressed people loitering on the sidewalks during their coffee breaks.

Taxes

A sales tax of 8.5% is added to all purchases except snack food. The hotel tax is 14%.

Taxis

Outside of Union Square, expect to have trouble hailing a cab on the street; you'll have to call for one instead. Try Yellow Cab (☎ 415-626-2345), Veteran's Cab (☎ 415-552-1300), Desoto Cab (☎ 415-970-1300), or Luxor Cabs (☎ 415-282-4141).

Time Zone

California is on Pacific standard time, three hours behind New York.

Transit Information

For Muni route information (cable cars, streetcars, and buses), call ☎ 415-673-6864. For BART (Bay Area Rapid Transit) information, call ☎ 415-992-2278. Calling ☎ 415-817-1717 connects you to all transit organizations.

Weather Updates

While in town, turn to one of the news stations on the radio (try KCBS 710 AM). Otherwise, www.bayarea.citysearch.com lists comprehensive forecasts.

Toll-Free Numbers and Web Sites

Major North American carriers

Air Canada
☎ 888-247-2262
www.aircanada.ca

Alaska Airlines
☎ 800-426-0333
www.alaskaair.com

America West Airlines
☎ 800-235-9292
www.americawest.com

American Airlines
☎ 800-433-7300
www.aa.com

Continental Airlines
☎ 800-525-0280
www.continental.com

Delta Air Lines
☎ 800-221-1212
www.delta-air.com

Hawaiian Airlines
☎ 800-367-5320
www.hawaiianair.com

Midwest Express
☎ 800-452-2022
www.midwestexpress.com

Northwest Airlines
☎ 800-225-2525
www.nwa.com

Southwest Airlines
☎ 800-435-9792
www.iflyswa.com

United Airlines
☎ 800-241-6522
www.ual.com

US Airways
☎ 800-428-4322
www.usairways.com

Major hotel and motel chains

Best Western International
☎ 800-528-1234
www.bestwestern.com

Clarion Hotels
☎ 800-CLARION
www.hotelchoice.com

Comfort Inns
☎ 800-228-5150
www.hotelchoice.com

Courtyard by Marriott
☎ 800-321-2211
www.courtyard.com

Crowne Plaza Hotels
☎ 800-227-6963
www.crowneplaza.com

Days Inn
☎ 800-325-2525
www.daysinn.com

Doubletree Hotels
☎ 800-222-TREE
www.doubletreehotels.com

Econo Lodges
☎ 800-55-ECONO
www.hotelchoice.com

Fairfield Inn by Marriott
☎ 800-228-2800
www.fairfieldinn.com

Hampton Inn
☎ 800-HAMPTON
www.hampton-inn.com

Hilton Hotels
☎ 800-HILTONS
www.hilton.com

Holiday Inn
☎ 800-HOLIDAY
www.basshotels.com

Howard Johnson
☎ 800-654-2000
www.hojo.com

Hyatt Hotels & Resorts
☎ 800-228-9000
www.hyatt.com

ITT Sheraton
☎ 800-325-3535
www.sheraton.com

La Quinta Motor Inns
☎ 800-531-5900
www.laquinta.com

Marriott Hotels
☎ 800-228-9290
www.marriott.com

Quality Inns
☎ 800-228-5151
www.hotelchoice.com

Radisson Hotels International
☎ 800-333-3333
www.radisson.com

Ramada Inns
☎ 800-2-RAMADA
www.ramada.com

Red Roof Inns
☎ 800-843-7663
www.redroof.com

Residence Inn by Marriott
☎ 800-331-3131
www.residenceinn.com

Ritz-Carlton
☎ 800-241-3333
www.ritzcarlton.com

Rodeway Inns
☎ 800-228-2000
www.hotelchoice.com

Super 8 Motels
☎ 800-800-8000
www.super8motels.com

Travelodge
☎ 800-255-3050
www.travelodge.com

Westin Hotels and Resorts
☎ 800-228-3000
www.westin.com

Wyndham Hotels and Resorts
☎ 800-822-4200 in Continental U.S. and
Canada
www.wyndham.com

Where to Get More Information

Visitor bureaus

San Francisco Convention and Visitors Bureau

P.O. Box 429097; 900 Market St.,
San Francisco, CA 94142-9097
(☎ 800-220-5747 or 415-391-2000;
Internet: www.sfvisitor.org).

Call or write the Convention and Visitors
Bureau if you'd like to receive a nifty booklet
with lots of useful information, including
maps of the city and a seasonal calendar of
events. Of course, the slant is toward the
advertisers, so take those glossy ads lightly.
There is a $3 mailing charge. If you have a
fax and a touch-tone phone, use the toll-free
number for automated 24-hour fax service
and "fast facts."

Napa Valley Conference and Visitors Bureau

1310 Napa Town Center, Napa, CA
94559 (☎ 707-226-7459; Internet: www.
napavalley.com).

This is the second-busiest visitor center in
California, which either says something
about our collective fondness for wine or
something about the beauty of the area
(or possibly both). They'll send you a free
brochure and a list of hotels on request;
for $10 (plastic accepted) they'll mail you a
120-page magazine, suggested itineraries,
and a handsome map of the area.

Information on the Web

www.bayarea.citysearch.com

A comprehensive, regularly updated site devoted to all things San Francisco, including arts, entertainment, dining, and attractions, with links to the hotel reservation network.

www.sfbg.com

The *San Francisco Bay Guardian* site with event listings and the lowdown on nightlife.

www.sfgate.com

The *San Francisco Chronicle* Web site. Read all about it.

www.qsanfrancisco.com

A Web site for gay and lesbian travelers.

www.sanfran.com

The Web site for *San Francisco* magazine. Includes dining recommendations and timely entertainment suggestions.

www.gocitykids.com

The Web site for families wondering what to do today. Lots of helpful info.

Print resources

Frommer's San Francisco

This popular guide covers all 46 square miles in great detail, including background on the sites, personalities, and neighborhoods that make San Francisco "everybody's favorite city."

Frommer's Memorable Walks in San Francisco, 4th Edition

This guide covers 12 easy-to-follow walking tours through San Francisco's most charming neighborhoods. Includes detailed maps.

San Francisco magazine

A monthly glossy with an events calendar, restaurant reviews, and features of local interest.

Transit information

Call ☎ 415-817-1717 for information on how to get anywhere in the Bay Area.

Making Dollars and Sense of It

Expense	Daily cost	x	Number of days	=	Total
Airfare					
Local transportation					
Car rental					
Lodging (with tax)					
Parking					
Breakfast					
Lunch					
Dinner					
Snacks					
Entertainment					
Babysitting					
Attractions					
Gifts & souvenirs					
Tips					
Other					
Grand Total					

Fare Game: Choosing an Airline

When looking for the best airfare, you should cover all your bases — 1) consult a trusted travel agent; 2) contact the airline directly, via the airline's toll-free number and/or Web site; 3) check out one of the travel-planning Web sites, such as www.frommers.com.

Travel Agency_____ Phone_____

Agent's Name_____ Quoted fare_____

Airline 1_____ Quoted fare_____

Toll-free number/Internet_____

Airline 2_____ Quoted fare_____

Toll-free number/Internet_____

Web site 1_____ Quoted fare_____

Web site 2_____ Quoted fare_____

Departure Schedule & Flight Information

Airline_____ Flight #_____ Confirmation #_____

Departs_____ Date_____ Time_____ a.m./p.m.

Arrives_____ Date_____ Time_____ a.m./p.m.

Connecting Flight (if any)

Amount of time between flights_____ hours/mins

Airline_____ Flight #_____ Confirmation #_____

Departs_____ Date_____ Time_____ a.m./p.m.

Arrives_____ Date_____ Time_____ a.m./p.m.

Return Trip Schedule & Flight Information

Airline_____ Flight #_____ Confirmation #_____

Departs_____ Date_____ Time_____ a.m./p.m.

Arrives_____ Date_____ Time_____ a.m./p.m.

Connecting Flight (if any)

Amount of time between flights_____ hours/mins

Airline_____ Flight #_____ Confirmation #_____

Departs_____ Date_____ Time_____ a.m./p.m.

Arrives_____ Date_____ Time_____ a.m./p.m.

Sweet Dreams: Choosing Your Hotel

Make a list of all the hotels where you'd like to stay and then check online and call the local and toll-free numbers to get the best price. You should also check with a travel agent, who may be able to get you a better rate.

Hotel & page	Location	Internet	Tel. (local)	Tel. (Toll-free)	Quoted rate

Hotel Checklist

Here's a checklist of things to inquire about when booking your room, depending on your needs and preferences.

- ❏ Smoking/smoke-free room
- ❏ Noise (if you prefer a quiet room, ask about proximity to elevator, bar/restaurant, pool, meeting facilities, renovations, and street)
- ❏ View
- ❏ Facilities for children (crib, roll-away cot, babysitting services)
- ❏ Facilities for travelers with disabilities
- ❏ Number and size of bed(s) (king, queen, double/full-size)
- ❏ Is breakfast included? (buffet, continental, or sit-down?)
- ❏ In-room amenities (hair dryer, iron/board, minibar, etc.)
- ❏ Other_____

Places to Go, People to See, Things to Do

Enter the attractions you would most like to see and decide how they'll fit into your schedule. Next, use the "Going My Way" worksheets that follow to sketch out your itinerary.

Attraction/activity	Page	Amount of time you expect to spend there	Best day and time to go

Going "My" Way

Day 1

Hotel _____ Tel. _____

Morning _____

_____

Lunch _____ Tel. _____

Afternoon _____

_____

Dinner _____ Tel. _____

Evening _____

_____

Day 2

Hotel _____ Tel. _____

Morning _____

_____

Lunch _____ Tel. _____

Afternoon _____

_____

Dinner _____ Tel. _____

Evening _____

_____

Day 3

Hotel _____ Tel. _____

Morning _____

_____

Lunch _____ Tel. _____

Afternoon _____

_____

Dinner _____ Tel. _____

Evening _____

_____

Going "My" Way

Day 4

Hotel _____ Tel. _____

Morning _____

_____

Lunch _____ Tel. _____

Afternoon _____

_____

Dinner _____ Tel. _____

Evening _____

_____

Day 5

Hotel _____ Tel. _____

Morning _____

_____

Lunch _____ Tel. _____

Afternoon _____

_____

Dinner _____ Tel. _____

Evening _____

_____

Day 6

Hotel _____ Tel. _____

Morning _____

_____

Lunch _____ Tel. _____

Afternoon _____

_____

Dinner _____ Tel. _____

Evening _____

_____

Index

• *D* •

• *Accommodations Index* •

• *Restaurant Index* •

FOR DUMMIES®

A world of resources to help you grow

TRAVEL

0-7645-5453-0

0-7645-5438-7

0-7645-5444-1

Also available:

America's National Parks For Dummies
(0-7645-6204-5)

Caribbean For Dummies
(0-7645-5445-X)

Cruise Vacations For Dummies 2003
(0-7645-5459-X)

Europe For Dummies
(0-7645-5456-5)

Ireland For Dummies
(0-7645-6199-5)

France For Dummies
(0-7645-6292-4)

Las Vegas For Dummies
(0-7645-5448-4)

London For Dummies
(0-7645-5416-6)

Mexico's Beach Resorts For Dummies
(0-7645-6262-2)

Paris For Dummies
(0-7645-5494-8)

RV Vacations For Dummies
(0-7645-5443-3)

EDUCATION & TEST PREPARATION

0-7645-5194-9

0-7645-5325-9

0-7645-5249-X

Also available:

The ACT For Dummies
(0-7645-5210-4)

Chemistry For Dummies
(0-7645-5430-1)

English Grammar For Dummies
(0-7645-5322-4)

French For Dummies
(0-7645-5193-0)

GMAT For Dummies
(0-7645-5251-1)

Inglés Para Dummies
(0-7645-5427-1)

Italian For Dummies
(0-7645-5196-5)

Research Papers For Dummies
(0-7645-5426-3)

SAT I For Dummies
(0-7645-5472-7)

U.S. History For Dummies
(0-7645-5249-X)

World History For Dummies
(0-7645-5242-2)

HEALTH, SELF-HELP & SPIRITUALITY

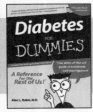

0-7645-5154-X

0-7645-5302-X

0-7645-5418-2

Also available:

The Bible For Dummies
(0-7645-5296-1)

Controlling Cholesterol For Dummies
(0-7645-5440-9)

Dating For Dummies
(0-7645-5072-1)

Dieting For Dummies
(0-7645-5126-4)

High Blood Pressure For Dummies
(0-7645-5424-7)

Judaism For Dummies
(0-7645-5299-6)

Menopause For Dummies
(0-7645-5458-1)

Nutrition For Dummies
(0-7645-5180-9)

Potty Training For Dummies
(0-7645-5417-4)

Pregnancy For Dummies
(0-7645-5074-8)

Rekindling Romance For Dummies
(0-7645-5303-8)

Religion For Dummies
(0-7645-5264-3)

Available wherever books are sold. Go to www.dummies.com or call 1-877-762-2974 to order direct

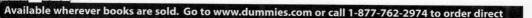

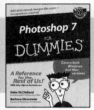